REFLECTIONS ON BODY
DYSMORPHIC DISORDER

REFLECTIONS ON BODY DYSMORPHIC DISORDER
Stories of Courage, Determination, and Hope

Edited by

Nicole Schnackenberg and Sergio Petro

with a Foreword by
Professor Katharine Phillips
and an Introduction by
Professor David Veale and Doctor Rob Willson

First published in 2016 by

The Body Dysmorphic Disorder Foundation
45b Stanford Road
London N11 3HY

Charity Registration Number: 1153753

Copyright © 2016 to The Body Dysmorphic Foundation

All rights reserved. No part of this publication may be reproduced, stored in a retrieval system, or transmitted, in any form or by any means, electronic, mechanical, photocopying, recording, or otherwise, without the prior written permission of the publisher.

Front cover image: *Girl Before a Mirror*, by Pablo Picasso. Reproduced by kind permission of the Design and Artists Copyright Society.

British Library Cataloguing in Publication data

A C.I.P. for this book is available from the British Library

ISBN 978-1-326-81741-1

Edited, designed, and typeset by Yvonne Doney Editorial Services: email: y.doney@tiscali.co.uk

Printed in Great Britain

CONTENTS

ACKNOWLEDGEMENTS   ix

FOREWORD by Professor Katharine Phillips   xi

INTRODUCTION by Professor David Veale and Doctor Rob Willson   xv

CORE THEMES by Nicole Schnackenberg

Genetics and Neurochemistry in BDD   3

Early Life Experiences   7

Mirror Gazing and Visual Processing   11

Artistic Propensity in BDD   15

Skin Picking in BDD   19

The Seeking of Cosmetic and Similar Procedures and Practices in BDD   23

Anxiety and Depression in BDD   27

Disordered Eating in the Context of BDD   31

Treatment Options for BDD   35

Recovery from BDD: A Very Real Possibility   39

STORIES

Why Share these Stories?   43

Amanda Hawkins   47

Andrew Hall   51

Annette Loren	59
Becca Forsyth	65
Ben Hilton	69
Beverley	75
Caroline	87
C. H. Handley	101
Carla Mark-Thompson	111
Charlotte	119
Danny Bowman	125
Dathen Bocabella	131
Dominic Edwards	143
E's Story, from the Perspective of her Mother	149
Ellen	155
Fiona	163
Frances Roberts: A Mother's Perspective	167
Hannah Lewis	171
Interlude Introduction	179
Interlude: Tina's Story, by John Martin	181
Helen Jackson	189
Joanna	193
J. W.	203
Laura Bexson	207
Lauren	215
Linzy	225
Liz Atkin	233

L's Story, by his Mum, Emma	239
Lucy Tattersall	245
Margaret	251
Megan Butcher	259
Minnie Iris	263
N: A Mother's Story	269
Peter's Story: Supporting a Child with BDD	275
Rachel Trewartha	279
Tony	285
Viktoria	293

RESOURCES

AVENUES OF SUPPORT AND FURTHER READING	301
REFERENCES	305

The stories contained herein share thoughts and opinions that are the property of the contributor. The BDD Foundation cannot, and does not, own or therefore endorse each of these thoughts and opinions, though fully commends each person for their courage in sharing their unique journey of living with BDD.

ACKNOWLEDGEMENTS

This book, quite simply, would not have been possible without the immense courage and goodwill of every person who has contributed their unique story, or that of their loved one, of living with body dysmorphic disorder (BDD). Some of our contributors have decided to remain anonymous or to use a pseudonym for a variety of completely understandable reasons, so we are unable to thank each person by name. The BDD Foundation, however, would like to extend sincere gratitude to all contributors and to their family members for sharing their journey with us all. This book is a rich and deeply inspirational compendium of the peculiarities and particularities of BDD, exploring how to move beyond this distressing psychological struggle and find a life beyond its agonising grip. Both hope and inspiration can be drawn from these pages which detail how numerous people have found a way through and beyond their BDD. Our intention, through the publication of this book, is to help you and your loved ones to find a way through, too.

Special thanks go to Professor Katharine Phillips, author of *The Broken Mirror*, patron of the Body Dysmorphic Disorder Foundation, and one of the world's leading experts on BDD, for contributing the Foreword to this volume. Immense gratitude also goes to Professor David Veale and

Doctor Rob Willson, two leading BDD specialists, researchers, and trustees of the BDD Foundation, for writing the Introduction and for their invaluable support and advice throughout the process of planning and editing this project. Thanks also go to the other trustees of the BDD Foundation, who have been instrumental in bringing this book to fruition, namely Amoreena Campbell, Alan Shooter, and Minnie Iris. Gratitude is also extended to Stuart Chandler for his ongoing support for the Foundation and to Steve Caplin for designing and creating the front cover.

Foreword

Professor Katharine Phillips, MD

I am deeply honoured to have the opportunity to write this Foreword. This is a landmark book – it is the first book on body dysmorphic disorder (BDD) that is written mostly by sufferers, family members, and carers of those who have struggled with this cruel disorder. Their perspective is invaluable, their voices are powerful, and they uniquely understand the experience of BDD. All of the contributors deserve our immense gratitude. They are courageous, generous, and tremendously inspiring.

BDD is a devastating illness. People with this condition believe that they look abnormal, ugly, or deformed, whereas others don't see them this way. They are preoccupied with their perceived physical flaws to the point where they experience significant emotional distress (such as anxiety or depression) or impairment in daily functioning – usually both. For example, the appearance preoccupations might make it difficult to go to school or work, concentrate on tasks, be around other people, care for others, or leave the house. BDD is often extremely challenging, and even heartbreaking, for family members and other loved ones. Of greatest concern, most people with BDD have suicidal thoughts, and many attempt suicide. Tragically, some kill themselves. BDD-related suffering is often the cause of suicidal thoughts and behaviours. BDD, especially more severe BDD, is one of the most debilitating of all mental disorders.

BDD is also common, affecting about 2% to 3% of the population, which translates into several hundred million people around the world. It is more common than many far better recognised disorders such as anorexia nervosa and obsessive–compulsive disorder.

How can it be that a disorder that is this severe and this common has gone unrecognised for so long? One reason is that until the 1990s, systematic scientific research studies had not been done to elucidate BDD's clinical features, prevalence, morbidity, causes, and other characteristics. Fortunately, this has changed. Another major reason is that people with this condition often suffer silently. Many are reluctant to talk about their appearance concerns; they feel ashamed, embarrassed, and worry that they will be considered vain.

But BDD is not vanity. Neither is BDD just normal appearance concerns, an "adolescent phase," a character flaw, or anyone's fault. Rather, BDD is a serious illness with complex causes. It probably results from a complicated combination of many neurobiological (brain-based), genetic, and environmental factors. As this book discusses, these factors could include aberrations in visual processing (over-focusing on detail and having difficulty seeing 'the big picture'), perhaps life experiences such as being teased, and possibly enhanced aesthetic sensitivity. More research studies are needed to better understand what causes BDD; in turn, this understanding may lead to even more treatment options and, ultimately, prevent BDD from occurring.

In the meantime, there is very good news. In less than three decades, we have found effective treatments that help the majority of people with BDD substantially improve and, in many cases, completely recover. One of these treatments is a class of medications called selective serotonin reuptake inhibitors (SSRIs), antidepressant medications that also help stop obsessions and repetitive behaviours such as mirror checking and comparing. These medications also often improve a broad range of other symptoms such as anxiety, social anxiety, and suicidal thinking. SSRIs are not habit forming or addictive, and, fortunately, they are usually well tolerated. The other effective treatment is cognitive–behavioural therapy (CBT), which helps people learn new, more helpful ways of thinking and skills to overcome their symptoms. CBT must be tailored to address BDD symptoms specifically. Scientific studies have shown that this treatment, too, often substantially improves BDD.

We are so fortunate to have two different treatments that are effective and usually well tolerated, when only several decades ago BDD was considered untreatable. No methodologically rigorous research studies have been done to determine which treatment is better. It is likely that they are about equally effective, and it's possible that they work even better in combination. Unfortunately, however, BDD is still under-diagnosed and undertreated. The majority of people with BDD do not receive treatment for this condition at all, and, when they do, it is usually inadequate. For example, most people receive medication other than SSRIs, take an SSRI for too brief a time, or take too low a dose (usually, high SSRI doses are needed). And many people receive therapy other than CBT, receive CBT that is not focused on BDD symptoms specifically, or have too few sessions. Harmful myths abound about both of these treatments, which, sadly, prevent many people from ever trying them, sometimes with tragic consequences. It is critically important to realise that when these treatments are properly administered, they help most people get better, and they can be lifesaving.

So many people from around the world deserve enormous thanks for advancing understanding of BDD, developing effective treatments, and spreading the word about BDD. People who have generously participated in BDD research studies deserve special thanks, as we would not have learnt about BDD without their participation. This book is an indispensable part of these amazing and remarkably fruitful efforts. I want to express my deep gratitude to the editors of this book, to the BDD Foundation for publishing this book, to Professor Veale and Doctor Willson for their indispensable role in the book and the Foundation, and, especially, to everyone who contributed to this book. It is a gift to all BDD sufferers and their loved ones.

I believe that the future is bright for those who have BDD. We have made tremendous progress, and effective treatments are already available. Research advances are accelerating at a rapid pace, so we will learn much more in the years to come. I am especially hopeful that new treatments will be developed, tested, and made widely available, so that even more people can overcome this disorder and live happy and fulfilling lives. And I hope that, like the courageous authors of this book, more people will come forward to describe their experience, reach out to others, and advocate on behalf of people with BDD.

To readers who think they might have BDD, please don't suffer in silence. Share your experience with others, and reach out for support. Remember that you are not alone and that help is available. Empower yourself by giving recommended treatments a try. Be persistent – if one treatment doesn't work, try another. Remember that most people can get better. And, most importantly, never give up hope!

Professor Katharine Phillips, November 2016.

Senior Research Scientist

Director, Body Dysmorphic Disorder Program

Director of Research for Adult Psychiatry
Rhode Island Hospital
Providence, Rhode Island

Private Practice of Psychiatry
134 East 93rd Street, New York, New York

Professor of Psychiatry and Human Behavior
Alpert Medical School of Brown University
Providence, Rhode Island

Introduction

We are hugely indebted to all those affected by body dysmorphic disorder (BDD) who have contributed to this book. Each of us has worked for well over twenty years on research and treatment for people who have BDD. As far as we are aware, this book is unique in providing a wide range of stories of people whose lives have been affected by the condition.

Contrary to the traditional view that BDD is rare and difficult to treat, the stories in this book provide tangible proof that BDD is, in fact, common, and can be improved or even overcome. This is the most important message of the book: there is hope.

As this book illustrates, the focus of an individual's BDD varies widely but the most common areas of concern are the skin, hair, nose, eyes, eyelids, mouth, lips, jaw, and chin. The crucial thing to understand about BDD is that it is not just 'dissatisfaction' with appearance, or even so-called 'imagined ugliness'. Studies have shown that a large number of people hold an unrealistically negative mental image of how they look and that many people are dissatisfied with aspects of their appearance. BDD is different. Despite its apparently superficial focus upon appearance, BDD is one of the most distressing, disabling, and destructive of all psychiatric disorders.

While often thought of as a 'modern disease', BDD was, in fact, first described 125 years ago, in 1891, by an Italian physician, Enrico Morselli. He described 'dysmorphophobia' as 'a subjective feeling of ugliness or physical defect which the patient feels is noticeable to others, although the appearance is within normal limits'. Fast-forward 125 years: BDD is now recognised in the World Health Organisation's *International Classification of Diseases (ICD-11)*. The essential features are:

- Persistent preoccupation (lasting at least one hour a day) with one or more perceived defects or flaws in appearance, or ugliness in general, that is either unnoticeable or only slightly noticeable to others.
- Excessive self-consciousness about the perceived defect(s) or flaw(s), often including ideas of self-reference: that is, the conviction that people are taking notice, judging, or talking about the perceived defect(s) or flaw(s).
- The preoccupation is manifest in any of the following:
  - repetitive and excessive behaviours, such as repeated examination of appearance generally or the severity of the perceived defect(s) or flaw(s) (e.g., by checks in reflective surfaces or by comparison of the relevant feature with that of others);
  - attempts to camouflage or alter the defect (e.g., by unnecessary cosmetic surgical procedures);
  - attempts to avoid social situations or triggers that increase distress about the perceived defect(s) or flaw(s).
- The symptoms result in significant distress or significant impairment in personal, family, social, educational, occupational, or other important areas of functioning.

BDD can affect both men and women and occurs in about 2% of the population. Onlookers such as family, friends, and even health care professionals are frequently perplexed because they can see nothing out of the ordinary in the person's appearance. BDD causes feelings of shame, anxiety, and depression and interferes substantially with the person's ability to function in important areas of his or her life. How BDD manifests itself can vary greatly; for example, some people might largely avoid social situations, whereas others might spend hours preparing or concealing their appearance before entering social situations. There are variations of BDD, such as 'muscle dysmorphia', sometimes referred to in the media as 'bigorexia', when an individual is preoccupied with the idea that his or her body build is too small or insufficiently muscular.

If you are reading this book because you think you might have BDD, it could be helpful to share the diagnostic criteria above with your doctor. Additionally, on the BDD Foundation website, www.bddfoundation.org, there is a questionnaire titled the Cosmetic Procedure Screening Scale (COPS) which can help to give an indication of whether you might have BDD. The BDD Foundation charity focuses on the idea that '*You are not alone*'. Please support it in whatever way you can to help maintain that reality.

Dr Rob Willson, Private Practice, North London. Chair of the BDD Foundation.

Professor David Veale, the South London and Maudsley NHS Foundation Trust and the Priory Hospital, North London. Trustee of the BDD Foundation.

In memory of David Petro

In honour of Joe Campbell

CORE THEMES

Nicole Schnackenberg

Genetics and Neurochemistry in Body Dysmorphic Disorder (BDD)

Genetics

The nature *versus* nurture debate is as old as the hills and continues to rage in both the scientific community and society at large. You will read many stories in this volume describing people's perceptions of their genetic predisposition to BDD and other stories of people who believe their BDD to be attributable not to their genetic makeup, but to their early life experiences of a variety of forms. As Caroline so imploringly asks herself in her story, 'Was I born with BDD? Is it in my DNA? Do my genes make me more susceptible to it? (I have always been a highly sensitive person.) Is it a result of a culmination of external life experiences which have caused me to turn inward?' Her questions are echoed by many others who share their courageous journey within these pages.

Regarding where we are in terms of understanding the role of genetics in BDD, the simple answer is that we still have an extremely long way to go. BDD is thought to be aetiologically related to obsessive–compulsive disorder (OCD) but the available evidence is incomplete. What we do know from the evidence is that BDD and OCD often co-occur (approximately 30% of people with BDD also meet the diagnosis for OCD) and that BDD tends to be more prevalent among first-degree relatives of people with OCD than among relatives of people without OCD. The extent, however, to which BDD shares a common genetic liability with OCD remains unknown.

There have been very few genetic studies related to BDD and the studies that have been conducted have been somewhat inconclusive. It has been found, for example, that 8% of people with a diagnosis of BDD have a family member who also has a diagnosis of BDD, which is a rate four to eight times higher than in the general population. Yet, it is uncertain whether this higher percentage is due to genetic predisposition or to shared environmental risk factors, learnt behaviour, and assimilated psychological anguish. In a study of female twins by Monzani and colleagues in 2012, genes were cited as being accounted for by 44% of the propensity for dysmorphic worries, while individual environmental factors and measurement error were found to account for the remaining variance of 56%. According to Monzani, the results indicate that unique environmental factors are also important in increasing the liability to develop severe dysmorphic concerns, since at least half of the variance in dysmorphic concern in this study was due to these unique environmental factors. People with BDD report more appearance- and competency-related teasing experiences in childhood than the general population and a higher prevalence of childhood abuse and neglect. According to Professor David Veale, adverse experiences such as these might contribute to the early formation of beliefs regarding the importance of appearance and/or interact with genetics to trigger dysmorphic concerns later in life.

Neurochemistry

As you will read about in more detail later in this initial section of the book, the two main treatment options recommended for BDD are cognitive–behavioural therapy (CBT) and selective serotonin reuptake inhibitors (SSRIs). SSRIs are prescribed on account of serotonin's perceived role in BDD. Neurochemical studies on BDD have primarily focused on how serotonin, which is a chemical in the brain, is related to nervous system function. One study, for example, found decreased serotonin binding densities in people with BDD compared to controls. Several treatment studies have also found that SSRIs decrease BDD symptoms overall. SSRIs have been found to reduce the severity and frequency of appearance worries, relieve emotional distress, reduce suicidal thinking, and improve insight. Yet, this does not prove that people with BDD have low serotonin levels or that low serotonin levels cause BDD, as some medical professionals and pharmaceutical companies have suggested. Rather, extensive additional research is needed to uncover what, if indeed any, neurochemical differences are causative factors in BDD. You will find within these pages stories of people with a diagnosis of BDD finding SSRI medication both helpful and unhelpful.

Early Life Experiences

A theme that comes up time and again in these stories is that of difficult early life experiences, usually taking place in childhood and adolescence. BDD would appear to be most typically embedded in low self-esteem, failing self-worth, and a sense that one's appearance is somehow a marker of intrinsic identity. In the context of a society within which happiness is sold as being achievable by obtaining a thin, 'beautiful' body if one is female and a toned, 'handsome' body if one is male, it is hardly surprising that so many of us come to entangle our self-worth up in how we look. This self-worth would appear often to be in question, in part, due to early life experiences that diminish, and sometimes even shatter, the sense in a person that they are good as they are.

An implicit theme in many of these stories is that of early attachment. Attachment describes the way in which we organise self-protective strategies within the relationships we have with others. When the attachment system is activated, we seek comfort and safety from people we view as stronger and wiser; early in our lives, these people are usually our parents or primary carers. When we have a secure attachment with our parents and primary carers we understand that our emotional needs can be, and are being, met and, thus, grow into a safe and certain sense of self. When the attachment is insecure in any way, we might come to view both ourselves and our primary carers with distrust and fear. We might go on to develop a false sense of self and an inability to notice our emotional needs or know how we can go about fulfilling them.

Attachment is an important consideration when attempting to understand appearance distress. Attachment can be conceptualised as two continuous dimensions: anxiety (monitoring the relationship and being sensitive to rejection or threats to security) and avoidance (avoiding closeness with the attachment figure). Secure attachment corresponds to low levels of both dimensions. It is important to note that secure attachment is related to body satisfaction. It could be that those with high attachment anxiety are more sensitive to socially relevant cues such as appearance. Furthermore, people without secure early attachments would appear, typically, to be more likely to be victimised and traumatised and can be, therefore, more likely to develop pervasive symptoms of shame and dissociation, which are two known correlates of BDD.

In addition to early experiences of insecure attachment, some of the stories in this book contain episodes of overt mistreatment in childhood, with Margaret's story and Beverley's stories being particularly poignant examples of this. In fact, in one study of individuals diagnosed with body dysmorphic disorder, more than three quarters reported a perception of childhood maltreatment, with emotional neglect being the most common form of such perceived maltreatment. A number of these stories speak about demanded perfectionism from adults, negative appraisals from primary carers and siblings, physical abuse, sexual abuse, emotional abuse, and early bullying experiences. These early life traumas can set the stage for BDD; BDD is commonly embedded, as we have already mentioned, in low self-esteem, a desire for predictability, emotional turmoil, high anxiety and, importantly, a seeking after identity. In many of these stories, you will come across people lamenting about how much they have longed to be accepted for who they are, desperate to feel as though they exist as a person who deserves to live and to be loved.

Within these pages, you will read many experiences of bullying of various forms and levels of intensity. You might come to notice many common threads, such as bullying focused on the physical appearance and bullying taking place at the most critical stages of personality and identity development (often during the adolescent years), such as is evident in the contributions made by Minnie, Andrew, and Danny among others. You will also read recounts of domestic abuse, divorce, neglect, transgenerational trauma, and a history of family mental health struggles. There are also numerous stories in this book of people who went on to develop BDD who had very secure, happy, and nurturing childhoods.

Of course, each of us will view the particular occurrences of our childhoods in our own unique way: Lucy, for example, describes her childhood as 'fabulous', despite mental health issues being present in her nuclear family. There is no firm trajectory, or set of clear circumstances or life experiences, that irrevocably lead to BDD. Confusingly, BDD is far more complex than this and can emerge in people with both difficult and validating childhoods alike. Yet, for the majority of the contributors to this volume, something happened at some point in their early lives that appeared to lead them to question their worth as a person. It might be useful, as you read these stories, to ask yourself what in your own life, or in the life of your loved one, prompted you/them to mistrust your/their self-worth and, therefore, to seek self-worth and identity in the appearance.

These stories are stories of incredible resilience, strength, and tenacity. They are stories of people who, despite often painful early life experiences, found a way through the confusion towards a place of greater self-acceptance, even self-love.

Mirror Gazing and Visual Processing in BDD

In research studies, people with a diagnosis of BDD have reported spending up to six consecutive hours in front of the mirror. Extensive checking and looking at oneself in the mirror, as you will read throughout these stories, is regularly a core feature of BDD. According to Phillips and colleagues (1993), mirror gazing occurs in about 80% of people with BDD, while the remainder tend to avoid mirrors either by covering them up or removing them in order to avoid the distress of seeing their reflection. In this book, you will read about how, at her worst, J. W. was checking herself in the mirror continuously for up to sixteen hours a day and about how Rachel would get 'lost in the mirror', completely unable to pull herself away. You will also read Ellen's description of her mirror avoidance: she explains, 'I became obsessed with avoiding mirrors and would go to the disabled toilet at work, as it was the only one where lights could be switched off and I couldn't see myself.' Some people report avoiding certain mirrors only; in a 2001 study by Veale and Riley, 67% of their BDD patients reported selectively avoiding only certain mirrors compared to 14% of the general population.

People with BDD are often secretive about their mirror gazing habits, often through fear of appearing vain or narcissistic, with significant experiences of shame being attached to these checking and gazing behaviours. In addition to experiences of shame and disgust, people with BDD frequently report seeing distortions in their appearance after focusing on their appearance in the mirror for an extended period of time and/or having unusual somatic sensations such as the tingling of the skin. Indeed, it is a regular occurrence in BDD support groups run by the BDD Foundation to hear stories of people seeing a part of their face, such as their nose, 'move' or change shape and size in front of their very eyes after an extended period of mirror gazing, as Annette speaks about in her story. It is also not unusual for people to report burning, itching, tingling, and pulsing areas of the body upon which they have been focusing in the looking glass.

It has been suggested that people with BDD might have perceptual distortions, given their discernment of appearance defects that are either unobservable or viewed as minor to the outside eye. Numerous studies have highlighted the acute propensity for people with BDD to process faces in detail as opposed to holistically; people with BDD would appear to focus on localised detail as opposed to processing faces globally. The 'face inversion effect' is further evidence for this local processing and describes the phenomenon within which the recognition of inverted (upside-down) faces is less accurate and slower relative to the recognition of upright faces, since we lack a holistic template for inverted faces. In a study by Feusner and colleagues (2010), people with BDD had a smaller inversion effect than controls, suggesting an imbalance in local *versus* global processing. Whereas controls tend to look at and process faces as a whole, people with BDD more commonly break faces up into their component parts and process them as these parts. In short, people with BDD have an increased tendency to engage in highly detailed processing of faces. In this book, you will read about C. H.'s uncanny ability to remember the exact location of moles on everyone's faces and Helen's explanation of a conclusion reached after a late night of mirror gazing; 'It has been staring me right in the face so to speak – it's my forehead; too small, too flat, not feminine enough. How had I not noticed this before, when all this time I thought it was my nose, which seems overly small now, after a botched nose job and a subsequent revision, but . . . maybe if I had a rounded forehead, it would give some definition to my profile, then, with the lip lift I am planning, I may look halfway decent.'

Mirror-gazing and mirror checking are areas covered by specialised CBT for BDD with the aim being to reduce safety behaviours including mirror checking, to reintroduce the mirror if it has been covered or avoided, and to promote a more holistic processing both of one's own face and that of others.

Artistic Propensity in BDD

It became astonishingly obvious during the editing of this book just how many of the contributors had chosen to study art or drama, painted as a hobby, worked in design and the arts, and/or have a particular eye for artistic detail. You will find some of the beautiful artwork made by the people who have so courageously contributed their stories peppered throughout this volume, which certainly adds a richness and depth to the messages being conveyed through these pages. You will read about Liz, who makes her living from painting and charcoals (and uses the practice of creating art to reduce her skin picking), Dathen's love of creative writing, about E, who discovered her artistic abilities during a hospital admission for BDD and whose self-portrait contained herein will undoubtedly stir your soul, Minnie's study of art and design and her work in art galleries as an adult, and Viktoria's extensive work in theatre, to name just a few. You will also read time and again about contributors' propensity for homing in on detail and noticing visual stimuli most others would fail to see.

It has been hypothesised by David Veale and Christina Lambrou (2002) that aesthetics might play a role in the development and maintenance of

BDD. The need for symmetry and precision in objects or activities is a known component, for example, of OCD, under which umbrella BDD is categorised in the *Diagnostic and Statistical Manual of Mental Disorders (DSM)*. According to Veale and Lambrou, the need for symmetry in people diagnosed with BDD may be focused on appearance as opposed to an object or activity. It could also be that people with BDD are more sensitive to subtle anomalies in facial symmetry than the general population, with the argument also being that people seeking cosmetic surgery are typically more aesthetically sensitive. A consequence of this aesthetic sensitivity is that a person might react more emotionally to perceived beauty or ugliness.

Another hypothesis is that people with a diagnosis of BDD are superior at appreciating art and beauty relative to others. As Caroline asks in her story, 'Maybe it is the artist in me? I see things differently and in great detail.' In research by Veale and Lambrou (2002), 20% of 100 patients with BDD had an education or occupation in art or design compared with 4% of 100 patients with depression, 3% of 100 people with OCD, and 0% of 100 people with post traumatic stress disorder (PTSD). Minnie makes a very interesting point in her story that her study of art and design in her late teens and early twenties seemed to somehow nurture the emergence of her BDD; as she learnt to develop a more critical eye and appreciation of aesthetics, she began to apply her new understandings to her appearance. She then set herself unrealistic aesthetic standards for her appearance, just as, indeed, she set incredibly high standards for her artistic endeavours.

So often, mental health labels are described in terms of deficits and unwanted thoughts and behaviours. A new wave of research, however, is beginning to appreciate the positive aspects of mental health presentations; each and every diagnosis comes with a particular set of positive skills, attributes, and resiliencies. The propensity for people with BDD to home in on visual detail, to process visual phenomena in terms of their minutiae as opposed to the bigger picture, and to notice and appreciate almost unperceivable aspects of objects including works of art, surely points to possible innate gifts and modes of expression available to people with BDD. Indeed, you will read in many of these stories how our contributors turned these artistic propensities to their advantage, even developing international art careers and achieving theatre acclaim. In these ways, the seeming 'curse' of razor-sharp visual focus in BDD can be seen as a gift worthy of self-esteem and offering to the world.

Skin Picking in BDD

Liz Akin's contribution to this book, in the form of her story and mesmeric artwork centred around the theme of skin picking, is incredibly moving and poignant. She certainly does not stand alone in her experiences. You will also read in this book about Lauren's compulsive skin picking and the pulling of hairs from different places on her body, of Hannah's use of skin camouflage to hide her skin-picking behaviours, and Fiona's popping and picking continuously at her pimples throughout the day, to cite just a few examples.

Skin picking, sometimes referred to as dermatillomania or excoriation, has been described as prevalent, disturbing, and difficult to treat, particularly when it occurs in the context of BDD. It is more common in females than males and is also a known correlate of OCD. The act of compulsively picking at the skin can produce scarring and skin infections; in rare cases, it has been reported to be nearly fatal. The psychological effects of skin picking can be extensive and far reaching and typically include feelings of shame, guilt, and embarrassment. Individuals with clinical levels of skin-picking disorder report spending a significant proportion of each day picking at their skin, with many finding that their skin picking takes up several hours of their day, which has certainly been the case for some of the contributors to this volume.

Triggers for skin picking can be multiple and various, with stress and anxiety being two of the most commonly cited precursors. Skin picking has been proposed by some to be an emotional regulation strategy, as a way of dealing with seemingly overwhelming emotions. Two kinds of skin picking have been identified by researchers. Automatic skin picking describes unconscious skin picking, which might happen while the person's attention is focused elsewhere or during a dissociative episode. Focused skin picking, on the other hand, describes conscious picking wherein the person is aware of what he or she is doing and is perhaps even actively and consciously choosing to pick. For many, picking typically begins unconsciously but becomes conscious after a period of time, which is similar to other body-focused repetitive behaviours such as hair pulling (trichotillomania).

As we will see from these stories, skin picking is a common correlate of BDD, particularly when the perceived physical defect is one's skin. BDD triggered by acne and other skin conditions can regularly lead to skin-picking behaviours in an attempt to 'smooth' the skin, as Joanna explains so eloquently in her story. Any alteration in our appearance, such as eczema or acne, can call to mind our sense of identity; who are we when the reflection in the mirror is no longer how we have historically viewed ourselves? The difficulty with skin conditions is that they can muddy the waters for a BDD diagnosis. BDD is diagnosed when the perceived defect is either slight or deemed to be a normal variation. Where, then, does this leave people with actual skin conditions of various forms and levels of intensity? Indeed, in one study, a significant proportion of people with moderate to severe acne met all other criteria for a BDD diagnosis, yet many of them had not received such a diagnosis due to the actual presence of their acne. Thankfully, clinicians are beginning to realise that people can indeed have BDD if they have an actual visible difference of some kind. You will come across a piece entitled 'A Mother's Story' in this book, for example, of a person born with a 'birth defect' who later went on to develop BDD.

In a bid to 'fix' the condition of the skin, many people in this book turned to skin picking in addition to various dermatological treatments, believing that when their skin cleared up everything would be all right. Sadly, this is rarely the case. More commonly in BDD, once the skin clears up, the focus of the BDD moves on to another aspect of the appearance, which makes perfect sense when we remember that BDD is a psychological problem, not a physical one.

Not everyone who has acne or other skin conditions goes on to develop BDD of course. In Dathen's compelling story you will read about how the greatest period of intensity of his BDD erupted *after* his acne cleared up. Dathen explains that he was in a much better state emotionally, in fact, when his skin was in a much poorer condition. BDD, at its heart, is not about appearances, which is a point we shall return to again and again in these stories. BDD is psychological and not physical in nature and is rooted, most commonly, in low self-esteem, insecure attachments, and traumas of a range of kinds.

Various treatment options and self-care practices are advised for compulsive skin picking, many of which centre on cognitive–behavioural therapy. CBT can help to raise awareness of what the skin-picking triggers might be and aid an ability to respond to these triggers in other ways. Other treatment options include acceptance and commitment therapy (ACT), medications such as SSRIs, and mindfulness-based practices including mindfulness-based cognitive therapy.

The Seeking of Cosmetic and Similar Procedures and Practices in BDD

In reading this book, you might notice that virtually all of the contributors describe the seeking of cosmetic products and/or medical procedures in order to 'fix' their perceived defect or defects. You will read about Minnie's surgery on her nose at the age of eighteen, Andrew's surgical 'pinning back' of his ears at the age of sixteen, and about Linzy's breast enlargement surgery (and her desire to have a second enlargement), among other similar stories. You will also read about the experiences of people being unable to think of little else aside from surgery and/or other cosmetic treatments. Helen describes being up until 4 a.m. researching cosmetic procedures on the internet and Hannah heartbreakingly explains how she yearned for cosmetic surgery as young as the age of nine in order to 'correct' her skin, to give just two examples.

It is unsurprising that people with a diagnosis of BDD, a facet of which is the wish to correct a perceived defect or defects, often seek out treatments such as these. In a 2001 study by Phillips and colleagues, 75% of a sample of 250 adults with BDD had sought cosmetic treatments and 66% had received them. Often the desire for these procedures brings with it a misplaced sense of hope; people with BDD regularly report immense hopefulness that the correction of their perceived defect(s) will enable them to experience less social anxiety, aid them in gaining greater self-esteem, and generally facilitate their ability to enjoy their lives. Sadly, these hopes more often than not fail to materialise following cosmetic and other similar procedures. In a 1993 study by Phillips and colleagues, only 4% of a sample of people with BDD who had received surgery felt that their procedure had been of any help to them. In another study, conducted by Veale in 2000, 16% of people with BDD who were questioned cited a worsening of their appearance-related distress after their cosmetic procedure. Shockingly, nine of the twenty-five participants in this study were so dissatisfied with the outcomes of their surgery that they went on to perform 'do-it-yourself' procedures at home.

Not everyone with BDD seeks out and receives cosmetic surgery, of course, although the figures are uncomfortably high. Dentistry and dermatology are two other frequently sought avenues. You will read about the time spent each day applying cream to his legs by Dominic during the height of his struggles, about how Danny started using whole tubs of anti-acne cream on a daily basis, and read Caroline's story of embarking on some invasive cosmetic dentistry to get rid of her self-called 'fangs', for example.

It is certainly worth repeating that cosmetic surgery and other cosmetic interventions such as dentistry and dermatology are rarely helpful to people struggling with BDD. Changing the physical appearance does not change the psychological issues underpinning BDD, which would have preceded any focus on the physical appearance. People with BDD would appear to become fixated on amending their physical appearance on account of pre-existing psychological battles such as low self-esteem, as we explored in the section on early childhood experiences. Most typically, the focus of the BDD shifts when one section of the appearance is deemed to have been 'fixed', or at least amended satisfactorily. You will read, for example, about how Minnie's focus of attention moved from her nose to her skin and hair after her cosmetic surgery, and about how Andrew also became acutely fixated on his skin following the pinning back of his ears.

A diagnosis of BDD points to the need for internal psychological and emotional struggles to be addressed and the BDD-associated behaviours to be amended. Once these areas have been attended to, people with a diagnosis of BDD report becoming more accepting, or even completely accepting, of their appearance and any defects they may have once believed, or even still believe, to be present, depending on their stage on the recovery journey. Indeed, one of the contributors to this volume, Carla-Mark Thompson, has even gone on to win beauty contests and to appear on national television. She explains, 'I now have the strength to say no to the negative thoughts and emotions before they escalate.'

Anxiety and Depression in BDD

Anxiety and depression often go hand-in-hand with BDD. In a 2004 study by Phillips and colleagues, people with BDD scored more highly on depression, anxiety, somatisation (the manifestation of psychological distress by the presentation of bodily symptoms), and anger–hostility than controls. People with BDD have high lifetime rates of psychiatric hospitalisation (48%), suicidal ideation (45–82%), and suicide attempts (22–24%). In the Interlude of the book you will read John's story about his mother-in-law, Tina, who took her own life after years of battling BDD. Such a story was an important inclusion in this volume to give an honest and complete picture of how severe BDD can become and to highlight the need for early diagnosis, intervention, and treatment. If you believe yourself or a loved one might be struggling with BDD, it is important, imperative even, to seek and receive help and support. Tina's story serves as a tragic reminder both that BDD has one of the highest suicide rates of any mental illness and that loved ones are left with a heartbreaking legacy of grief and confusion. BDD absolutely can be moved beyond, as the rest of the stories in this volume so hopefully point to, yet BDD is not something to be taken lightly, to be swept under the carpet, or to be ignored.

The phenomenon of depression is currently divided up into several diagnostic categories in the *Diagnostic and Statistical Manual for Mental Disorders*. Clinical depression, or major depressive disorder, describes acute feelings of sadness, loss of interest in activities, sleep and appetite changes, guilt and hopelessness, fatigue or restlessness, difficulty with concentration, and suicidal ideation that persists for most of the day, almost every day, for at least two weeks. Experiences of depression, however, are on a spectrum and people with BDD could have anything from mild to major (clinical) depression. It is rare for people with BDD not to have any symptoms of depression at all. According to a 2002 study by Nierenberg and colleagues, BDD is frequently co-morbid with major depression and is associated with an earlier age of onset of depression and longer duration of depressive episodes.

You will come across numerous stories of people struggling with depression, alongside and intertwined with their BDD, in this book. For example, you will read a mother's account of her daughter, who, soon after her twelfth birthday, began to struggle with depression and eating issues which later seemed to lead to her BDD, though it could have equally been the case that the BDD was there from the beginning and itself was a precursor to the depression and eating issues. You will also read about how Ben's viewing of himself in the mirror would lead to severe bouts of depression and about how Megan was diagnosed with BDD at the age of fifteen after years of depression beforehand.

Anxiety is another common correlate of BDD. Anxiety is described as a feeling of unease, such as worry or fear, that can be mild, severe, or anything in between. Everyone has feelings of anxiety at some point in their lives but when this anxiety becomes overwhelming and/or constant enough to affect daily life, it may be diagnosed as an anxiety disorder such as generalised anxiety disorder (GAD). Anxiety is the main symptom of several other diagnoses, including panic disorder, phobias, post traumatic stress disorder (PTSD), and social anxiety disorder. Anxiety comprises both physical and psychological symptoms, which vary considerably between people, but often include feelings of worry and restlessness, difficulties in concentration, insomnia, heart palpitations, and dizziness, to name just a few. Again, you will read many examples in these stories of anxiety going hand-in-hand with BDD. You will read about how Rachel's social anxiety was intensely tangled up with her BDD and about how Andrew's bullying experiences led to a spiralling of his anxiety, which then fed into his BDD, to give just two examples.

Given the core features of BDD, it is perhaps unsurprising that anxiety and depression should be so commonly interwoven with this struggle. The notion of an unacceptable appearance defect, which is often experienced by the person as making them unworthy of attention and love, can cause immense feelings of despair and catastrophic episodes of anxiety at the thought of having to face people with the perceived defect. In order to avoid the anxiety of other people seeing and judging their appearance, a person with BDD might become completely housebound, or hide away for extended periods of the week, month, or year. Others use clothing and/or camouflage techniques such as make-up, or only come out after daylight hours, as was the case for Charlotte, who writes movingly about only socialising in the dark in her story. Self-isolation can further feed into feelings of depression that might already be there, thus becoming a self-amplifying cycle. Support for people with BDD, therefore, would seemingly do well to address any anxiety and depression present. It is often the case that as the BDD-associated behaviours are tackled, anxiety and depression diminish over time. It is important to mention, however, that anxiety can initially be heightened in the early stages of treatment, particularly through exposure exercises, though this is a temporary increase that rapidly decreases when the person's fears are not realised. It is also commonly the case that if the anxiety and depression are addressed and diminished, the BDD-associated behaviours, thoughts, and rituals tend to reduce also.

Disordered Eating in the Context of BDD

In her compelling contribution to this book, Caroline explains how she was anorexic for a brief period of her life and then bulimic before going on to develop BDD. Beverley also describes a similar journey. This relationship between disordered eating behaviours and BDD comes up repeatedly in these stories and it is often astounding at BDD support groups just how many people are also currently attending eating disorder support groups elsewhere, or have struggled with an eating disorder in the past.

There are many diagnosable categories of disordered eating behaviour and many people engage in aberrant eating behaviours without ever receiving a formal diagnosis. Given the high levels of shame so often embedded within these behaviours, many people could fail to seek and receive the help they need in much the same way that BDD can regularly go undiagnosed for many years. Carla, for example, describes her intense battle with calorie restriction, excessive exercise, and binge–purge cycles in her story, for which she never received help on account of how carefully she kept her behaviours hidden.

The scope of this book does not allow for an in-depth discussion about the various presentations of eating disorders, which are numerous, highly complex, and multi-faceted. What follows, therefore, is a very brief summary of some of the most common of the eating disorder diagnoses. Anorexia is categorised by calorie restriction leading to a significant loss of body weight. Excessive exercise in a bid to further burn up calories is a common correlate. In bulimia, individuals attempt to intentionally remove calories from the body via various purging behaviours, such as self-induced vomiting and excessive exercise. Often, people with this diagnosis remain at a "safe" weight. Binge-eating disorder is diagnosed when an individual repeatedly eats large quantities of food in short periods of time without attempting to remove the calories from the body. Orthorexia, a newer diagnosis which is becoming more common in our health and appearance obsessed society, is characterised by the cutting out of entire food groups in a bid to eat 'cleanly' or 'healthily'. Emotional distress is present in each of these diagnoses, which are only the tip of the iceberg in terms both of categories of eating disorders and individual presentations of these struggles.

It is perhaps unsurprising that BDD and disordered eating would have such a close relationship, given that they are both focused on the physical appearance while concurrently being steeped in shame and low self-esteem. While some of the contributors to this book restricted or amended their food intake to achieve a different weight or level of muscle mass, others moved towards distressing eating habits for other reasons, such as to ensure that their skin remained clear. The avoidance of food in particular can also serve, as Lauren explains so succinctly, as a means of taking some control over one's life and a method of distracting oneself from painful feelings related to the BDD.

Research by Joshua Hrabosky and colleagues (2009) indicates that there might be some key similarities and differences in the presentation of eating disorders and BDD. Both disorders are characterised by similar levels of body dissatisfaction and preoccupation and sufferers of each are more likely than controls to engage in maladaptive coping strategies for managing body image distress. The main difference comes, however, with the focus of distress. People diagnosed with eating disorders are more likely to be distressed by their weight and shape, while people with BDD are typically more focused on other, non-weight related, aspects of their appearance. There can, however, be multiple overlaps, as these stories so strongly testify to.

In a study conducted in 1998 by Rosen and Ramirez, forty-five women with a diagnosis of anorexia or bulimia were compared with fifty-one men and women with a diagnosis of BDD and fifty non-clinical controls. Again, the people diagnosed with eating disorders were mainly preoccupied with weight and shape, while the people with BDD had more diverse preoccupations and reported more negative self-evaluation and avoidance due to appearance. Importantly, however, both groups showed equally severe body image symptoms overall and experienced similar levels of low self-esteem, which were significantly higher or lower, respectively, in comparison to controls.

The invitation is, perhaps, to ask ourselves if the labels of 'eating disorder' and 'body dysmorphic disorder' are the important elements of this discussion. The vital point is, rather, perhaps, the emotions and self-beliefs underpinning the need to somehow change or 'perfect' the physical appearance. While the aim in many eating disorders is most commonly to reduce the weight of the body or to enhance musculature and the aim in BDD is to 'fix' a perceived defect or defects, the underlying agony is ultimately the same: the belief that one's physical appearance is something to be ashamed of, the notion that one is not good enough as one is, and the conviction that by somehow changing the physical body, one can become more 'beautiful', more accepted as a human being, and more worthy of love.

Treatment Options for BDD

People with BDD are often highly ashamed of their appearance-focused thoughts and behaviours. They might hide or deny their struggles and fail to seek psychiatric help on account of believing their issue to be an appearance-based and not a psychological one. People with BDD, therefore, are rarely diagnosed in a timely manner. When treatment is sought and received, however, outcomes can be extremely positive, which is something you will read about often throughout the stories contained in this volume.

The National Institute for Clinical Excellence (NICE) offers very clear guidelines for the treatment of BDD, which comes under the umbrella of obsessive–compulsive disorder (OCD) in the *Diagnostic and Statistical Manual for Mental Disorders (DSM)*. Two clear treatments for BDD are recommended by NICE: cognitive–behavioural therapy and selective serotonin reuptake inhibitors (SSRIs). As David Veale, the UK's leading expert in BDD, points out, there have not yet been any controlled trials to compare different treatments to determine which is the most effective or which treatment best suits which person. Trial and error, therefore, typically need to be employed in many, if not most, cases in terms of combinations of treatment, length and intensity of CBT, and level of medication.

Cognitive–behavioural therapy

Cognitive–behavioural therapy (CBT) is the gold standard psychosocial treatment for BDD in adults and has shown promise in adolescents. It is based on a structured programme of self-help so that a person can learn to change the way he thinks and acts. Unfortunately, many of the contributors to this volume were referred for general CBT in the first instance, as opposed to BDD-focused CBT. There are clear differences. Receiving the correct BDD-focused treatment is an absolutely vital element in terms of the odds of positive outcomes. In BDD-focused CBT, the person is helped to refocus his attention away from his physical appearance and to give up comparing his appearance with others while reducing his perpetual rumination. Through graded exposure exercises, people are helped to confront their fears without camouflage of any kind and to stop rituals and safety behaviours such as mirror-checking and excessive grooming. As one might expect, levels of anxiety often increase in the short term as the person is helped to move completely outside of his comfort zone. Over time, however, confronting the fears becomes easier and the anxiety, thus, gradually subsides.

CBT requires high levels of commitment and engagement, with extensive homework exercises, including exposure exercises (exposing oneself to one's fears, for example, leaving the house without sunglasses on) being the order of the day. As Tony explains in his story, he plans to have another round of CBT and really give the homework sessions one hundred per cent of his energy and attention, as he wonders if his lack of engagement was a primary reason his first round of CBT was felt to be largely unsuccessful. BDD-specific CBT is delivered as part of a stepped care approach, which aims to provide the most effective, but least intrusive, treatments appropriate to a person's needs. It assumes that the course of the disorder is monitored and referral to the appropriate level of care is made depending on the person's difficulties. Each step introduces additional interventions. The steps laid out by the NICE guidelines are shared below (more detail can be obtained from the NICE website).

Step One –   Awareness and Recognition;
Step Two –   Assessment;
Steps Three to Five –   Treatment Options (brief, individual CBT or group CBT, SSRIs or more intensive CBT, SSRIs and CBT combined).

Anti-depressant medication

Selective serotonin reuptake inhibitors (SSRIs) are the recommended medication option for people struggling with BDD. According to Katharine Phillips among other experts, the dose often needs to be in the high range and taken daily for at least twelve weeks to determine its effectiveness. At the first International Conference for BDD in May 2015, Phillips explained that the most common reason for SSRI medication being ineffective in BDD is that the dose is set too low. SSRIs are a type of anti-depressant medication and can, therefore, also improve levels of motivation and engagement in CBT. People are strongly advised to stop medication only under medical advice and supervision.

A number of people in this book cite SSRI medication as having been useful to them: Hannah describes how she needed to try a number of SSRIs before she found one that worked for her, while an anonymous contributor noticed a clear improvement in her son after trying SSRIs for the first time. Lucy describes how medication, CBT, and the support from her family and friends resulted in her BDD thoughts and related depression slowly diminishing, and Joanna also found the combination of CBT and medication very helpful. Amanda explains, 'For me, the key to treatment was finding the right medication accompanied by having a good therapist.' Other people explain how they found medication useful initially, with its benefits diminishing over time, such as Annette, who writes about the 'massive difference' she initially felt with fluoxetine, then experiencing the 'wearing off' over time, as she puts it. Again, it is useful, perhaps, to remember that medication needs to be at the right dose to be effective and that different SSRIs work in different ways for different people. As David Veale points out, medication might also have side effects for some people. In these cases, the dose can be adjusted or an alternative drug may be prescribed.

You will also read stories in this volume of other treatment options or self-care practices being very useful to people battling BDD. Joanna perceives yoga to have been the most important element in her emergence from BDD, for example, while Minnie was greatly supported by self-help books on both the subject of BDD and on self-acceptance in general. Liz found greatest solace in creating artwork, Beverley a deep sense of homecoming in Christian healing and compassion-focused therapy, while Danny describes a great sense of transformation in serving and supporting others, to cite just a few of the inspiring examples expounded in these pages.

* * *

The NICE guidelines clearly state that, in the treatment of people with BDD, sufferers, family members, or carers should be provided with good information, both verbal and written, about the disorder, its likely causes, its course and its treatment. The stories in this volume sadly show that such information-sharing is rarely the case, perhaps given the relative unknownness of BDD in comparison to other mental health disorders and the lack of knowledge and training in BDD for GPs, who are often the first port of call for struggling families. You can find a leaflet describing BDD and the treatment options available, which can be taken to GPs and other medical professionals, in the Avenues of Support and Further Reading section at the back of this book.

Recovery from BDD:
A Very Real Possibility

A point of discussion that often comes up in BDD support groups is whether BDD is something a person must learn to live with or whether full recovery is truly possible. You will come across differing opinions within the stories contained in this book. While some of the contributors believe that their BDD will always be with them to some extent and the best they can hope for is to be increasingly able to manage their condition, others believe that full recovery from BDD is absolutely possible and would, indeed, describe themselves as recovered from BDD.

Mental health professionals working in the area of BDD also have contrary opinions on this subject, with some believing that the ultimate aim of therapy for BDD is to find ways of best living with the condition while others hold a firm conviction that BDD can be moved beyond entirely. Given the stories of those who believe they are recovered in this book, it feels reasonable to assume that absolute recovery from BDD is indeed possible. This would appear to entail a reversal of the belief in any perceived defect or defects, or a complete alteration in levels of distress related to the perceived defect(s), and a return to a sense that one's physical appearance is acceptable and even pleasing to the self and to others.

We warmly invite you to welcome the possibility that full recovery from BDD is possible as you read through the stories in this volume. If some of our contributors were able to completely move beyond their struggle with BDD, often after many years of suffering, there is no reason to believe that such a possibility does not exist for you or for your loved one also.

THE STORIES

Why Share these Stories?

In the midst of a battle with body dysmorphic disorder (BDD), it would appear to be, in many cases, all too easy to lose hope. The stories in this book poignantly demonstrate, however, that it is wholly possible to move beyond BDD and learn once again to respect and love yourself and fully enjoy your life.

These are stories of courage, of gutsy determination, and of heroic refusal to give in or give up. Within these pages you will meet people who might have some similar experiences to yourself or to someone you love with BDD. They might have experienced self-loathing, obsessional thoughts and behaviours, unrealistic perceptions, overwhelming emotions, social anxieties, self-inflicted isolation, and the gripping fear that so often accompanies BDD. In so many ways, each of their stories is entirely unique and yet you will find many common threads and facets of these stories that particularly echo your own. Too many of us for too long have felt like the only monster in a world full of princes and princesses, perhaps finding it difficult to imagine that anyone else could possibly understand how we feel or appreciate the intense pain of our existence. Yet, there are many others who would also give anything to feel visually acceptable and, therefore, worthy of attention and love. The core message of this book is that you are not alone.

To receive a diagnosis of BDD, a person must be extensively preoccupied with a perceived defect or defects in their appearance for more than one hour each day, which present to the outside eye as imperceptible or nothing more than a normal physical variation. Such diagnostic criteria, however, is only the tip of the iceberg, a fact to which these stories bear such powerful testimony. BDD is most commonly focused around the face (especially the nose, facial skin, hair, eyes, mouth, jaw, and chin), although any body part may be involved, with the preoccupation often extending to more than one area of the body. One is almost equally likely to be diagnosed with BDD whether male or female, and such a diagnosis sadly equates to catastrophically high levels of distress, chronically low mood, and crippling anxiety. Tragically, BDD has one of the highest suicide rates of any mental illness, although many people, as we shall see throughout these pages, find a way to manage and even overcome their BDD and go on to live happy and deeply fulfilling lives.

At support groups run by the Body Dysmorphic Disorder Foundation, a common lamentation is that many health professionals have a limited understanding of BDD and its correlates, with a significant number seeming to have no knowledge of the disorder at all. It can take immense amounts of courage and emotional strength to ask for help and be particularly tormenting to have one's experiences brushed aside or attributed to vanity. BDD, rather, is the polar opposite to vanity, with sufferers commonly abhorring their appearance to such an extent that shame permeates the very essence of their existence.

Many people with BDD seek help from other professionals before they come to the attention of mental health services, due to poor insight about the nature of their condition, which is commonly viewed by the sufferer as being of a physical as opposed to psychological origin. As we have already discussed, people with BDD typically believe their intense anxiety and sadness to be due to the appearance of their physical body, while the true root of their distress is psychological in nature, embedded within various life experiences and anomalous self-beliefs.

A key theme you will find running through the entirety of this book is that of a move away from attributing one's suffering to the physical appearance of the body and gradually coming to realise that the perceived ugliness and accompanying self-identified defect(s) are not, in fact, reality. The reality of the situation of BDD, rather, is that a person sees defects and physical hideousness where none exists, or that those perceived 'defects' are simply attributable to normal variation. Every person, whoever he or she is and whatever his or her history, has unique physical attributes that *could* be viewed as abhorrent, yet not every person tumbles into the topsy-turvy world of BDD. BDD is not about acne, crooked noses, dark circles under the eyes, thinning hair, bowed legs, or any other such thing. BDD is about painfully low self-esteem, identity struggles, undermining life experiences and a sense that one is unlovable no matter what one does and no matter how hard one tries.

If you feel overwhelmed by a sense of your own physical defect or defects and believe these appearance phenomena to be the source of your pain, we ask humbly that you entertain the possibility that you might be mistaken as you read through these stories. Allow the jury to be momentarily out, enable an alternative possible reality to stand side by side with your current schemas for the duration of these pages. The people whose voices speak through these chapters were, too, once fully convinced that every iota of their suffering would evaporate if their physical appearance changed. They came gradually to understand, however, as you shall read, that such a belief is only ever a decoy from a deeper pain that has absolutely nothing to do with the size of one's nose or the state of one's skin. When we tackle BDD as a problem that is emotional and psychological in nature, we engage with the true source of our tears and afford ourselves the opportunity to find an identity beyond the reflection we see in the mirror. The possibility then opens up for us to experience freedom from BDD and a broader, truer sense of self.

'The face in the mirror', by Liane Piper.

Amanda Hawkins

Nothing traumatic happened in my childhood and I had a good upbringing. When I started getting feelings of anxiety and engaging in safety behaviours, such as wearing the same clothes every day, I wasn't sure where it had come from. I have often heard in support groups that people's BDD had stemmed from childhood trauma, but this wasn't the case for me. When I was thirteen, it all got too much. I stopped going to school and was diagnosed with BDD as well as social anxiety. My school was a highly competitive and pressured environment and that, on top of my feelings of ugliness and panic, tipped me over the edge. However, my BDD seemed to have stemmed from primary school. I got acne earlier than anyone else in my school, which made me feel different to everybody else. I also had a fringe straight across my forehead, which no one else had. This was the first time I became aware of my appearance and felt different to others. At that time the 'popular' group of girls were bullying others, calling them ugly. Although I was not directly targeted, I think this experience introduced me to the fact that people could be judgemental and that people notice how others look.

The main areas of focus for my BDD have been my hair, skin, facial features, and clothes. Although clothes are not a part of my body *per se*, my

BDD made me obsessed with wearing the same outfit every day, sometimes for six months at a time. I constantly had to check my appearance and clothing in mirrors, shop windows, and the reflection of my phone screen. For a while I left the house only when I was going to therapy. I became very isolated, but fortunately had a few good friends that I kept in contact with from school. I returned to school with very poor attendance but managed to complete my GCSEs. Avoidance has always been my go-to safety behaviour. In the short term it seems like a good solution. It temporarily makes the anxiety go away and I feel as though I can breathe again. But in the long term, it perpetuates the BDD, making the anxiety even worse the next time. Avoidance is still something I am working on today.

Nothing my mum said to comfort me would help. I would just get angry with her every time she said, 'You look beautiful', or when she would disagree with me when I was complaining about my appearance. There was nothing she could say that would make me feel better or change my mind. My relationship with my parents became strained and my mum left her job to tend to my needs full-time.

Our first port of call was the GP, who then referred me for cognitive–behavioural therapy (CBT) through the National Health Service (NHS). Instead, I saw a therapist privately, as the waiting list on the NHS was so long; this is, unfortunately, all too often the case. I have seen a number of therapists, some good, some not so good, and some really not very good at all. Looking back, I would recommend that anyone looking for a therapist should make sure the one they choose is familiar with BDD and has some experience in treating it. Some therapists, and especially a lot of GPs, still haven't heard of BDD. I have also seen psychiatrists and been on a number of medications. For me, the key to treatment was finding the right medication accompanied by having a good therapist and doing the homework they set. I felt hopeless for a long time, wanting a magic pill to make me better. It took me over two years to recognise that if I wanted things to change, I was the only one who could make those changes happen. That meant really participating in therapy, which is not easy! Cognitive–behavioural therapy is the most commonly recommended treatment for BDD and it has helped me considerably; however, I am currently working with a therapist who combines a number of different treatment approaches. Once I noticed that I had made some recovery, it was such a relief. I finally felt that I might actually be able to get better and would not necessarily have to resort to suicide.

Telling people that I had, and still have, BDD has elicited mixed responses. Very few people seem to have even heard of it. I have heard from other sufferers that some people see it as vanity or self-obsession. Other people seem to dismiss the problem, saying, 'Just get over it.' However, the majority of people I have told have responded very positively and supportively. Sharing my problems with others has helped them to understand what I'm going through. It is good to have their support, even if they're just there to listen or to distract me. From sharing what I was going through, I discovered that a vast amount of others I knew had been dealing with mental health problems themselves.

I now see my BDD as a mental illness rather than thinking I am truly ugly. Regardless of how I actually look, believing that I am ugly is not helpful to me and is only hurting me. Thanks to some steady recovery, I now feel better about my appearance. Some days I am still not able to leave the house, but other days I actually like how I look, which in the early stages of treatment I would have never expected! I am now eighteen years old and in college. I have a good relationship with my family and my boyfriend and am able to enjoy some aspects of life. I am still struggling, but I have come a long way and will, I hope, continue to do so. I am now looking forward to my future, and hope to go into clinical psychology as a career.

To others who have BDD, I definitely would say that I feel for you. BDD is a bully and I do not underestimate how awful you might feel. As hard as it is to do, recovery can only happen if you try your utmost and agree to try to tackle it. Good treatment is important. Going to face-to-face support groups run by the BDD Foundation and online groups run by OCD Action has also been very helpful for me over the past year. It has made me feel less alone and has introduced me to people who understand what I'm going through, on a level that people without BDD can't. As they often say in the support groups, 'Together we are stronger.'

Amanda Hawkins.

Andrew Hall

I was raised in a loving, supportive home by my parents, Louise and Steve, and shared a playful and mischievous childhood with my sister, Becky. While closer to my mother during my younger years, I grew to develop an excellent bond with my father during my adolescence, from whom I've learnt numerous life lessons and who has always provided me with cherished perspective. We were very lucky to be raised in financial security, and our small family has always been very stable, functioning as a solid base for me from which to launch into adult life.

While I always enjoyed school and took great pride in my academic achievements, I look back and realise that in reality I suffered extensive bullying related to my ears from primary school through to my A-levels. I would hear certain phrases every day, from the good old-fashioned 'big ears', to 'bat ears', or even the inventive 'FA Cup' (accompanied at least once with being dragged off my feet in a faux 'celebration', one ear in each hand). I wonder if, over time, I simply got used to such treatment; it was such a frequent occurrence that, all truth being told, I never really considered it abnormal.

Despite these experiences, I have always had many friends. Although there have been those that have come and gone, my friendships have always proved an enormous help to me during times of need. One of my saddest memories during recovery from BDD, however, was meeting my favourite secondary school teacher in the street. She seemed to completely disregard my illness in favour of telling me that I must go to university as it was 'the most important thing.' My brain, however, certainly disagreed.

I can distinctly remember the moment my BDD 'began', so to speak. I decided when I began my A-levels at sixteen that I would have my ears surgically pinned back as I wanted to cut my hair, which I had always worn long as a 'shield' in a bid to fit in. After the surgery, when the bandages were removed, I remember immediately thinking that something was not right as I stared into the mirror, flooded with feelings of disappointment and confusion. I had honestly believed this surgery would fix all of my problems, but the reality was that it opened a door to something far darker than I could have ever anticipated. Prior to this point, while I didn't like my ears, I simply hid them and went about my days. Once the surgery was over, and my dissatisfaction began to take root, the obsessions and the compulsions began. Things developed slowly at first. I would slip out of lessons just to look at myself in the mirror, checking my ears, and rapidly became more obsessed with my hair. I would always be late for school, as I would be flitting about in front of a mirror, or several mirrors, trying to make things 'perfect'. I became highly receptive to people's comments and criticisms, and any grey areas would, of course, be deemed insults. What magnified the issue further was an irrational belief that I would 'rule the school', as I had believed I had done at secondary (which, in reality, was just rose-tinted, wishful thinking). As my surgery had made things so much worse and my 'rise to power' had never occurred, I began to be more and more aware of how alienated I felt. I became jealous of old school friends who had moved beyond me socially. I was continuously comparing my appearance to that of my friends in order to fit in, with hopes of matching them on the social hierarchy. It never happened, and I sacrificed a great deal of integrity: I changed the way I spoke, the way I stood, the clothes I wore. But, looking back, the people I envied and those whose company I craved were really, in all honesty, not my cup of tea!

Interestingly, at the time, I remember distinctly believing that I was just a little bit more concerned with my appearance than other people. I had never heard of body dysmorphic disorder and was blissfully ignorant of the reality. In terms of emotions, I felt frustrated, deeply embarrassed, and ashamed of my obsessions. I thought I was vain, and people would tell me so when they caught me stealing a look at my appearance in the mirror. Children and young people, who, of course, know no better, can be so cruel. I have distinct memories of seemingly endless jibes concerning the critique of my hairstyle, my clothes, and almost every aspect of identity. It felt relentless, and my anxiety began to spiral as a consequence.

Aside from the surgery (I had a second surgery at the age of twenty-one), I would engage in numerous concealment behaviours, ranging from hiding the primary perceived flaw with hair of varying styles (washing it, styling, rewashing it again and repeating until my head was raw) to attempting to 'fix' other aspects of my appearance that would temporarily become targeted (such as my skin), or making changes as a means of desperately attempting to improve my overall satisfaction. I would meticulously clean and cleanse my skin, using various magnifying mirrors to seek out any imperfections. I would fake-tan my skin to appear less pallid, and then, of course, become horrified at the thought that somebody might notice. I would also use my mother's or sister's concealer and foundation at times, due to acne or just in an attempt to look 'healthier'. I had my teeth corrected with invisible braces at the age of twenty-one, as I felt that my clustered teeth restricted me from smiling freely. When I was at breaking point I remember spending a total of eight cumulative hours throughout the day checking my appearance and comparing myself to others, checking and re-checking, going through Facebook pictures of myself and other people, seeking out celebrity images to copy, all in an endless cycle that would leave me both exhausted and distressed.

In the past, my romantic life has been limited. This was undoubtedly due to low self-confidence and poor self-esteem. My only long-term relationship, which took place when I was eighteen, was, in reality, quite a reprieve from my symptoms. However, I can remember asking my girlfriend at the time various questions about what she thought of me, at which she would become frustrated, or just simply bewildered. My academics suffered as well. I simply couldn't focus on my A-levels, and my weekend work, while also a great distraction, was a minefield for my BDD. Any strenuous activity or heated environment would lead to the onset of panic. As I worked in a bakery, this proved extremely challenging. My friendships and family relationships, however, did not suffer in the same way. While some friendships dissipated due to my behaviour, I have undoubtedly formed some of the closest bonds of my life with those whom I shared my recovery with. My family, especially my father, were everything I needed and more, with their willpower, patience, and tremendous compassion.

I shared my concerns frequently with my family. Some people, of course, did not understand, and the clichés of 'get over it' or 'snap out of it' were uttered once or twice. One of my closest friends at Sixth Form told me that I was weird when I confided in him. Looking back, I don't blame other people for being who they were and reacting as they did, especially as so many of my friends were teenagers, and BDD is relatively unheard of in the mainstream to this day. However, there were, of course, those diamonds in the rough who held me up and provided support whenever I needed it. I am eternally grateful to them all, as they fanned the flames and helped me to focus on moving forward.

I went to several GPs over the course of my recovery, from initial contact and understanding my condition (I was formally diagnosed with BDD and general anxiety) to later specific referrals from consultants and psychiatrists. The experience was, of course, daunting at first. I felt that what I was divulging was so personal and specific that I would surely look ridiculous and might even be sectioned. However, it transpired that everything I was saying had been heard before and it was an overwhelming relief to be told that I was suffering from an illness that could be treated. It made me feel safe, assured, and hopeful. As time went by I built a strong relationship with my doctors, and, as a result, was able to tackle my illness with a powerful support network at my fingertips.

I received a wide variety of CBT treatments, from basic NHS 'Step 2' and 'Step 3' therapy, to more refined BDD-specific treatment. The initial and basic NHS therapy took place over six months and, while not especially effective in targeting the BDD symptoms, was very good at helping me come to terms with other areas of anxiety in my life. The private therapy I sought in the months afterwards lasted for only around eight to ten sessions before I realised that it was not going to be effective. However, the fact that I had received two sets of treatment and was taking simultaneous medication meant that, when it came to being referred for specialised NHS therapy soon after, I met the criteria. The following year I went to the University of Bath's specialist anxiety clinic, which proved to be highly effective. I learnt many useful techniques: flooding (such as washing my hair and leaving it as it was, or going out in public with my 'shields down'), systematic desensitisation (tackling a fear hierarchy), and exposure (having my appearance critiqued via video feedback from other students, and finding out that my fears weren't recognised). These techniques were all pivotal in my escape from the most distressing elements of my BDD. In fact, the work at Bath and the personal and highly specific approach to treatment meant that within three months I was on the road to long-term recovery. This therapy ended two years ago and I have continued to benefit from, adapt, and build on the treatment outcomes.

Many things have contributed to my recovery, and continue to contribute to my health today. Medication brought me to a level of functioning where I was able to effectively access life-changing CBT. I still take medication periodically to maintain a balanced state during times of stress, and this feels very good and healthy to me. Mindfulness, meditation, and talking with friends and family all help me to focus my mind on my simplest needs (breathing, relaxing), on the positive aspects of my life, and to vent my frustrations.

I researched BDD extensively, and while this may not have been entirely helpful due to the somewhat cold nature of literature on the internet, the insight proved essential in helping me to properly communicate my distress and subsequent needs to those around me. The bespoke anxiety therapy I received from Bath proved a challenging process; waiting, hoping, facing setbacks and disappointments but, ultimately, the wait proved worthwhile and the outcome has been life changing. I deeply believe that the journey itself was essential, as it has helped to shape me into a resilient and informed human being, with a passion for helping others both like and unlike myself.

After much reflection, I now believe that I developed BDD as a result of the bullying I suffered in childhood and adolescence. The plastic surgery I later received acted as a trigger as it highlighted my dissatisfaction with my personal appearance, and a subsequent need to remedy the situation. In this sense, the surgery did not work, and as a result I felt cheated, and that my appearance was not as 'perfect' as I thought it should be post surgery. This pushed my symptoms into full throttle and began a vicious and self-destructive downward spiral.

However, following the unforeseen negative consequences of my second surgery, I began to realise that the psychological aspect was the definitive problem, that unhelpful past experiences were clouding my insight, and that maintenance behaviours were exacerbating/perpetuating a problem beyond measure or reason. Support from friends, family, and professionals, alongside informational resources, helped me to identify what I was suffering from (down to the specific thought and behavioural patterns) and to find ways to remedy the problem.

These days, I am now far, far more satisfied with my appearance. The therapy I have received has significantly realigned my sense of reality. I can now confidently say that I feel as if I am an attractive person far more often than not, but I also clearly see how important I am as an individual in other, deeper, and far more meaningful ways! While there are those days when BDD 'blips' interfere, everyone has those moments to some degree and I now know that they will pass. I am more than just ears, skin, and teeth. I am a human being with empathy, passion, compassion, love, and worth.

Where BDD or any mental illness is concerned, awareness is key. It is essential. The stigma surrounding mental health and body image must be challenged if change is to occur. Too often people are seen as vain, when in reality the opposite is true. I find this ironic and frustrating in equal measure, as we live in a society defined by obsessional beauty standards, endless advertising and sensory overload. Our society demands perfection, yet, when people become obsessed, they are treated as vain, self-absorbed, and often ridiculed. While I cannot force society to change, I think it is extremely important to raise awareness of the consequences, campaign for change, and offer compassion and hope to those affected.

I am older now, a bit wiser, far more informed, and, above all, rational. I understand what happened to me in youth to cause my illness, and I understand how to manage residual symptoms. I have always been interested in psychology, and I am now close to completing my degree. My comprehension of how the brain works has helped me to understand myself and others to a higher degree. Sometimes, when I struggle, I keep this in mind (although these times are so rare now!). These days I pursue education, work, hobbies, and relationships (both romantic and otherwise) with far greater ease than ever before. My therapy can be applied in so many ways, and gives me so much strength in those darker moments, which are far lighter than before.

I am proud of myself for continuing to challenge my insecurities and problems, and for seeking out ways to better myself. I think it is especially important to embrace the understanding that mental health is just like any other illness and it should not be ignored. You cannot ignore wobbles: it is a challenge to face them, but it is worth the struggle!

I am so grateful for those I love, as they offer me so much love in return. It is all about using your experiences to better yourself and others, seeing the positive aspects of what we experience and applying this to our daily lives.

I am looking forward to graduating, possibly pursuing a career in education (potentially in relation to mental health), having my own home, and eventually a family. I am also far more open to experiences than ever before. I look forward to seeing what adventures today and tomorrow brings, keeping in mind that you never know who you might meet, or what might be around the corner. I know that sometimes we all have difficult moments, but there is always tomorrow!

Do not give up. You are not alone, and you can do this. 'Thoughts do not mean facts': your brain and all of its chemistry can confuse you and convince you that life is hopeless or that you cannot survive this. I did, and you most certainly can. Fight against the depression, keep yourself busy and build up from the little things piece by piece (the little things are the most important). If something seems too much, come back to it later. Rest, eat, have a nice warm shower, read a book, or watch a film. Become engrossed in reality, not illness. Go and be with nature, as a very influential therapist once told me. Spend some time with animals, with loved ones, friends. Remember that sometimes people won't understand, but give them time. People change, you change. Give yourself time to recover, reflect, and, most importantly, to move forward. Some people say that they don't need medication or therapy, but I think it is worth exploring different options. Try different approaches, and never give up! You are worth it; we are all worth it. I promise you that.

Andrew Hall with his father, Stephen.

Annette Loren

I grew up in a family home with my mum, dad, and two older brothers. I attended an all-girls' private school and was very happy there until around the age of seven, at which time my mum and dad split up. Up until that point, I don't really recall any unhappy memories.

My mum was always there for us and was an immensely devoted mother. My dad was very work-orientated and I don't really have many childhood memories of him other than his driving me to school. When my parents split up I was too young, I think, to understand what was going on. What I do know is that my mum left my dad for my step-dad, who we later moved in with. My brothers stayed with my dad at the family home.

I believe that my problems started to build from this early point in my life, although at times I do wonder if I was somehow born with BDD already dormant within me.

My step-dad bullied me from the very beginning. He criticised me and put me down until I moved out of home at the age of twenty-six. It started off with name-calling: 'sparrow legs' and 'elephant' were two common ones. He also made fun of my name. He would purposefully leave me out and belittle me in front of others. He used to play mind games with me and would even scare me by saying that I was making my mum seriously ill. He suppressed my personality and darkened every room he walked into. I lived in constant dread of seeing or being around him. I could go on forever about his many unkindnesses, but I imagine you get the idea.

My brother was hospitalised with severe OCD at some point after the split. He moved in with us and was extremely poorly. He was obsessed with looking in the mirror and was constantly comparing himself with me. He asked for reassurance continually and I found that I had to grow up very fast in order to cope with his illness. I did my very best to look after him. I would help him when he self-harmed in particular. My brother was my idol and I absolutely adored him. When he was taken into hospital I was utterly devastated. Furthermore, I was left to deal with my step-dad on my own.

I moved to a new school after the break-up. It was a mixed-sex state school and different in every way to the private school I had previously attended. Many aspects took a great deal of getting used to. I was very sensitive throughout school and struggled a lot with friendship groups. I was often bullied and easily influenced by my peers. At around the age of thirteen, I became part of a popular group at school and found a bit of confidence in myself. I became very sociable and had a string of boyfriends. I have memories of keeping a daily diary about wanting and needing to be liked.

It is hard to be exact but I think I remember having my first obsessional thought at around the age of seven or eight. My dad, my step-mum and step-sister and I were on holiday in Cephalonia and I was sharing a bedroom with my step-sister. There was a large mirror in the room and I remember catching sight of my step-sister's reflection and feeling a pinch of worry flood over me as we didn't look quite the same. I was very bony and my bones protruded in comparison to hers. I instantly felt as though something must be wrong with me and became fascinated with female appearances and the bodies of celebrities from that moment onwards.

Very quickly, make-up became my new best friend. I spent so much money on face creams and lotions even when I was very young. I remember having my hair permed (it was very fashionable at the time) and putting a lot of mousse and hairspray on it, trying to make it perfect. I am unsure of what I did wrong, but I remember my step-father hiding all of my hair-styling products on one occasion for a whole week as a punishment. I was a wreck. I suddenly felt so small and embarrassed leaving the house and was acutely aware of how I looked, feeling the need to explain to everyone why I looked the way I did.

My concentration has been affected my whole life by BDD. School and work alike have suffered due to my inability to take in outside information, since I am constantly processing the BDD thoughts and compulsions, which take up so much mental energy. I have actually nearly crashed my car on several occasions due to having to check my appearance in the car mirror. As a passenger in a car, I find it almost impossible to stop pulling the visor down to look into the mirror and check how I look.

On average, I think about 90% of my day is spent thinking about how I look. I still try to function as normally as I can, especially now that I have a two-year-old child. When I had my baby two years ago, I genuinely thought that my BDD thoughts would subside as I wouldn't physically have time to worry about my appearance. Somehow, the BDD thoughts still manage to fit themselves in, which can make life overwhelming at times. I am very aware that life is short and so very precious. Despite this, I still spend much of my spare time researching corrective surgery and fad pills and creams.

I am not somebody who plays the victim. In fact, I can count on one hand the number of people I have confided in and, even when I do share with the people who are close to me, I hold back on expressing the severity of it all. I am very worried about people thinking that I am vain when in fact the opposite is true. My rational mind knows that it is not achieving anything by constantly looking into the mirror, but the BDD side of me cannot ignore or let go of the obsession with my appearance. I spend hours staring and picking at my skin. Sometimes I worry myself so much about how I look that I make myself sick and have panic attacks. I see so many beautiful women around me and am always looking out for people with the same physical faults as I perceive myself to have, but I cannot find anyone. Without even realising it, I can sometimes badger my friends and family for reassurance but there is no right answer they can give since BDD is not pacified by rationality.

I'm thirty-four years old now and have a fear of what getting older will do to my appearance. I am scared of my wrinkles worsening, my face drooping and my eyes sagging. Sometimes the aspects I focus on are changing all the time. Today, for example, I am struggling with the appearance of my forehead but tomorrow it might be something else. Today I feel that my forehead is too big, that I should perhaps get a fringe. I also notice today that my eyes are dark and have bags under them, that my skin is too pale, and that the lines from my nose to my mouth are deeper. My teeth also look more yellow than they did yesterday. There is little break from these BDD thoughts. Most nights I even dream about my appearance. I'm haunted day and night and my brain is so tired. I have so many family and friends and yet so often I feel completely isolated, entirely alone.

I have found that keeping busy does help to keep my mind distracted from my appearance somewhat. The task has to be very captivating, otherwise the BDD thoughts creep in and I cannot concentrate.

I have attempted to confide in my mum and husband but it is just too difficult for them to understand. I try to reason with myself that I have a psychological problem and not a physical one. Sometimes I can actually see my features change in front of my eyes while looking into the mirror. This can be very strange and frightening indeed.

Even when I was having contractions while in labour I topped up my make-up, crazy as this might sound to the outside ear. Sometimes I am actually scared that I might somehow pass this illness on to my child. He is my life and I recognise how deeply beautiful he is, yet sometimes I find myself worrying about his appearance and am afraid that he will come to look more like me as he gets older. I must admit to crying as I write these words about my gorgeous little child.

Over the years I have seen a number of hypnotherapists, psychotherapists, and independent counsellors. My personal experience with different GPs has been awful, as they had no knowledge of BDD. Even the CBT therapist I was referred to by the GP was not familiar with BDD and I had to educate her about its symptoms. The therapist I saw for a year while I was pregnant, however, was a great help to me. I don't believe she cured me in any way, but being able to speak about my appearance struggles with someone who was completely impartial was a huge relief. After trying what I knew to be every available avenue to me, I finally resorted to medication – fluoxetine. Initially, I felt a massive difference. I started taking it in September 2015 and in the October I went on a family holiday. For the first time for as long as I can remember I was able to go into the swimming pool. I even walked to the edge without a towel wrapped around me. I wasn't even waist-deep (I hate my hips) and I played in the splash pool with my son. It was one of the happiest times of my life. My husband was in complete shock.

I wanted that holiday and those feelings of freedom to last forever. Sadly, the early effects of the medication have worn off, although it does continue to make some difference and things are better than they were at my lowest times. I have now at least had a glimpse into what life can be like without a constant battle with BDD and I have hope that I can return to this place of greater recovery.

It took a lot of bravery, but recently I went to an open support group. I'm glad that I went and found, again, that talking helped a lot. It was not a BDD-specific group and I was the only one there with BDD, which made it much harder. Again, I found myself having to explain the illness, all the while worrying that people would not understand.

I strive to be a positive role model for my son and to teach him never to give up. We have to believe in ourselves and know that we can get through anything. I hope and dream to be able to educate others and to help them through this crippling illness. I also dream, one day, to see what others say they can see in me – beauty, inside and out.

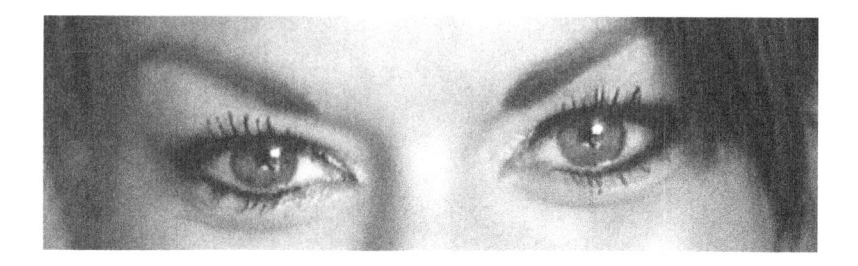

Annette Loren – eyes.

Becca Forsyth

What is BDD? What does BDD feel like? These are two questions I am often asked when I begin to tell people about this evil illness I suffer with.

I will often answer their questions by asking them if they can see a black cat beside me. They cannot of course. 'There is nothing there', they say. I explain that this is what BDD is like for me. I see something that nobody else can see. To me the black cat is real but, to everyone else, it is nothing more than a mirage.

I see the deformed Becca, the ugly Becca, the less-than-perfect Becca. Others insist that the things I see are not there, that they are not real. Often this leads me to question myself. Am I mad? Or are people lying to me?

BDD is an evil and sad illness that has taken me to the point of contemplating suicide. The BDD voice inside my head tells me that I don't deserve to live. It whispers that I am unworthy of love and will be alone forever.

Accepting that I have this illness is not easy some days. Sometimes I think I'm not ill and am just ugly.

I was officially diagnosed with BDD when I was twenty-four years old. My troubles, however, began from the early age of fourteen when I developed bulimia nervosa. I started to control my food in order to deal with some very emotional circumstances at the time. To me, it seems that both my bulimia and my BDD stem from a combination of emotional factors, rooted in the particular ways in which my mind seems to work. It is my understanding that I was born with certain characteristics that predisposed me to BDD. It just took a trigger to ignite the flame, a series of emotional circumstances I found impossible to cope with.

I can clearly remember being obsessed with my hips in particular during my adolescent years. I still have huge issues with this part of my body, often feeling as though my hips are too big and don't fit with the rest of my body.

The first thing I think of when I wake up and the last thing before I sleep is how I look. It rules my day and my life. I have cried myself to sleep so many times. I've prayed for something to take this away from me.

BDD has taken everything from me: friendships, relationships, and so many possible happy memories. In their place have been many years, suicidal thoughts, difficult emotions and tremendous pain.

It really is a terrible illness that has not only had a huge impact on me but on my wonderful family and friends too.

I'm very lucky to have an amazing mum and dad who, through everything, have never given up on me or stopped believing that one day I will be free. I can't even begin to imagine how much harder my life would be without their support. My illness has affected them deeply. There is nothing they want more than to see me happy.

There have been times, of course, when my friends and family have been frustrated. It is a difficult illness to understand and I do often try to imagine how it must be for them.

I suppose I sometimes get angry because if I had a physical illness such as cancer, I wouldn't be questioned and might even have some sympathy. There seems to be very little sympathy out there for BDD. It can be hard for some people to believe that it is a real illness. Along the way I have been called vain, selfish and an attention-seeker. I wonder why this illness should be seen as any different to any other.

When I finally found a support group at the Priory Hospital I finally found people who were speaking my language. As I looked around the room I couldn't believe how normal everyone looked and how much pain they were in on account of their BDD. They had the very same fears as me, centred around the belief that they were not ill but simply ugly. Meeting these people has helped me to know for certain that BDD is a real illness and absolutely exists.

It seems to me that meeting others with the same struggles can be the best kind of therapy. How can you understand something you haven't experienced yourself?

So, where do I stand today? I accept (most days) that I do have an illness and know that I will have to continue to fight for some time. BDD makes me a very strong person who has to fight for my place in this world. I know there is a part of me, the ill part, that doesn't want me to live and enjoy my life. Yet the more I get up and keep going, the more I realise how beautiful life can be.

If I could offer some advice to people with BDD I would say, most importantly, to remember that it is not your fault. This is very much a real illness and you did not ask for it. If you can, find a friend or family member you trust and confide in. It may help to look up some information about BDD on the internet and print it off for them as a starting point; BDD truly can be very difficult for loved ones to understand and comprehend. Try to be patient and don't get frustrated if they don't seem to get it straight away. Sometimes, the best you can hope for is for someone to say that they accept you are ill and will support you. I would also recommend going to see your doctor, who will hopefully be able to refer you for treatment. Again, prepare yourself for the possibility that your doctor may also struggle to understand and may not have heard of BDD. You can print some information off the internet for them too!

I was told by one doctor when I turned up in floods of tears that I was a beautiful girl and he didn't know what I was going on about! This is not what I wanted to hear when I already thought I was going mad.

I would also strongly implore you to go along to a BDD support group and meet others like you. It will help you to realise that you are not alone.

Take life a day at a time and allow yourself to have bad days; don't beat yourself up for days such as this. We are all human beings at the end of the day and each and every one of us is full of complicated emotions.

To finish, I would like to share one of my favourite quotes with you, by Vivian Greene: 'Life isn't about waiting for the storm to pass ... it's about learning to dance in the rain!'

To me this means that, even if I continue to struggle, I know if I just keep going and occasionally go out to 'dance in the rain' I can get through life. I truly believe that you can too.

Becca as a small child.

Ben Hilton

I can remember the exact moment when my issues first came to light. I was eighteen and sat in my bedroom at university. I looked in the mirror and noticed that something was different. It was only slight, only subtle, but my nose looked different to how I had seen it before. From that moment onwards mirrors would play a significant role in my life over the next fifteen years.

That first moment of seeing my flaw gradually developed into something I struggled to manage. I started to spend more and more time looking in the mirror, worrying that something had changed. Soon one mirror wasn't enough, I would need at least two to see my nose from different angles.

It soon developed into an obsession. I went from being someone who had never really worried about the way I looked to becoming increasingly self-conscious. I had a very happy childhood with amazing parents and three brothers of whom I was the third out of four. I was a fairly quiet child and continue to be introverted by nature but adventurous at the same time. I was lucky enough to have a large group of close friends and was never the victim of any kind of bullying. I had girlfriends and generally enjoyed my time at school. Looking back I can't think of any particular moment or period of time that seemed to lead to my issues with BDD in later life, it just seemed to creep up on me.

I started to spend more and more time looking at myself in the mirror, using different lights and different angles to try to get a better perspective and in an attempt to work out exactly how bad my nose was. I gradually became unable to walk past a car or a shop without looking at my reflection in the window and I almost never liked what I saw.

Whenever I saw my reflection I got this feeling in my stomach, a knot that was accompanied by a feeling that something was seriously wrong with the way I looked. It soon became the most important thing in my life. This developed into an anxiety that would later lead to serious bouts of depression.

Throughout all of this, however, I was still able to lead a relatively normal life, finishing university and going travelling before trying to concentrate on starting a career. But my preoccupation with my appearance was never far from my mind. I lived with a constant feeling of dread and started to compare myself to everyone around me. I began to mentally study other people's appearances and their noses in particular. Almost everyone looked better than me. No matter how hard I tried to rationalise my thoughts and put them into perspective, it never helped. My appearance was the most important thing.

Photographs became unbearable and I would spend hours studying photos of myself and then throw them away. My iPhone became my worst enemy. I felt a compulsion to photograph and video myself from different angles and then spend hours studying them. I hated what I saw but I felt that I had to get an understanding of just how bad my nose was.

I went through periods during which it was more manageable and my preoccupations with my appearance would fade into the background for a while. But they would always come back . . . and they came back stronger than ever. I was consumed by the thought that my nose was changing, that it was growing. Over time the problem became worse and worse.

For ten years I never told anyone about the way I felt or what I was going through. Relationships failed because I wasn't prepared to talk about my issues. When going through a dark period I would shut myself away and become completely withdrawn. Because I couldn't talk about what was really affecting me my girlfriend would assume that it was her fault, but I couldn't even begin to think about what I would say. I didn't even understand it myself. I started to Google the way I felt and came across the condition of BDD and suddenly things seemed to fit in to place. I was reading in black and white the exact things I had experienced over the past ten years. I think this was the start of being able to do something about it. Things had got to the stage where I just couldn't go on the way I was. Something had to change, something had to give.

I finally decided to speak to my mum and then my dad about it. I was embarrassed to talk about it and found it difficult to articulate how I felt but they were totally understanding and helped me to begin to fight back.

I went to see my GP in order to finally seek some professional help. I was given medication and referred to a therapist for CBT, which would continue intermittently over the next eighteen months. It was helpful to talk about my issues and try to make sense of them but I didn't feel that I was making enough progress towards getting better. I went through several different exercises during my therapy, all centred on CBT. They focused on trying to change my obsessive thought processes and reduce my compulsive routines. I would keep a diary of what I was doing during the day and the extent of my preoccupation and distress. In all honesty, however, I don't feel that CBT was much help for me. It was good in theory and when I was going through good periods it all made sense. The problem was that when I went through a dark period it would all go out of the window and all the coping mechanisms I had practised were put aside because it was all I could do to just get through that period. For CBT to be effective you have to be proactive with it and practise the coping mechanisms when you're feeling all right as well as when you are going through a difficult period. You have to be open-minded and throw yourself into it. You have to be disciplined to practise the techniques. I think that was why it didn't work for me, because I didn't have the self-discipline at the time.

One of the most important questions I was asked during my therapy was, 'If you were stranded alone on a desert island would you still worry about your appearance?' My answer was, 'yes.' My concerns were never really about how other people saw me but about how I saw myself. I did sometimes worry about what other people thought of my appearance, girls in particular, and my confidence in relationships was definitely shot to pieces, but the problem was still how I saw myself. My appearance just wasn't acceptable to me. At that time I thought that if I was alone on a desert island I would be just as worried about my appearance as I would be about surviving.

I went through some very dark periods as my anxieties turned into serious depression. I just couldn't accept the way I looked and I had this feeling of total desperation that there was nothing I could do about it.

I had thought many times about cosmetic surgery to try to address my concerns about my nose but the stigma attached to cosmetic surgery always made it seem like an impossibility. Over time, as my problem became worse, my desire to correct my flaw increased and I finally decided to go ahead with a rhinoplasty procedure. I was realistic about my expectations and knew that it wasn't going to solve all of my problems but I honestly believed that it was the only option I had. On waking up after the procedure I spent the evening in hospital with a sense of disbelief that I had found myself in this position.

It took some time to get used to how I looked after the operation but I was reasonably happy with it and thought that this was the start of finally getting rid of my obsession with my appearance. But the thoughts that I had and the way I perceived my appearance hadn't gone away. I went through more periods of extreme anxiety and depression over the coming two years. I thought that my nose looked better than it did but it still wasn't enough. I still hated the way I looked. I never regretted having the operation though, and I often wonder where I would be now if I had not had it done. I would never want to advocate cosmetic surgery for BDD sufferers though, because the problem ultimately lies within the mind, but I guess every case is different. My problems persisted beyond my operation and I even went as far as having a consultation for a second operation because I still thought that my nose was too big. I never went through with it, however. I wondered why I couldn't just accept this perceived flaw of mine. I could easily accept flaws in other areas, physical or otherwise, but my nose felt like the most important thing in the world to me.

I continued with my medication and sought further therapy privately. I also eventually managed to speak to some friends about my issues. The importance of speaking about what you're going through cannot be overestimated. I've always been a very private person and generally reluctant to talk about personal things but I found, quite quickly, that being able to talk about what I was going through helped massively. Likewise with the therapy I had, the opportunity to talk to a complete stranger about things was very beneficial. I found that I didn't have to live a double life, appearing outwardly to be happy and content but inwardly being in great distress. Very gradually my compulsive behaviours and ruminations decreased and

I started to manage my issues better. I would go through longer periods of feeling good and, while there would be frequent setbacks and the dark periods would creep back in, they were more manageable than before. I became able to put things into perspective and realised that the problem I felt controlled my life had been created in my mind. I finally realised that it was my thought processes, and not my appearance, that needed to change.

I am now at a stage where I can live with my BDD, function as normal and live a good life without the constant distraction of thoughts about my appearance. They've not gone away completely and I still have my moments, but I am able to accept BDD as an unfortunate part of who I am.

I have thought many times about why I have been affected by BDD and I think it is a combination of factors. I am a natural-born worrier, a deep thinker, and place importance on aesthetics and on how things look generally. I also have compulsive tendencies and so I think that these factors alongside each other have made me more susceptible to a condition like BDD.

However, despite all that has happened to me, I feel that BDD has helped me to better understand myself and appreciate that there's much more to me than just a nose.

My advice to other sufferers would be to seek help. Speak to friends and family because it's too much to handle on your own. Try a combination of therapy and medication. Meditate. Think very carefully about your desire to have cosmetic surgery, as it isn't a cure for BDD. Although I do not regret having surgery, and feel that it helped me in a certain way, it can often push the problem to another area. You need to address the cause of your thoughts and not your perceived flaw. Try to allow yourself to believe that your flaw is only in your head. Above all else, stay strong in your dark moments and just ride them out. Accept that BDD is a part of you but understand that it doesn't control you. We all have our dark periods and there's a million people who have been where you are and got better.

'Because tomorrow the sun will rise, who knows what the tide could bring . . .' (William Broyles, 2000).

Beverley

I am the eldest of two girls. My sister, who is twenty months younger, was fair, petite, and ever so pretty as a child, while I felt that I was really plain, heavily built, and had dark hair. I always thought that my sister was the favourite and that she was loved more than me because of the way she looked. I was intensely jealous of her and, sadly, hated her because of it; I felt so unloved and unattractive. We argued and fought constantly. My parents were unaffectionate towards us, as well as towards each other, although they never rowed and I believed they loved each other.

My parents were heavily involved in the occult throughout our childhood, in which they involved both my sister and me. It was a completely terrifying environment. We were told we weren't allowed to tell anybody outside the family home what was going on because others wouldn't understand. My parents told us that we were special because we knew the truth, but it meant that we grew up having to keep a secret without anywhere or anyone to turn to. I longed to run away because of the overwhelming fear but I couldn't understand the loneliness and unhappiness I was feeling because I didn't know anything else. I didn't know that what we were being exposed to was wrong and abusive. I was brought up to accept that my experiences were normal so I thought that my fear of it must be abnormal and that there was, therefore, something wrong with me because of it. I thought that my parents would love me even less if I let them see how scared I was, so I had to pretend to be brave. At night I couldn't sleep on account of the fear and night after night I lay awake too afraid to shut my eyes, hugging my knees to my chest in an attempt to make myself as small as possible, and praying that God would protect me.

Alongside this, my uncle was a serial paedophile and routinely abused very young boys who were occasionally brought to our house. Nobody ever did anything to stop it, which felt confusing and very upsetting. This was another thing we had to keep secret from the outside world, and another burden that weighed very heavily on my heart. He eventually went to prison, but not until old age.

My mum had been a semi-professional dancer and my father a singer, as well as being a company director, and both of them were attractive people and conscious of their bodies. My sister and I had several dancing classes a week while growing up but I never felt good enough and felt extremely uncomfortable in a leotard because I didn't believe I had a good enough body to be a dancer.

I felt very unattractive at school and was very shy and nervous of others. I compared parts of my body constantly with others around me, which was obsessive and debilitating, taking up a lot of my thought life and causing considerable distress and unhappiness. I was actually quite isolated and traumatised by everything that was going on at home with the occult activities but, instead, I became increasingly more preoccupied with my body and comparing it to others. I felt different and was bullied because of this, but it was probably more to do with the fact that I was behaving differently; I was withdrawn as a consequence of the trauma rather than it being anything to do with the way I looked. To me, however, the bullying always seemed to focus on my appearance and I was routinely being picked on for being too fat and being left out of games because I was fat, even though I also knew that some who were not excluded were bigger than me.

It felt to me as though I wasn't ever good enough in any area of my life, although I tried extremely hard and was very competitive and won several awards at school for academic achievement. However, I gradually became increasingly more isolated as I became more obsessed with the way I looked and comparing myself to others, just as I had done with my sister since as early as I can remember. I was particularly obsessed and upset about the size and appearance of my thighs, tummy, face, and genital area, which I considered to be fat, ugly, completely unattractive and unfeminine. I felt unloved, and was sick with jealousy over my sister, whom I constantly saw as loved more because of her appearance.

I started to wear a lot of make-up from about the age of thirteen. I regularly got told to wash my face at school but I couldn't because it became a mask that I couldn't go out without, so I would try to avoid certain teachers and hide. I spent hours doing my make-up and constantly compared the size of my legs to those of other people.

When I was fourteen years old I discovered that my mum was having an affair and we went through a very traumatic and messy divorce process, during which time I stopped eating and developed anorexia because life was horrendous at home. I initially felt that if I was able to make my parents happy they would stay together, and then I blamed myself because I couldn't do anything about their problems. Of course, I was already depressed with everything that had been going on for years by then. The affair was the final straw and I just gave up. I stopped eating completely for a while, lost a huge amount of weight, lost interest at school, and gave up trying any more. I ran away from home at the age of seventeen, got married at nineteen, and was divorced by the time I was twenty-three.

Between the ages of fourteen and twenty-four I spent a lot of time in and out of hospital very ill from anorexia, but my fears and obsessions over appearance weren't just about size and weight. I was also obsessed with the other parts of my body, which I never told anybody about. Everything about me felt unattractive and I had even tried to mutilate and alter the appearance of the more personal parts of my body with razor blades. I now understand that because I saw myself as so ugly and unattractive I was not only venting this anger on those parts of me that made me female, but also because I had been sexually abused; because of the way I had been touched and looked at I wanted to change and destroy this part of me too, because it made me unhappy and reinforced those feelings of disgust. I attempted suicide several times throughout my twenties and thirties and hated myself, my body, and my life.

I was often sectioned and once had a long spell on a secure unit because of the severity of my anorexia and suicidal behaviour. I was addicted to more than 130 laxatives a day and had to spend long periods of time on a punishment–reward programme in hospital. They took away my make-up, my clothes, books, jewellery, no visitors or phone calls, and I wasn't allowed to use the toilet or go to the bathroom to wash – absolutely everything was stripped away and they made me stay in a room with a nurse by the bed twenty-four hours a day to force me to eat. The rationale was that if I ate I would get rewarded with something, such as a bath, but I wanted my make-up back more than anything because I couldn't cope without it. When they realised how much I wanted my make-up back, having been reduced to complete hysteria and after pleading with them to give it back, they merely said it would be the last thing I could have back, thinking that they had found something I would fight for. Instead, I refused to let them put the lights on in my room, insisted on complete darkness, and faced the wall and wouldn't look at any of them because I felt crippling shame if anybody looked at me and saw my face. I felt so humiliated and degraded that I didn't fight to get my stuff back and just gave up. Nobody considered this to be a symptom of BDD, and I'd never heard of it then.

I was twenty-four when I came out of the secure unit and started suffering with frequent flashbacks which I dealt with by cutting. This was a new experience and one I blamed solely on the degradation and humiliation of the punishment–reward programme in the hospital. My arms became covered in cuts and badly misshapen.

I had nowhere to live when I came out of hospital because my husband had left me for somebody else while I was having treatment and so I was taken in by a church. I became a Christian and the church took over caring for me. They placed me in the home of a young family and were very strict about what I could and couldn't do, which was hard as I had been living independently since the age of seventeen and had never experienced a normal family life. My new-found faith, however, gave me hope, the will to live, and was the motivation I needed to get better. I slowly started to eat and gain weight. I was helped by a surgeon at the church who performed reconstructive surgery on my arms, and I managed to recover from anorexia eventually but continued to be upset over certain body parts, in particular my thighs, and avoided swimming or wearing clothes that would have shown my legs. I very rarely wore jeans or trousers (unless with a long top to conceal my legs), and certainly never wore shorts! I would take forever to get dressed and would get undressed over and over again every day as I checked my appearance repeatedly. I continued to wear a lot of make-up and would never spend even a day in the house on my own without wearing it. I certainly would never have let anybody see me without make-up on. I would usually reapply it before going to bed and would then get up early before my husband woke to reapply it in the morning so he didn't see me without it on. I have also had botox and fillers several times, and insisted on wearing a wig for a while. There are very few photos of me and I avoided looking in mirrors apart from the dressing ritual every day. I deliberately avoided catching my reflection in shop windows. Everywhere I went I found myself constantly comparing the size of my legs to others as I walked down the street, and especially when sitting in a room with others. I would check how much of the chair my legs covered in comparison to theirs. Sometimes I could see that other people were considerably bigger than me in their upper body, but I still saw my thighs as bigger than theirs, which felt confusing and I couldn't make sense of what I was seeing.

All of this was very distressing but I never told anybody what I was doing and did not seek help for it, because I thought it was all residual thinking and behaviour which was part and parcel of the old anorexic behaviour, even though I had recovered from anorexia.

Then, two years ago, I suffered a labral tear in my hip that required surgery. I was beside myself with anxiety at the thought of my pelvic area and legs being looked at, touched, uncovered and naked in front of a room of people in the operating theatre while I was under general anaesthetic. I was convinced that all those in the operating theatre would sneer and laugh at me, and would discuss between themselves their disgust at the state of my legs, and I felt very ashamed. Alongside this I had a phobia of doctors, which I linked to the punishment–reward programme and to being sectioned. I couldn't even visit my GP without having a panic attack, so the prospect of hip surgery became a complete nightmare for me. Four weeks after the surgery I fell and re-tore my hip, which meant that I had to have the surgery done all over again. This was simply too much to cope with and I started to become very unwell from the stress of it.

While this aspect of my life was debilitating, other aspects had improved considerably over the years. I had remarried, and had two wonderful sons who have done very well. I had been involved in Christian ministry for a number of years and was running a Christian therapeutic community programme for people with complex mental health issues called Still the Hunger. Some time earlier, while training as a psychotherapist, I had read a paper on BDD and I had wondered at the time if I had BDD, but I hadn't heard much about it before and had certainly never considered that this might be behind the stress with the surgery. I conducted some research on the internet and came across a website. I sent an email to the Priory to find out more and to see if I could get help with getting through the next operation. The fear of my legs being looked at was getting out of control, and my dread of doctors was making the whole thing impossible. It basically felt like a total mess and very confusing and I was fighting to keep this part of my life a secret, particularly with my work. I was then amazed to be diagnosed with BDD at the age of forty-nine and, even more, to discover that others felt the way I had throughout my childhood and I wasn't alone with these thoughts and feelings.

The thought of further surgery at that point, however, was causing me so much anxiety that it was very difficult to look at these issues and I started to become more physically unwell from all of the stress. The anti-inflammatories I was taking for my hips caused stomach erosion, which led to terrible nausea and pain and I lost four stones in weight. It was a very confusing time because it was hard to know whether I was just physically sick from the gastritis, or whether the emotional strain of what I was going through was playing a part in destroying my stomach. Also, it became impossible to know whether historical anorexic behaviours were kicking in or whether the weight loss was purely down to the physical pain and sickness alone. I was, however, getting increasingly more depressed and struggling with the secrecy of it all. Secrets had always been a factor in my life.

In the midst of all this I was suddenly told by my therapist that I needed to address the sexual abuse I had experienced at the hands of a doctor over twenty-five years earlier, which I had never disclosed to anyone, not even my husband. The thought of talking about it was incredibly difficult. We attempted to do some image rescripting work, but after all these years of repressing what had happened, finally bringing it to the surface and reliving it was too much, as it brought it alive and into the present. I couldn't cope with it and overdosed on the morphine I was taking for pain. I was then diagnosed with complex post traumatic stress disorder (C-PTSD) on top of everything else and it was explained that I was primarily traumatised by my occult childhood experiences and needed to work on this, which I thought had long since been resolved. I imagined that it would be easy to do some rescripting of this, but I was wrong and this turned out to be even worse than trying to face the abuse by the doctor. Another serious overdose followed this therapy session.

Meanwhile, I had fallen again while waiting for my hip to be redone and I had torn the other hip as well, so both were torn and needing surgery simultaneously. I was being so sick that I was referred to the upper GI surgeons as well, who suspected cancer and sent me for a CT scan and an endoscopy, which felt like another violation and assault upon my body. The CT scan showed up a solid mass in my liver which they thought looked like possible secondary cancer and I was assigned a specialist liver nurse. I was so traumatised by this time because I was spending several days a week at various hospitals, which all added to the anxiety.

Eventually I found the courage to go to the police to report the sexual abuse by the doctor, which my consultant and church supported me through. It was all a massive struggle and extremely stressful and traumatic.

During all of this I learnt about compassion focused therapy and the consultant I was seeing at the Priory tried to help me to see how I was hurting myself, and how all of the stress was affecting my body and making me sick. I did some reading on compassion and combined this with my own Christian faith. Despite my own difficulties, I continued with my work at Still the Hunger and I started to teach compassion to them as I was learning it myself. We began to see interesting breakthroughs here as well as I also grappled with the whole idea of treating myself with more love and respect.

I wasn't able to deal with any of the issues at the root of the BDD as an outpatient because it was too triggering and risky for me, and my consultant wanted to admit me to the Anxiety Disorders Residential Unit (ADRU) where it could be managed within a safe environment. This felt like a complete backward step, and one that I couldn't get my head around with the fear of doctors still being a massive difficulty. I had also been suffering with symptoms of dissociative identity disorder (DID) for many years, which was also deteriorating massively at this time. Throughout the day the fragmented child personalities would keep crying out for mummy, which I had no control over whatsoever. This was confusing and very distressing, with child voices taking over my body, speaking through my own mouth, that I had no control over but could still hear. Generally they were triggered by flashbacks to things that made me feel ashamed but I was experiencing flashbacks all the time. These voices were by far the most difficult symptoms to ask for help with because of the feelings of acute shame surrounding this, although this caused the greatest sense of hopelessness and despair because I didn't think anybody would understand what was happening to me. It was yet another secret I felt I was forced to carry.

I was told that I could not be admitted if my weight was too low and if I continued to starve, as I wouldn't be able to do the CBT, and it was through the compassion work that I gradually managed to address my eating and gain a stone and a half on my own in preparation for the next phase of the treatment. It was explained that I was a long way off dealing with the BDD and a lot of work had to be done on the other areas before we would come to the BDD itself.

The whole referral process took several months and was so incredibly frustrating and complicated; it caused an awful lot more stress on top of an already difficult situation. It seemed that neither my GP nor my local Community Mental Health Team (CMHT) knew how to make a referral to a specialist out of area service, and nobody understood how to apply to the Clinical Commissioning Group (CCG) for the funding approval. I had no other support whatsoever locally as they were not able to provide the intensive therapy needed. It seemed to be one waiting list after another while I was very unwell. A year after the initial recommendation by the consultant for admission I still hadn't received funding approval from the CCG, despite the CMHT agreeing to it, so I had still not even had an assessment at the unit and I never got on to their waiting list.

Meanwhile, I attended a Christian healing conference and received prayer for healing for my BDD, DID, PTSD, the shame I was carrying, as well as prayer that the stress of the police investigation would be lifted off me. I was healed that weekend, praise God! Three weeks after the healing I returned to see my consultant to tell him that I no longer needed to be admitted because I had been healed. I thought that he would think I was even madder than before and that I was trying to avoid going into hospital because of my fear of doctors. He was well aware that I had been going round and round in circles panicking about how I was going to cope with being admitted to a hospital again, assuming it would cause even more anxiety, and I thought he would see this as a massive excuse. But I knew that something amazing had happened and I desperately hoped that he would be able to see this too, although I didn't expect him to believe me.

Instead, to my amazement, he said that he was completely astonished and had never seen anything like it before in his life. He asked me to draw another picture of how I saw myself now and, when we compared this to my original drawing, he said that in itself was all the proof he needed. I had drawn a picture of myself with everything in the right proportions, nothing was distorted or disfigured, and it was a far more accurate representation than before. I told him what had happened at the conference, and while he said that he had no scientific explanation for it, he confirmed that there were no longer any symptoms of BDD, body shame, or dissociative symptoms.

I can now wear jeans – and have even worn shorts – without having to cover up my legs with a long cardigan, despite having gained some more weight. My mind is more peaceful from all of the destructive and obsessive thinking. I feel happy for the first time ever. I have stopped looking at how much space my legs take up on chairs, and never even think to compare mine to the next person. I do not spend ages checking the size of my legs or tummy in multiple outfits every day and I just put on the clothes I want to wear that day. I treat myself with respect and kindness and think about looking after myself in the way I eat and behave and manage my time each day. Compassion-focused work has become a big part of what we offer now at Still the Hunger too, and I think this whole area is crucial in recovery, particularly when combined alongside faith.

I think that my experience of BDD started very early on in life because I misinterpreted my parents' lack of affection towards me as being related to my appearance. This caused me to begin comparing myself unhealthily with my sister, which then extended out beyond the family to my peers. I believe this actually created a distraction for what was really going on at home with the occult activities, which I couldn't cope with at all. So I turned all of this fear and confusion into an obsession with my body as a means of distraction. This became so much a pattern of thinking that, when the stress got worse during my parents' divorce, I again put all of the focus on to my body by starving myself, thereby creating an even deeper, ingrained obsession to distract myself from all of the fear and confusion at home. The anorexia then prevented me from seeking any help over the years for the BDD symptoms because I just thought it was residual anorexic thought patterns. In fact, I now believe that the BDD had been there first.

I feel that I am very fortunate to have found a way out of this, but am saddened by the lack of support available for people with BDD. I would never have even come across it as a diagnosis if it were not for my own studies as a psychotherapist and the reading of a single seminar paper on it. I have no doubt that if I hadn't read this paper I would, in all probability, have still assumed I was struggling with old anorexic thinking patterns. Yet it has taken me until the age of fifty-one to understand this horrible condition and, through my faith and new-found understanding of compassion, to walk free of the need to distract myself in this terribly sad and distorted way from the things that really mattered and which I couldn't bear to look at as a child.

All I ever really needed was to feel safe and loved and that was the one thing I didn't ever feel, despite being happily married with two now grown-up boys whom I adore. We have always been very close, so it is a shame that there are so few photos of me with the children as they were growing up, or with my husband, but we will, I hope, have a few more now that this is behind us. I now know that I was never plain or fat. My legs were in normal proportion to the rest of me but my distorted thinking performed a function by distracting me from the really distressing stuff going on in my life. It was these areas that I was running away from, but which are now finally in the past.

Since then I have noticed on a couple of occasions that when I have looked in the mirror I have been surprised to see the original distorted appearance of my legs materialise before me. On those occasions I've been able to analyse the fact that I was probably feeling stressed and could tell myself that what I was seeing was not an accurate representation of my legs. I remember the video shown at the BDD conference in 2015 and can say that the experience was very similar to this in the way my body appeared to distort and morph into something else in front of my eyes. Before the healing I would have disagreed with what seemed like a sensationalised interpretation of how BDD is experienced in this video because I had only ever seen the distorted ugly image, so I would have insisted that was what I was actually seeing. Now that I have seen a true appearance, I am able to hold on to this and tell myself that the distorted image I occasionally see isn't true and then have encouraged myself to ignore it. It hasn't then disturbed me any further, so I would consider myself to be doing all right now.

I suppose I ought to mention make-up though . . . This has become a way of life for me now at the age of fifty-one. I would never attempt to go out without it, even if it was suggested in the course of treatment, as other brave people have attempted. I would not open the door to the postman, or spend a day on my own at home without having it on even if I didn't have to go anywhere all day, although it is lighter than it used to be. Having had it forcibly removed on so many occasions, I'm not even attempting this one. However, I have found great comfort in the words of Psalm 139:

[14] I praise you because I am fearfully and wonderfully made; your works are wonderful, I know that full well. [15] My frame was not hidden from you when I was made in the secret place, when I was woven together in the depths of the earth. [16] Your eyes saw my unformed body; . . .
[17] How precious to me are your thoughts, God!

With regard to the other issues, the cancer diagnosis turned out to be a mistake and I am physically much better, although have continued to suffer with hip problems which require ongoing surgery. Unfortunately, coinciding with a further labral tear, I had taken on a new client at the charity who went on to disclose personal sexual abuse at the hands of her father, who had been a GP. I was advised that this would be too triggering for me and I shouldn't get involved, but others disagreed, believing that as I had been healed of this that I would be the right person to help her. While the client did well with our support, I personally found the work very difficult when I was approaching surgery again and my original fear of doctors was reignited; the surgery was again an extremely traumatic experience for me.

After the surgery I initially felt completely unable to see my GP, return to physio, or even have the stitches out because it all felt abusive and traumatic. The flashbacks returned with a vengeance. I was disappointed to hear myself describing myself as a victim of PTSD again, which forced me to think through the original healing experience and finally claim this healing back. I chose to turn my back on the PTSD, and to focus on thanking God for all that He had previously done and to step back into a place of peace. Yet again the flashbacks receded and I have been able to resume my rehabilitation with physio. I am still considering with my GP and consultant whether it would be wise to engage in some specific CBT for PTSD at either the Maudsley or the ADRU for the abuse by the doctor and what happened in the secure unit and on the punishment–reward programme because this never happened in the end, or whether to just leave it alone and focus on going forwards now.

I am, however, able to look forward to the future with my husband and children – and am happy to include here a photo of me wearing shorts!

Beverley in shorts.

Caroline

'There is a crack in everything.
That's how the light gets in.'
(Leonard Cohen, 1992)

I don't claim to have totally beaten this crippling condition but I have learnt to manage it. I have survived over thirty-five years of daily self-loathing with regular suicidal thoughts. I was living in an abusive relationship but I couldn't leave because the abuser was myself. It was a permanent battle with my own mind. As well as it being incredibly cathartic for me to write this I also hope that it will help fellow sufferers in some way, perhaps aiding them in feeling less alone in their inner turmoil and realising that BDD is nothing to be ashamed of. I felt immense shame and kept all of it inside. I assumed that most people would think that my thoughts and behaviours were just selfish and nothing more than self-obsessed vanity. In a world full of suffering I knew there were people with much 'bigger' problems but still I couldn't shake it. The guilt, the isolation and feeling so misunderstood can be such a huge hurdle. I hope that by telling our stories we will reach the people who need it and help them to move forwards with their lives.

Was I born with BDD? Is it in my DNA? Do my genes make me more susceptible to it? (I have always been a highly sensitive person.) Is it a result of a culmination of external life experiences that have caused me to turn inward? Depression certainly goes hand-in-hand with BDD, at least for me anyway. Did the depression come first or the BDD? As a toddler I didn't feel disgusted with myself but then I didn't look in the mirror or see photos of myself – I was free for a while. As a child I recall feeling inferior to my sister and my friends. I began to compare. ALWAYS comparing. I remember being repulsed at any school or family photos of myself, especially the holiday photographs with burnt red skin and freckles galore. It felt like the main object of our holidays was to get a tan, so I always came home feeling like a failure. In fact, one of my first 'boyfriends' dumped me because he didn't like my extra freckles on returning from some time away! Maybe my insecurities started when the hormones kicked in? They certainly intensified around that time. Am I just a big teenager who never managed to grow up? Is it self-inflicted punishment because I didn't feel good enough, hence I jumped in first with the criticism before anyone else had a chance to do so? Maybe it is the artist in me? I see things differently and in great detail. Colours are accentuated and shapes are more defined. Some people are born with the gift of synaesthesia where there is a union of the senses. I wonder if all BDD sufferers are born with a distorted perception of themselves.

If you go down the spiritual route one might wonder if it could be a memory from a previous life? Maybe I had my teeth knocked out in a medieval battle? Perhaps I am mentally picking up on other people's thoughts? For a long time all of these ruminations were going on inside my head as well as the BDD itself!

I cannot count the number of times I have become so worked up while getting ready to go out. Not even for the office party or some important meeting but just down to the local shops. The more frustrated I got with my hair and my reflection the redder I would go in the face, eventually breaking down in tears. This would often result in one of my horrific nosebleeds. I'd be an irrational ball on the floor, covered in blood and pulling my hair out with frustration. Why can't I be normal? I would ask myself. Why did I have to be this ugly? I just want to go to the bloody shop! Why is such a simple thing so incredibly difficult?

In a meditative state I could gaze at myself in the mirror and my face would distort right before my eyes. It took many forms. But I always looked so old, so tired, and so incredibly sad.

One thing I know for sure is that the more you focus on something, the more energy you feed it and the more it grows. At one time, every waking moment became a living nightmare and sometimes I couldn't even escape it in my sleep. BDD can be all consuming and sap the very essence of life out of you.

In my darkest moments I would try to put a first layer of make-up and mascara on without a mirror so as to avoid getting upset at that first sight of myself in the morning, especially if I was in unfamiliar surroundings where the lighting wasn't right. I didn't really seek reassurance from others as I didn't want to draw attention to my flaws. I wouldn't have believed any positive comments anyway. When I did receive any reassurance I just felt as though people were just trying to be nice. I was so uncomfortable in my own skin that I decided quite early on that I was unlovable. I decided that I wouldn't be getting married, having children and doing all of that stuff. Besides, I was too ugly to give birth in front of strangers. I even worried about people seeing me when I was dead. I HAD to be financially independent, self-reliant, and vigilant at all times. I couldn't allow myself to need anyone. I didn't like my reflection in the mirror and so assumed that no one else liked my appearance either. I couldn't trust anyone. I was going to be doing this life alone. Back then I hadn't figured it out that to have a successful career I would *also* need to love myself.

I was anorexic for a short period in my life . . . then bulimic. It was a time when I felt I had no control over my life during the second year of my seemingly pointless degree. I had also just split up with a boyfriend of nine months who suddenly announced he had just become a father. So I found some semblance of comfort in being in control of my weight. Losing weight so quickly gave me a great sense of achievement but then the weight loss slowed down. Then there was the fear of putting it all back on again – that would be FAILURE. The fact is that no matter how thin I was I still wanted to lose more. I felt clean with nothing inside of me. The scales told me that I was underweight but the reflection in the mirror said otherwise.

I was born with ginger hair and pale, freckly, transparent skin. I was once told that I had blue ink on my face, but it was actually one of my veins! Are all thick-skinned people blessed with a more resilient personality? And do 'thin-skinned' people have a weaker immune system to external negative experiences? That's where the term 'thick-skinned' came from – right? I'm sure there are many of you out there with thick skin who would disagree but, at this time, this is how my mind worked.

I felt I was a disappointment when I was born a female. My very pretty older sister was welcomed with open arms, especially by my grandmother as she was the first girl in the family for a long time. Yet their second child was supposed to be the boy. Everyone wants one of each don't they? I definitely felt as though I was the runt of the litter. The ugly sister. My sister often pointed out various imperfections in me that subsequently lowered my self-esteem. I took everything she said very much to heart.

My hair faded to strawberry blonde, or 'nicotine stained', as it was once described by some cruel boy on the back seat of a bus to his friends. My eyelashes and brows are practically invisible, not white like some blondes, but sort of translucent. When I was about twelve I had a friend around to stay. She was aghast when she saw me with no mascara on. 'You look totally different!' she exclaimed. For as long as I can remember I have never left the house without mascara and make-up on. I've often wondered how on earth I could have coped if I was male. For holidays or swimming I used those home eyelash dye kits. Even to this day if I have a house guest I will leave my mascara on overnight just in case they see me first thing in the morning.

After graduating with a first class honours degree in graphic design and illustration I had to return home to my parents while waiting for an operation on my back due to a bad fall I had when I was anorexic; there was no cushioning there to take the impact of the fall. In preparation for job-hunting I also embarked on some invasive cosmetic dentistry to get rid of my 'fangs'. It went wrong. I withdrew and became a recluse for most of my twenties. I had no social life and was totally introverted. I spent most of my spare time painting, riding, walking the dog, and exercising in my room. I also spent a fortune on home teeth whitening kits and facial creams that were supposed to fade my ginger freckles. My poor, poor parents just didn't know what to do with me. Nothing they said helped. I was like a broken record. One day, after I'd had two totally unnecessary tooth extractions, I was breaking down in my bedroom. This was the final straw for my mum and she called the doctor round. The doctor suggested that it would be a good idea to admit myself voluntarily to a psychiatric ward to give my parents a break. So I went. I don't remember receiving any therapy there. I just remember being handed my pills, waiting for permission to have a bath and just lying there wondering what the hell I was going to do. A few long days later my father came to take me home with tears in his eyes saying, 'You shouldn't be here.'

Later, after two stepping-stone jobs, I managed to find a reasonably good job and buy my own small house. I enjoyed the work and spent most of my evenings at the gym – great for getting out of the house while not having to talk to people! Also great for the endorphin kick and keeping trim. As I was approaching thirty I felt that any chances of having a successful career had vanished. I didn't fit into the clique at work. They were all very family-orientated and couldn't understand why I remained single with no children. I was different – a weird misfit. I suddenly realised that if I wanted to find a partner and go on to have a family like 'normal' people then I would need to change my reclusive method of surviving.

I was raped at the age of sixteen, a sort of date rape although we weren't on a date and were at a house party. My friend had deserted me and this guy was pestering me. 'It was my fault. I shouldn't have got myself into that position,' is how I explained it to myself. The guy ignored my repeats of NO! I didn't tell anyone but blocked it out of my mind.

At college, when I was nineteen, about a week after the aforementioned boyfriend split, I was sexually abused and threatened by a very forceful human being. The students I shared a house with allowed many visitors into the house and he was one of them. I later discovered that he was fresh out of jail. I was still upset about the break-up and ended up being rude to this guy who was being extremely pushy. He just wasn't getting the message. His evil eyes stared into mine, with his big sweaty forehead pressed against mine. It felt as though it would never end. Eventually he left saying, 'Your nightmare's over.'

I blocked it out of my mind and busied myself with my studies and the anorexia.

I told myself 'It MUST be me. It happened again.'

The sound of laughter often deeply saddened me – I know that probably sounds very strange and wrong. Christmas was especially difficult. People chattering and laughing with ease and with joy. What must it be like to be completely in the moment with people? Without that sabotaging voice telling you, 'You're making a fool of yourself; you're too ugly; they all think you are a waste of space and would rather you weren't there; don't smile and show your horrible teeth; you can never be happy; you are a disgusting, revolting, UGLY BITCH!' It is something I felt was unachievable – to be happy. Always analysing, questioning people's sincerity and feeling so estranged and alienated.

So I sought help. I felt misunderstood by my GP but, because they knew my long history, they realised it wasn't just a short episode of depression. After many consultations, at the age of around twenty-eight, I was finally diagnosed with BDD (which I had never even heard of). I was offered SSRIs and CBT at Newcastle University, which was a forty-minute train journey away. Back then there was only the one book recommendation – *The Broken Mirror*, by Katharine Phillips.

'I haven't got BDD – other people might – but not me – I'm just plain ugly – end of!'

I didn't know if anyone else thought this. That's the fear of change, fear of a huge battle on our hands, fear that we might find out we've been wrong all these years and THEN having to forgive ourselves for wasting so many years of our lives.

Despite the denial, in many ways it was a relief to have a diagnosis, not just for me, but for my parents. But what to do with this knowledge? I asked my workplace if I could take an afternoon off unpaid every other week to travel up to Newcastle for about six months for treatment. This resulted in the inclusion of a new question in their questionnaire for prospective employees, which was 'Have you ever suffered from a mental health illness?' This definitely put a full stop to any prospect of development in my role there. I was ostracised and labelled a 'nutter'. I wanted to *live to work* not *work to live* but felt that my managers wouldn't allow me to do so.

My CBT therapist once suggested that I go to my next appointment with no make-up on. I plucked up the courage. I felt so exposed on the train journey and walking through the city centre to the university. I felt such a freak and as though everyone was staring at me. I might as well have been naked, so exposed did I feel. When I got there I perceived a look of shock in my therapist's eyes (I *do* look completely different). I broke down in tears and ended up having a nosebleed for the whole of the session. Needless to say, I put my mask on for the journey back home! This aside, I did find the CBT very effective indeed. I just wish I could have had it outside of work hours.

I also sought out more cosmetic dentistry to put right the first attempt. I know – probably not a wise move. But I had brainwashed myself that I could only have a life if I could sort my teeth out. I was totally obsessed with other people's teeth. While watching television I wouldn't be watching the programme, but rather be zooming in on their teeth and getting depressed. That was the main feature I would look at to compare myself with and bring myself down. After trying a few local dentists with no luck I ended up being referred to a clinic on London's Harley Street. I made numerous expensive trips there over a span of more than four years. I underwent bone and gum grafting and implants but the treatment partially failed. So roughly £15k and a few more wasted years down the line I gave up and asked a local dentist to do what he could with it so that I could try and forget about it once and for all. By that time I'd realised that even if I ever did manage to achieve a healthy looking full set of teeth I would still not be happy with my skin, my hair, my body, my voice, my height, etc.

I'd like to point out that by no means could I afford all of these expensive treatments but, for me, it was a matter of life or death. That hard-earned money should have gone towards a mortgage or further education. The dentist did his best but I now have to wear a piece of prosthetic gum to hide the bone loss and gum recession. So I'm far from happy with it but enough is enough. At the age of forty-three I realised that my dream of a 'happy ever after' was over. Another wasted decade of my life.

Relationships

There had been two or three significant relationships in my life but they were very short lived due to my hang-ups. Then, at the age of thirty-seven, during one of the Harley Street visits when I still had hope, I reunited with my ex-boyfriend from my college days. We had always kept in touch and had both matured a great deal since then. It felt like we were soul mates and unbreakable this time. Still trusting the dentist's promise and aware that I didn't have much time left to start a family I rushed into it. I sold my house and we bought a house together nine years ago. Things didn't go to plan. Hindsight is a wonderful thing. It turns out that we wanted different things and slowly drifted apart. Although no longer together romantically, we still share the same house as friends until one or both of us move on. Tied together in negative equity rather than Holy Matrimony!

My parents sold up and moved to Spain about fifteen years ago. The distance between us has actually greatly improved our relationship with regular emails but there is no other family left around here any more. The village I grew up in is full of strangers. It is as if I'm a ghost that cannot move on. I find it quite hard to get my head around the fact that I have remained stagnant in my home town when I was the one who most wanted to get away.

Unexpected reflections and photographs still catch me out but I manage not to dwell on it too much. At one time I'd want the ground to swallow me up if I caught my reflection somewhere out in public. That reflection never felt like me. Even a glance in the rear-view mirror could make me want to go straight back home. I can only recall going to the hairdressers about three times in my adult life. My hair is so difficult that I feel sorry for the stylist having to try to do something with it. You will see from my photo that my mum also couldn't do anything with it! To sit in front of a mirror and talk to your stylist through the mirror is one of my worst nightmares. It's one thing to deal with the reflection but if I have to chat I will also see my teeth. I feel sick just thinking about it. Note to self: it is just a thought that is making me feel this way and thoughts can be changed (with pure and utter determination!) This is one of my challenges to myself in the near future. After cutting my own hair for so long I could do with a top stylist to sort me out!

On reflection, after reading through this, I can see that I have mentioned quite a few outside influences and experiences that have had an internal impact on me. There have been many more. I remembered EVERY negative (or perceived negative) comment made to me and quickly rebuffed any compliments. This is a key point that my CBT therapist made. Taking on board compliments for me is like trying to fit a square peg into a round hole.

In my early forties I feared that things were only going to get worse as I aged. Just recently in the media there was a discussion about a woman in her fifties being granted the right to die because she felt she had lost her 'sparkle' and didn't want to get old. How sad. Is this what modern society has brought us to?

I also had to come to terms with the fact that I would never have my children and be part of a family unit. I realised that life had passed me by and my position at work had gone so rapidly downhill that I had become invisible there. For a short period in my life I fell into another coping mechanism – my secret alcohol consumption. Thankfully, I managed to put a stop to it and have not touched a drop for nearly two years. However, stopping the drinking brought the issues I'd been masking to the forefront. I had a bit of a meltdown at work one day and some totally unreasonable and hurtful things were said to me. For example, I was told that I needed sectioning and that I wasn't liked as a person. I actually managed to air my grievances quite assertively while under attack but, nevertheless, I will never feel part of the team at work again. I went back on the SSRIs to help me out of the black hole I found myself back in.

So, at forty-seven years old, what now?

Earlier this year I decided to be brave, to put myself out there and search for alternative employment. I suppose my CV looks quite good on paper so, to my surprise, I have had a fair amount of interest, a few job interviews and one job offer so far. The job offer wasn't quite right but very encouraging none the less, so I will continue with my search. I would possibly even consider a complete career change. I'd love to work with animals or birds or do something to help our environment. Nature has been my saviour so I'd like to give something back. My future is a blank canvas, which is quite a good position to be in. I also have a bunch of paintings inside of me bursting to get out but I need the time, confidence, energy, and a good-sized art studio!

I have made some truly inspirational virtual friends initially through a private 'childless by circumstances' Google Plus Community and we have shared so much of ourselves with each other. This would not have been possible for me if it were a face-to-face group. A few of us formed a separate private community that is not so much about the childlessness any more. We have been there to chat, laugh, support, advise and encourage each other and recently met up in London even though three are from different countries. I was so nervous but I couldn't be the only one of us not attending. I haven't actually had a close friend for nearly thirty years so this has made a massive difference.

I now seem to have found some inner strength, some self-compassion and self-support. I don't really care what others think any more. Did I just say that?! I am ME – unique – just like each and every one of us. I can take the rubbish out with wet hair and no make-up! That might seem like a small thing but there was once a time when I wouldn't answer the door if I wasn't made-up, not even to the postman. Now I am learning to embrace my authentic self. Who wants to be the same as everyone else anyway? The gap between how low I rate myself and how highly I rate others is closing. I have one 'safe' mirror in my home that I can use and I'm actually beginning to see physical aspects of myself that I like as well as the lovable attributes of my true self (my soul). I still make comparisons, unfortunately. But now it's not so much with people's teeth, skin, hair, legs, etc. I now make more comparisons with things such as people's ability to speak confidently in public, their intelligence, their status, their children and the fancy houses they live in. Sometimes I get overwhelmed with regrets about the wasted years. The missed opportunities and offers of friendship I've backed away from. People stop asking eventually. But if I beat myself up about this it will only set me back and imprison me once again. I now have a deep hunger for knowledge and a burning desire to find a much more fulfilling life.

Thank goodness for the internet. It wasn't around when I was first battling with this. There are now so many resources out there and it's a great way to connect with people from all over the world. BDD is not a new condition. Imagine what it must have been like centuries ago. Possibly ending up in a lunatic asylum or burnt at the stake. Thankfully, there is a much greater awareness of mental health issues nowadays, but there is still a very long way to go.

There are things you can do to move beyond your BDD. If, like me, you feel compelled to wear make-up all the time but find it a chore, then take small steps by applying lighter layers or by going make-up free at home when you know you won't have any visitors. When I have a housework day I do this. I would advise you to refrain from checking the mirror – just go about your day as you would normally. You'll begin to get used to it and enjoy the freedom. If I need to check myself before going out I find it good practice to stand back from the mirror and see the whole me; just a quick glance and a cheeky smile. That is how others will see me. They won't be zooming in and scrutinising my every feature (unless maybe they are a fellow sufferer . . . and then they will probably be focusing on my good points to make themselves feel worse).

Even though, in some ways, I feel I've made a profound breakthrough I also still have trouble talking to people close up and in daylight. I am aware of people observing my imperfections such as my teeth when I speak. I see their eyes move around my face judging me. I used to avoid eye contact. I worried that people would see the sadness in my eyes – a bit like the deep sorrow I often saw in my mother's eyes. Now I'm learning to engage more by using my eyes to aid communication. I hope that then the person will really hear me and relationships can be more easily formed.

So it's still very much work in progress. People will always judge, I can't change that, but I can reduce the importance of external judgement through my own self compassion. Even if I think people might be noticing how ugly I am I manage to carry on saying what I need to say, hopefully with increasing confidence in the future. Practice makes perfect! *If I believe the whole world is out to get me then that will be my experience.* I now see it as a challenge in this game of life. If I flunk a social interaction – so what? – I didn't die and I can pick myself back up again because I have a new best friend – me! I've never spoken to a friend or colleague in the cruel way I've been talking to myself for all these years.

The Inner Bitch is still present. She's only trying to protect me after all but I keep asking her to try a new way as the old way doesn't work. There is no longer an inner battle going on, it is more like a dialogue with gentle persuasion. It is comforting for me to know that I can 'do' being alone quite well – that is what I'm used to and the only time I am truly relaxed – but I am also now able to try something different, to go out of my comfort zone and dip my toes in the water, so to speak, and reach out to others. It's really been quite a lonely life so far so I've got nothing to lose and everything to gain.

I also believe it is a quality to show our vulnerability. We are only human and we all make mistakes. I am learning to embrace my imperfections. None of us is perfect in society but we are all perfectly ourselves.

Kintsugi/Kintsukuroi

'Not only is there no attempt to hide the damage, but the repair is literally illuminated ... a kind of physical expression of the spirit of mushin ... Mushin is often literally translated as 'no mind,' but carries connotations of fully existing within the moment, of non-attachment, of equanimity amid changing conditions ... The vicissitudes of existence over time, to which all humans are susceptible, could not be clearer than in the breaks, the knocks, and the shattering to which ceramic ware too is subject. This poignancy or aesthetic of existence has been known in Japan as mono no aware, a compassionate sensitivity, or perhaps identification with, [things] outside oneself.'

(Christy Bartlett, *Flickwerk: The Aesthetics of Mended Japanese Ceramics*, 2008).

Earlier last year I was over the moon to see a feature on the BBC News about BDD and thrilled to hear that the BDD Foundation had been established. Finally some validation! The isolation dissipates and there is a sense of connection on hearing of others with BDD bravely sharing their stories through the media. Human connectedness is a great healer rather than me/you against the world. Greater awareness will also help the families and loved ones of BDD sufferers as they struggle with their feelings of helplessness.

Persistent negative thoughts are as detrimental to your wellbeing as smoking. The sooner you can work on breaking the habit the better. This could be the hardest challenge you ever face. It is certainly no walk in the park to change something that has been one's default for so long. It is imperative that we never give up. BDD is no way to live. I'm so grateful for the chance to be a part of this project and if there is anyone out there who can relate then please try to get all the help you can to fight this thing. You are important and so worthy of a happy, fulfilled life.

'Don't hide your light under a bushel'

Regarding my grief for my unborn children – well, I *do* have a child to love and care for; she's my inner child. That little girl below needs all the love I can give her. I keep her in my heart. She deserves better now. She didn't do anything wrong.

I'll leave you with this quote, which I find incredibly empowering. Religious or not, the message is the same . . .

> 'Our deepest fear is not that we are inadequate. Our deepest fear is that we are powerful beyond measure. It is our light, not our darkness that most frightens us. We ask ourselves, Who am I to be brilliant, gorgeous, talented, fabulous? Actually, who are you not to be? You are a child of God. Your playing small doesn't serve the world. There is nothing enlightened about shrinking so that other people won't feel insecure around you. We are all meant to shine, as children do. We were born to make manifest the glory of God that is within us. It's not just in some of us; it's in every-

one. And as we let our own light shine, we unconsciously give other people permission to do the same. As we are liberated from our own fear, our presence automatically liberates others.' (Marianne Williamson, 2006)

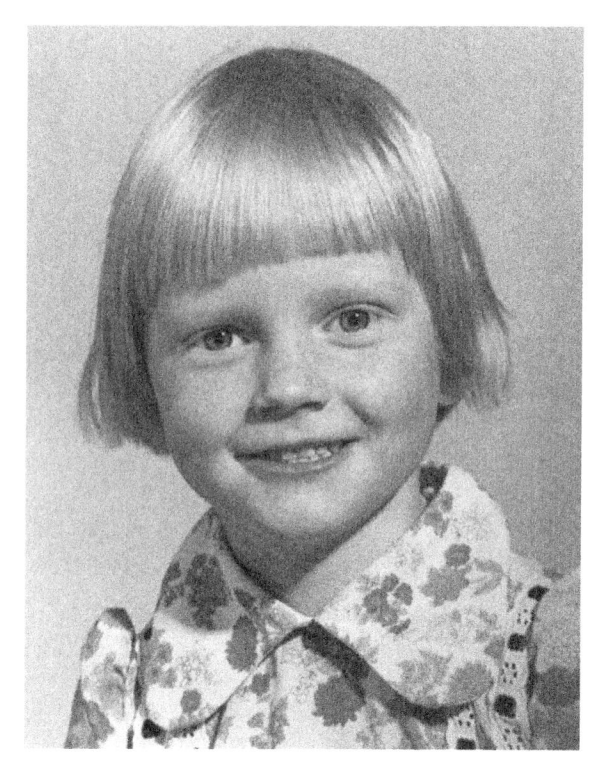

Caroline as a little girl.

C. H. Handley

Glass Darkly

'For now we see through a glass, darkly; but then face to face: now I know in part; but then shall I know even as also I am known'. (1 Corinthians 13:12 KJV)

From when I was a small child, and really up until the onset of early middle age, I had an eerily good memory for people's names. If an acquaintance were to mention their mother's maiden name in natural conversation, I could remember it years later. I felt puzzled that others couldn't.

There was another area of my memory that was unsettlingly good. I had the ability to remember the appearance and whereabouts of blemishes and spots, moles and lumps on the faces of everyone I knew. I was a bit horrified by freckles and moles, finding them at once fascinating and repulsive. My own moles were a source of revulsion and fear to me. I remember standing out in the rain with my face turned up to the sky, trying to terrify my sister and myself by saying that every raindrop that landed on our faces would turn into a mole.

I have a memory of sitting in front of a mirror, aged seven, staring at my face and wishing desperately that it could be pretty. My hope was that, through some form of magic, my face would become distractingly beautiful by the time I reached adulthood. I wondered if this could really happen. It seemed unlikely. It's worth saying that although I felt my appearance was incredibly insufficient, I did have a sense at that moment that I was in some way special. Not everything has been hard and miserable.

There's much I could say about my childhood home and experiences. There was nothing particularly remarkable from the outside. I had a loving mum and dad and a big sister with whom I was great friends. My internal life was painful, though. I felt unattractive in looks and personality, but had strong enough willpower to bluff my way through most things. I thought my parents didn't like my personality even though I knew they loved me. I knew my father thought looks were important and my mum took great care over her appearance. They told me that I was good-looking and had good features. For years I have felt the curse of having 'good features' (not really anything to complain about, I know!). For some reason I interpreted the 'having good features' verdict as having a good framework to my face, just with none of the prettiness to fill it in. I envied girls with small features. I have large eyes, nose, and mouth, which can give a very striking impact but not necessarily a pretty or feminine one.

My father was strict and incredibly intelligent and my mum, sister, and I adored him. When I was eleven I lost my dearly loved grandmother; she died slowly and painfully of ovarian cancer in our house over a number of months. From the age of seven or eight I had been gripped with a fear of the supernatural when alone or at night-time, after doing a series of lessons on 'real ghost stories' at school. At the age of six I had to move school to one I was very afraid of, which coincided with my mum going back to college – I missed her very much. I mention these things to give an idea of my internal thought-life and emotions throughout early childhood. My childhood in many ways was very privileged and stable.

The year my grandmother died we moved house, which was something of a relief. My sister and I were delighted to be allowed a dog. We now lived in a large modern house at the other end of town. At the age of fourteen I moved from an all-girls school to the local comprehensive. It was new to me to mix with boys, and it quickly became obvious that they did not count me amongst the group of girls known for their good looks.

They nicknamed me 'Panda' due to the dark circles visible under my eyes. I so longed to be part of the 'pretty pack' – to have the boys' approval. I felt it was my responsibility to be good-looking and I was failing badly. I felt, and honestly have felt throughout the years, that I am responsible, perhaps even morally responsible, for my own looks. Somehow it was my duty to be pretty. Yet I thought I was so very unattractive. My 'good featured' face was hollow in some sense and incomplete. My looks made me morally unacceptable. I felt totally powerless to do anything about it.

My sister and I were walking the dog one afternoon in diagonal sheets of scudding rain. My cagoule hood was on my head, forming the tunnel-effect peep-hole created by drawing the hood strings tight. We walked past some boys who, despite our sartorial androgyny, had managed to work out that we were female and therefore felt compelled to make suggestive comments. One boy approached me and, peering into my tube-hood to assess my looks, turned and said to his friends, 'Nah, don't bother, it's a dog.'

A crushing evaluation, a moment in time where what I feared in the silence of my heart to be true turned out to be true, or so it seemed, objectively. A dog. A panda. A non-human. It didn't occur to me at that age not to listen to the unkind words of an immature adolescent. The words may have been unkind but he was a truth-teller in my mind. The problem of my inhuman ugliness rooted deeply into my psyche. It was an impossible problem I was going to have to find a magical solution to. I had to achieve the impossible; I had to be pretty in order to be acceptable and morally all right. It was an unachievable goal. Yet it felt like a totally necessary one.

One afternoon I was fiddling about with my mum's make-up, and tried some of her thick foundation. I dolloped some on the dark patches beneath my eyes and spread it out and marvelled at the transformation. No dark circles under my eyes. No 'shopping bags' as my best friend's brother called them. I looked almost normal. The impossible problem had been remedied, well, at least for the daytime, and that was a relief. I found that if I applied eye-liner and mascara I looked even more normal. No more alien ghost-dog during daylight hours.

So from then on I was never seen without make-up. The boys at school stopped calling me Panda. I became more popular. Boys began to show a real interest in me. I had temporarily 'made it'. Life was bearable.

When I got to Sixth Form College the interest from boys seemed to accelerate. Unfathomably, I now had become 'beautiful' and an object of desire seemingly for many boys and men. It was intoxicating. It was petrifying. How could alien-dog have blossomed into film actress beauty? I knew the answer. Make-up. I knew alien-dog was alive and ailing under the thick layer of foundation. She was a thing of the night. She was kept well hidden.

Looking back, Sixth Form College was profoundly painful. On the one hand I was pleased to be getting attention, on the other hand I was crippled with fear and anguish, just waiting for the day that alien-dog would be exposed. It was a deeply shameful secret and exposure would feel like death. I don't think I exaggerate. Having left the panda moniker behind, I was now heavily criticised by some people for wearing too much make-up. I agreed. Yet I didn't know how to cope without it. I was ashamed of my face and ashamed of the mask I wore to cover it. I felt I had a moral duty to be pretty and would be a let-down to my family if I was not. However, I knew my father disapproved of the amount of make-up I wore. Which disapproval would I choose? No contest. The make-up stayed on.

Into my late teens, out to work and then on to university, alien-dog remained concealed. From everyone – even my close family by this time. I had to get up jarringly early each morning to carefully cover my dark circles, and check from different angles how visible they were. Checking and camouflaging my dark circles took a healthy chunk out of each day. I just accepted that this was the way it had to be. My eye make-up and lipstick application was a lengthy process too. I still desperately wanted to look normal, but by this stage I felt I also had to live up to the beautiful ideal. I had been called beautiful and I had to keep that reputation up. I was in an ugly/beautiful dichotomy; it felt extreme, shameful and lonely.

Once or twice in my teens and early twenties I had been glimpsed without any make-up on. A male friend saw me bare-faced when I was about fifteen or sixteen and said, 'I can see why you wear all that make-up now.' I knew he was not trying to hurt me; he was just speaking the truth.

The one or two other occasions I was 'seen', things did not go well. I became very, very careful.

I quickly developed a pattern in romantic relationships. I had a string of long-ish term boyfriends who were highly intelligent, and who thought I was breathtakingly beautiful – but not much else. In other words, they dated me for my beauty. And I knew the beauty was not real. I could not reveal my unmade-up face to my boyfriends, and they took little interest. Of course, alien-dog's natural habitat was night-time when all make-up generally comes off for sleep. This posed an excruciating problem when I stayed the night with a boyfriend. There was no alternative but to keep alien-dog stuffed down and stay as Beauty with the make-up left intact. It was about this time that I had recurring eye infections. The cleanliness advice for removing make-up at night time was proving demonstrably correct.

On to university and a philosophy degree. I had very little confidence in my abilities and only began working really hard in my third year when I realised I might be a bit cleverer than I had thought; I came two marks away from achieving a First. I loved philosophy. At last something that made sense. Something deep, imaginative, yet wonderfully clean and logical. University is a sweetly painful memory for me. I met people with whom I could much more be myself, although Beauty was still in play. For a short while I had a boyfriend who actually liked *me* and cooked me lovely dinners and made up songs about me. Alien-dog was squashed inside and I could almost forget her. Beauty seemed far more real during those days.

University life was so much better than Sixth Form or at work. I struggled, though, with serious migraines and bouts of depression. In my final year I started dating a young man who really did care about how much make-up I wore. Unbelievably, perhaps, he was the first boyfriend I had who really seemed to properly notice that I was hiding my face from him and would never appear unmade-up, even at bedtime. I had learnt by then never to talk about my fears to anyone. Alien-dog was so shameful she could not be spoken of. Although I took great care to hide her every day, and to check often and thoroughly whether she was at all visible, in a weird sort of way my belief in her existence had faded. She was so well managed she didn't really exist.

But with new boyfriend pecking away at my defences it became apparent that she really did exist. New boyfriend was deep and philosophical like me. He was complex and brilliant intellectually. He was at once tender and passionate and frighteningly bad-tempered and jealous. We were hooked on each other. New boyfriend really did want to get beneath the make-up, and he wasn't going to take no for an answer. After many months he finally persuaded me to go to the bathroom with him and wash all of my make-up off. I looked up at him, face bare. Boyfriend said, 'That is the most beautiful face I have ever seen.'

A moment of profound healing. I am so grateful for that moment in my life. For although Boyfriend was controlling, jealous, and darn scary, that night he handed me a shard of light. The tiniest inkling of the beginning of a belief that I could be wrong about alien-dog. Sure the relationship went badly wrong, both of us were deeply unhappy together, the arguments were unbearable. It took years to recover from the pain of it. Boyfriend gave me a sore heart and belittled confidence. But he also gave me the smallest beginning of a sense of something that looked like a nanoscopic grain of hope.

Some time in my twenties I saw a television programme about a young woman who thought she was unacceptably ugly. In this case the woman thought that her eyes were plain and 'piggy'. The programme followed her progress through therapy, and the slow, painful steps she took to be able to go out without wearing make-up. I was absolutely staggered at her bravery. I could never ever do that, I thought. But then, I reasoned, she only *thinks* she is ugly. My problem is that I am genuinely too ugly to be seen. Her problem is therefore not the same as my problem. I didn't forget the programme, though.

My depression grew worse and by the time I was twenty-five I had begun a series of counselling sessions. I deliberately chose a Christian counsellor so that I could fire grumpy questions at her about the Christian faith. Since I was small, I had a sense of God's reality. I wasn't a Christian as such and I had never met anyone who talked about God as if he were actually real. Until I met this counsellor.

I was very resistant to begin taking anti-depressants, and held off until the depression became completely unmanageable. I've met many people since, depressed and reluctant to take anti-depressant medication. I wish I had started anti-depressants earlier, because they did help. Life was a bit more manageable. The counselling sessions focused mainly on my childhood. I once tried to express the fears I had about being too ugly to be seen without make-up. I did not emphasise this problem very much because I was deeply ashamed of it and it was really very difficult to bring it up in conversation at all. My counsellor suggested that many women found going about without make-up a difficult thing. We left the problem to one side. Neither I nor my counsellor recognised how key this problem was to my depressive symptoms.

By my mid-twenties I had become a Christian and an authentic change had occurred within me. I always thought that believing in God would be a sketchy, vague experience, a flickering flame that could blow out if the wind got too strong. I was surprised to find that after making a commitment to Christ, in whom I was making little effort to believe, the conviction of his existence and my relationship with him inescapably settled in my heart. This was, and is, a great joy. Now broken emotionally and immovably convinced of my hidden ugliness, I joined the Christian community.

At church I became close to the vicar and his wife, who were very kind and loving towards me. They somehow knew I was sad. I didn't give them any details and they didn't ask. They just loved me. Because of the love of these good people and the support from my counsellor I think I was able to let go of some of the effort of trying to hold it altogether. I had to give up work; I was unwell with depression and losing the ability to be seen to be managing. With the help of my counsellor I pinpointed something that may be helpful – with a loan I was able to go back to university and study for a Master's degree in philosophy. I moved away. Time to start again.

At university for the second time, I settled down to hard work. Before long I met my future husband, our relationship surprising to me because it was actually nice, pleasant, and healthy. Did such relationships really exist? I took a risk and slowly allowed him to see me with less and less make-up. To my amazement he didn't even seem to notice. I was too fearful and ashamed and tired of alien-dog to talk about her much. But I did let him know that this was a problem for me, and he kindly let me know that my problem wasn't a problem for him. He thought (thinks) I am beautiful. He would prefer that I never wear any make-up at all. This still seems too dizzying a concept to actually believe! My husband thinks I am beautiful. His constant gentle reassurance and belief in me is the springboard from which I can explore getting better. His words were, and still are, healing, yet alien-dog stubbornly refused to budge.

Body dysmorphic disorder is so painful and so intractable. Out of the depressed feelings and broken hearts and bereavement I have experienced, I am still ashamed to say that BDD for me has been the worst experience of all. But I am not hopeless.

Throughout my married life and having a (surprising!) number of children I have been marvellously distracted from dwelling on alien-dog. Life just got in her way. True to say, even when our four children were under all the age of five (aged four, two, and baby twins) I got up early each morning (5 a.m. or earlier) to apply under-eye concealer, so that I wasn't too shocking to be seen around the housing estate where we live. I wore very little other make-up, though. The experience was freeing, yet I still felt ugly. I made a special exception for my husband thinking I was beautiful. My logic is something like – well, he tends to see things differently from anyone else. He has a different viewpoint. He is unique and thank God for him! This was, and is, my view.

Over these past years I have been very involved with church, both pastorally and preaching. I love to speak on philosophical and Christian topics. These things have given me purpose and some insight into my own faulty thinking. Two years ago, while praying, I sensed God saying to me that I should tell some close friends about alien-dog. I had long since given up talking about her. I just managed her. I didn't talk to my husband about her. I still camouflaged but I didn't check my face obsessively any more; in fact, I avoided looking in mirrors at all unless I absolutely had to. I was pretty annoyed that God was bringing all of this up again.

It was interesting timing, actually, because some time before this my doctor had increased the dose of my anti-depressants. This had been very helpful since I struggled still with depressive thoughts. With the increased dose I felt better, more 'normal', more able to cope. A friend dropped round to see me and left me with the Bible verse, 'Do not call anything impure that I have made clean' (Acts 10:15 NIV). I thought it was time for me to tell someone about alien-dog.

It's been two years since I let the dog out. Husband and close friends were the first to know. I was astonished and delighted at their response: none of them judged me or failed to take me seriously. I thought that uncovering the existence of alien-dog would invite hatred but the opposite happened. These precious people have given me the courage to look into getting further help. Some days now I can almost believe it's possible to get better. That's progress.

Letting that dog out has been a turning point for me, really. To summarise where I am now, I can talk about the good things and the not-so-good things:

Good things

- The love and acceptance of my friends and husband has been indescribably helpful.

- Most days I am willing to believe I have BDD, rather than thinking I am actually ugly.
- On 25th April last year I spent a whole day with no make-up on. I was seen by real human beings, some I knew very well, some I didn't. On the sight of me no one collapsed in a dead faint or was spontaneously sick. I took this as an encouragement.
- My GP has diagnosed me with BDD. Now any treatment I receive is directed more towards BDD than towards depression. Although I don't think the two things are mutually exclusive, I do feel better knowing that the response can be more targeted.
- With the support of friends I attended the first BDD International Conference last year. I was overwhelmed by compassion for everyone there and had to smile inwardly at the larger than average representation of drop-dead gorgeous attendees.
- I feel more integrated with alien-dog. There is no longer a huge split between 'outwardly seen me' and 'me seen behind closed doors'.
- I've realised that keeping alien-dog a secret all these years only strengthened the sense of shame in my life. It is much nicer to bask in the warm sunshine of my friends' and husband's acceptance and love.

Difficult things

- This dratted condition hangs around. It has less power over me, but I have bad days.
- I still feel the need to camouflage each day, though now with very little make-up.
- Having exposed my dark circles to the world and, to my knowledge at least, caused no one instantaneous cardiac arrest, I have started to worry about other features on my face, thinking they might be noticeably grotesque.
- I *would* dearly like to kick this condition into the rubbish bin where it belongs. But I can't find a CBT counsellor in my area with a good understanding of BDD. I'm not willing to go back into therapy that is not BDD targeted.
- Very few people seem to 'get' BDD. I am very careful who I talk to about it.

- Long-term anti-depressant medication? Is it a good thing? I don't know.

I am profoundly grateful for the progress I have made. And I am daring to hope for the future now, with the glint of a possibility that one day, I'll be completely over this thing. That would seem like heaven.

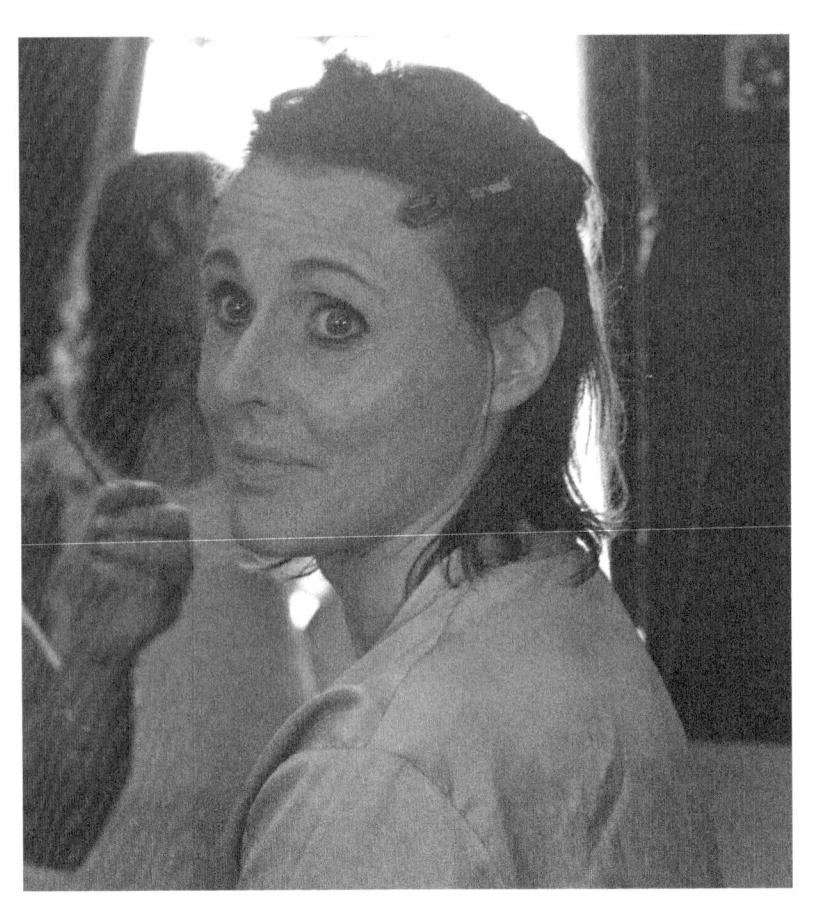

C. H. Handley.

Carla Mark-Thompson

My childhood was one that was full of love and was nurturing. I never went without and I truly believe that my parents did all they could have possibly done for me. I grew up in a household with my two older siblings and my mum and dad, so the house was always full. We had regular family time, especially on Sundays when my dad would take us on boat rides on the River Thames. I feel, however, that my family became rather dysfunctional over time as the breakdown of my mother and father's relationship became evident, stemming from alcohol abuse and infidelity. I don't think my parents really knew how painful this was for me to witness because I was only around seven years of age and they probably assumed that I would be unaware of what was going on. My dad eventually left the household and, although I still had a relationship with him, insecurity and inadequacy gradually began to plant itself within me. I never really realised the effect that it was going to have on me for the years to come. As I got older, the relationship that I had with my mum slowly began to deteriorate. We would argue a lot and I never really went to her for help or advice about anything.

I would never want to relive my years at secondary school. I was beginning to feel really self-conscious at that time, comparing myself to the other girls in my year group from the age of eleven; then, from the age of thirteen, this gradually got worse. Most people would describe these feelings and behaviours as normal because of puberty, but with me I never seemed to grow out of feeling this way. I always felt frustrated because it seemed to me as though I was the only one this was happening to. Everyone seemed as though they were happy with their appearance and I guess a part of me envied all the girls who I thought liked the way they looked. Despite the self-hatred that started to manifest within my mind, I managed to keep a big circle of friends at school and was popular with everyone. It was as if I was living a double life. I could be the loud 'confident' Carla that every-one wanted to be friends with but inside I was disgusted with what I looked like and wasn't actually as confident as people might have perceived me to be. I always admired my friends and wished that I could look like them. I just always felt as if I wasn't really pretty enough.

I had specific things that I didn't really like about myself, mainly my face and my teeth. I eventually had my teeth fixed cosmetically through my dentist. I didn't like having direct eye contact with people because I felt uncomfortable if people stared at me for too long. In my mind, I believed they were staring at me and thinking that I was really ugly, which is the view I had of myself. After all, this is what I told myself every day so it was hard to understand why anyone would think otherwise. School photo days would give me the greatest anxiety. I dreaded the day I would get the photos back because it reconfirmed how terrible I looked. When I did get them back I would rip them up and throw them away and just try to forget about them ... which is why I have no official school photos of myself from year nine onwards. This anxiety wasn't just with school photos but with all photos and videos. I would usually avoid having my picture taken. If I ever did have a photo taken it would always be from an awkward side-angle. In truth, I never liked people taking photos of me at all and preferred to take them myself. I would ask for reassurance from my cousin before I uploaded any photos on social media. I always needed her opinion in order to put up any photos of myself. I lived based on what I thought other people's opinions of me were.

Things gradually got worse for me and, by the age of fourteen, I remember an incident when a boy at school was going through all of the girls he thought were pretty; he casually told me that I didn't make it into that category. I felt really bad. It felt like a confirmation of what was already in my head. Things started to spiral out of control at this point. My face was a major issue for me, as I believed it was really big and fat and I felt the need to change it. I started a strenuous exercise regime to lose weight and developed an unhealthy relationship with food as I began counting every calorie I consumed. This became an obsession. I experienced a huge amount of guilt when I ate, so I would binge-eat and then make myself sick. I would lie to my friends and tell them I was going to use the toilet – but I was really going to force myself to throw up what I had just eaten. No one knew anything. It was a dark secret that I was ashamed of. My body, however, did begin to change, though I still felt ugly. I lost masses of weight and people began to notice that I wasn't myself any more. A girl in my year group at school with whom I had fallen out embarrassed me in front of my whole year group by shouting out that I made myself sick and that I was ugly with fat lips. I felt betrayed, as she had told me that I could open up to her when we were friends. (She also shared with me that she, too, struggled with what she ate and how she felt about herself.) Around this time I was also in an emotionally abusive relationship that lasted for three years.

Some days were worse than others. I would cry, feel depressed, have suicidal thoughts and just want to stay in bed all day and hide away from everyone. At times I even pretended to be unwell because I just couldn't face getting up and going to school.

Over time I developed a lot of safety behaviours. A major one was that I would avoid mirrors in public spaces to the point that I would only look at my reflection in the cubicles where the shiny metal toilet flusher was. At home I had a special mirror in the bathroom that I would do my hair and make-up in because I believed that all the other mirrors in the house made me look ugly and highlighted all of my imperfections. I wouldn't look in the mirror with anyone around me because I had a fear that they would be negatively judging me. I would also usually would wear entirely black clothes to avoid attracting any attention on the days that that I felt really down. When I did leave the house I would repeatedly look in the mirror before I felt comfortable enough to go out, which often made me late for school and then work as I got older. I also remember times when I would do my make-up and just stare at myself really close up in the mirror and feel awful. I would take my make-up off and keep redoing it to make myself feel less unattractive, but I would still feel the same and often ended up staying at home. There were also times when I had anxiety getting on the bus because I felt like people were staring at me thinking that I was ugly. I would always keep my head down and avoid eye contact.

All of this was becoming physically and emotionally draining. It hindered me going to the hairdressers and even into changing rooms because of the mirrors. When I would go out to parties I always looked down and hated bright lights as I felt they would reveal my flaws. In public my posture was always bad, walking with my head firmly down. I was emotionally unstable and would often be moody or tearful because I felt as though no one understood what was going on in my mind. It was very frustrating and, on top of all of this, I was being dragged further down by the emotional abuse I was receiving from my boyfriend. I truly depended on others for validation because I never knew my own worth. I would allow people to treat me badly, especially men, because I didn't have any self-value or self-esteem to believe that I deserved any better.

I never knew what body dysmorphic disorder was. I just thought that I perhaps lacked confidence. As time went on, however, I began to understand that I was experiencing something very abnormal and more severe than just low confidence. Many people around me could see that something wasn't right but I was always told the same thing, 'Don't worry, you will grow out of it, it's just a phase'. I would look online and type in things like, 'Why do I feel so ugly?' and there would just be articles on how to not feel ugly, which were focused mainly on exterior solutions and things like affirmations. But none of this ever worked for me. I was so scared that I would feel ugly for the rest of my life and remember praying to God and asking him whether one day I could just feel normal like everyone else.

By the age of twenty I came to a point in my life where I was really sick and tired of the darkness that I was living in. BDD was crippling me and I was desperate to live a life within which I wasn't so preoccupied with my reflection. I had been to my GP on one occasion and she wasn't really helpful, but simply told me that I was probably experiencing hormonal emotions due to my menstrual cycle. I told her my symptoms and she advised me to take oil of evening primrose. It was devastating because I really thought I must be going crazy. Even seeking professional help didn't seem to help at this point. It left me really embarrassed that I had been so open with how I was feeling and had been told that I was just vain and narcissistic in response. I didn't give up, however. About two years later I decided to go back to the GP a second time. I broke down, telling the same doctor that I wasn't lying or exaggerating and that I seriously needed help. This time she referred me to be examined by a psychologist. I was then offered cognitive–behavioural therapy for three months.

I was filled with hope at this point but also a lot of fear. I thought to myself that this could finally be the end of my suffering, but I also had a lot of reservations. What if the cognitive–behavioural therapy didn't work? What would I do then?

I began to regularly attend weekly CBT sessions, which I feel really helped me to see that a lot of what I was experiencing was within my mind and not actually the truth. I learnt a lot of practical strategies, which I had to adapt to, that helped me to break my safety behaviours over time. I faced a lot of my fears during therapy. There were a lot of tears but also a lot of progression. I was really determined to win my struggle with BDD. I knew that it was going to be hard but I started to develop a fighting spirit within me. Once my therapy was over, it was time to stand on my own two feet. I had been equipped with all that I needed to move on and get better and now had to choose to take responsibility if my progress were to continue. I knew in my heart there would be tough days, but I never wanted to experience a relapse so I began to fight to stay on track.

I realised that BDD would always be with me but also knew that I now had the power to silence it. I still have days when I don't feel that great but I don't beat myself up about it any more and BDD no longer rules my life. I now have the strength to say no to the negative thoughts and emotions before they escalate. A major thing I have learnt about my experience with BDD is that, in order for me to continue getting better and stronger, I need to continually step outside of my comfort zone. I started to do a lot of things that scared me. For example, I paid to have professional photos of myself taken. Although I cried and felt really anxious, I felt I needed to do it to get better (and at the end of it I was still alive so it wasn't that bad!) I also took part in the 'Miss Caribbean UK' beauty pageant for the first time in November 2014. This was a huge step for me and with all of my doubts and fears of not being good enough I realised that if I wanted to keep getting stronger I needed to keep throwing myself in at the deep end by doing things I never thought I would be able to do. I also wanted to show other women that anything is possible and that a negative self-image can be changed and used to empower others. I did not win a place in 'Miss Caribbean UK' 2014 but in April 2016 I decided to try again at the 'Mr and Miss Black Beauty Pageant' and I won First Runner Up, which was amazing. My aim is to use this platform to continue raising awareness of mental illness. It was really awesome to see how much I had grown. Many people could also see the massive transformation I had gone through.

I feel that cognitive–behavioural therapy helped me a lot but the fundamental thing that got me through it, and that still helps me to this day, is my relationship with God. I find so much strength in my faith and draw on that to keep me going. I have finally come to accept that my face will never change and have learnt to work with what I have and to appreciate it. Not many people know what BDD is and, from my perspective, it needs to be taken much more seriously. It is such a serious mental illness and there is not enough being done about it. It is not vanity. It is a mental disorder just as significant as OCD, depression, and other mental illnesses. I'm not embarrassed and I don't pity myself. I see it instead as empowering because I can now educate others and use my experience to support and encourage fellow sufferers, to be a voice for those suffering in silence.

I believe that my purpose on this Earth is to use the pain of my past to uplift and change the lives of people all over the world. I feel that everything happens for a reason. Although what I went through was devastating at times, I now have a duty to dedicate my life to helping others, especially by encouraging and speaking up for those who feel that they cannot.

My advice to others who are suffering with BDD would be to try and think of it as a battle that you are determined to try to win. Please do not be ashamed about how you feel. You are not alone in this. Do not be afraid to seek professional help. It is a step-by-step process and every step, no matter how small, can really help to push you closer to recovery.

I can understand the fear and how uncomfortable it may be for you. It is not an overnight process, but the more you confront your fears and break down your safety behaviours, the closer you will get to recovering and the happier you will become. If I recovered, so can you!

Carla Mark-Thompson.

Charlotte

I first experienced BDD, although I didn't know it was called BDD then, when I was around fourteen years old. It started gradually, slowly building up inside of me. Little did I know it would stay with me for years. I remember starting to get spots at this age. I didn't take much notice of them at first as they didn't seem to bother me that much. However, when they did not go away and stayed for months and months, people started commenting on them at school. I would get called 'spotty' and 'ugly' and get asked questions such as, 'Why do you have so many spots?' or 'What's that on your face?' When I first heard someone call me 'spotty' the pain was indescribable. I felt hideous and deeply crushed. From then on all I wanted to do was hide and cover up my face.

Back then there was nothing more satisfying than getting through a day without someone commenting on my face. When the name-calling continued, I developed an obsession with my spots and would count them individually, writing the numbers down day by day, spending hours in the mirror closely monitoring each and every one of them. I used anything I could to cover them and picked at them incessantly in an attempt to make them go away. I started to arrive late to school and lessons most days and would constantly have my head down, trying to hide. I would spend so much time staring in the mirrors in the bathroom at school that I wouldn't even realise the time. I would then walk into lessons late, which made me extremely anxious and nervous because I knew there was no one I could tell about what had been keeping me. I would make up lies and my behaviour didn't go unnoticed. Some days I was running so late that my anxiety would kick in and I wouldn't feel brave enough to enter a classroom full of people, so I didn't go. I was getting into lots of trouble for truanting at school and my mum would get very mad with me. I had to make up so many excuses and was starting to look like a liar. I was far too embarrassed to even think of telling anyone the truth, as I knew that no one would understand.

I started to feel very depressed because I felt so ugly. I would panic about going anywhere that people were going to see me or where any attention might be drawn to me. I avoided all school assemblies, PE lessons, and would only socialise in the dark. I began to hate myself and my confidence just got worse and worse. Some days I wouldn't even go to school and bunked off the whole day. I was becoming such an angry and agitated person that I began arguing with more and more people and this led to me only having a small number of friends. That's when the bullying began. I was especially agitated when I thought people were looking at my face and my spots, leading me often to walk away without explanation from that person or take all my anger out on them. I argued with the people that were most popular and, of course, this led to people I didn't even have arguments with to hate me. At the time I never realised why I was so angry and so agitated with everyone. But now it all makes a lot more sense and I understand that the strong feelings of irritation and anger were all about my own issues and little to do with anyone else. I actually had no reason to be angry with other people. A lot of it was jealously, I suppose. I was angry with myself, but took it out on everyone else. I would try to find reasons to be angry with people just so that I could let my frustrations out. Sometimes I would get into arguments with teachers just so they would send me out of class and I could hide in the toilets. If someone even looked at me in what I considered to be a 'funny' way I would scream at them. No one could understand why I was so angry and there was no way I was ever going to explain. So I just let them all think I was just 'doing it for attention', which in fact was the complete opposite to the truth. I actually wanted to hide, for the whole world to leave me alone, for nobody to notice me at all.

Not knowing what to do with me, my school organised a counsellor for me to talk to. Looking back now I realise that she never once mentioned anything to do with any mental issues or feelings. All the questions were mainly around home and my behaviours; 'Is everything OK at home?' and 'Why are you arguing with people?' I didn't have the perfect family life; however, my parents were still together and that was all that mattered to them. As I grew older I learnt that mental health problems actually ran in my family. My aunty suffers with a large number of mental health issues and rarely leaves the house, my uncle committed suicide, my nan was on anti-depressants for years, my mum suffers with OCD, and my cousin has mental health issues. At the time I thought I was so alone and 'weird' for having these feelings, but I was not alone at all. It wasn't until I grew older and left school that I learnt just how many people suffer with mental health problems.

As the years went on I spent hundreds of pounds on many different types of products for skin care and tons of make-up products. This eventually ruined my skin all the more by leaving scars. To this day I still have some scars left and I hate the fact I used so many different strong, abrasive products that actually caused more damage to my skin. It makes me realise how desperate I was at the time for my skin to get better and to be covered up. I did try to explain my feelings to my mum and various doctors many times but I don't think they really understood the extent of what I went through. It was the hardest thing I have ever had to try to explain. When I went for counselling, I was so desperate not make myself look vain or stupid for being upset over my looks. I wrote down my feelings for the counsellor to read and have never felt more embarrassed than when she was reading it. She kept reassuring me that I was beautiful but, for some reason, I just felt so stupid that I never went back. Counselling never helped me personally, probably because I kept giving up on it and never really gave it a chance.

It is so hard to explain to a counsellor, doctor or even a family member that I hate myself and the way I look and that I am obsessed with my facial features. How to explain the days I would spend researching everything and anything possible that would resolve my skin issues? I just couldn't bring myself to be honest with anyone about the emotional turmoil I was going through. Instead of sharing my worries, I kept spending days doing more research on what foods I could eat to help my skin, what hygiene tips might clear my skin up, what skin care routines I could try, where the cosmetic surgery clinics were, what I could drink for clear skin, how to protect my skin in the weather, and so on and so on. Every time I felt as if I was getting somewhere and my skin started to improve, it would just go downhill again and I would feel rubbish again.

After talking to my mum, I knew she didn't understand why I was feeling like this and thought my feelings were abnormal. I could tell by her facial expressions and responses. However, she was extremely supportive and helped in every way she could. Eventually I went back to the doctors and just broke down in tears and told them the counselling wasn't helping. This is when I was prescribed an anti-depressant. I was eighteen years old when I started taking them and nineteen when I finished. This helped me so much and I don't believe I would be here today without them. I promised myself that I wouldn't get addicted to them, yet little did I know how hard it would be to come off them. Taking them felt as if a massive weight had been lifted off my shoulders and for a long time I felt happier and a bit more carefree. They gave me the boost of confidence I desperately needed. When things were more settled in my life and I had a boyfriend, I was thinking about coming off them for a while. So I started gradually to take them less often and it was extremely hard because I had major anger and agitation issues to the point where I was starting to get into massive arguments with the people around me. I began to self-help myself with these feelings by going on long walks when I was feeling angry or doing workouts which relieved my stresses. Gradually it got better and I was managing to control my feelings.

I fell pregnant and knew I had to stop the medication for good. It felt weird at first when I stopped taking the anti-depressants but, honestly, I soon felt fine again. Throughout my whole pregnancy I felt very chilled, calm and happy, which I was surprised by. My mental health since I've had a baby has definitely been up and down, mainly because of stress. I have suffered with stress very badly and at times it has got the better of me. I think sleep plays a massive part in mental health and this has certainly been my downfall. I feel so much better and can cope with things much more effectively when I have slept and am rested.

I definitely believe that the older you get the wiser you are. I still suffer on and off with the BDD and there are still days I spend wishing I was pretty, but I know how to deal with it now. One of the most helpful things I have done is to stop comparing myself to other people. I used to be extremely jealous of any girl I saw who was pretty and had clear skin and this would make me so depressed. Now I believe I am who I am and that everything happens for a reason. There are plenty of people out there suffering on a daily basis from this condition and that makes me feel as if I am not alone, and it also makes me want to reach out to others and help them. I taught myself to overcome my feelings of BDD. I have learnt that the best way to process my anger, frustrations, agitation, and general feelings of self-hate is to exercise. I do at least a ten-minute high intensity workout daily now and this honestly makes me feel so much better. My mind feels less clogged up, more free and generally less stressed. I do this every morning and I know it works because if I don't do it I feel awful for the rest of the day. I also make sure that I have fresh air every day, always going for a walk; this seems to relieve any bad feelings inside.

I think it is also important to do something you love doing at least once a week, mine being to write, read, or blog, as this makes me feel as though I have achieved something and makes me feel happy. Last, I believe you should socialise at least once a week with a friend or a family member at the weekend, going to the cinema, a restaurant, a show or something you enjoy because this feels like a nice, stress-free break. Don't get me wrong, I still have my off days when I get a huge spot and don't want to leave the house, but then I kick myself into the right mind frame and think, 'right, get over it, do something that is going to make you feel better'. I then venture out without having a care in the world about what people think and who sees me.

'Gradually Daniel began to become conscious of his appearance and the clothes he wore. He started using face creams and spending longer periods getting ready to go out. There was nothing immediately alarming about this, as it seemed to be a feature of his age group. Hanging out with girls from neighbouring schools was a regular after-school occurrence.

'Over time Daniel's behaviours deteriorated. He became rude, anxious, and was often agitated. He was convinced that he had serious acne when, in reality, he would simply experience the odd blemish or spot, which was certainly not abnormal for his age. The GP, however, prescribed anti-acne medication and told him that it could take up to six months for the tablets to work. What followed were six months of sheer distress. Daniel began to control what he ate as he was told that certain foods decreased the effectiveness of the prescribed tablets. Additionally, he made himself stand up for two hours after taking them as he had read somewhere that this increased their effectiveness. He refused to leave the house, dropped out of education, and lost contact with all friends. His waking time was focused on seeking reassurance about his appearance. If you told him that his skin was clear he would accuse you of lying. If you said there was a slight blemish he would collapse into tears. He took copious numbers of photographs of different aspects of his appearance in different lights and would check different mirrors, carrying them into the garden to check his skin in the sunlight. Sadly, Daniel attempted to overdose and his high levels of distress and agitation made his behaviours towards himself dangerous and unpredictable. Our main concern was keeping him safe. It wasn't unusual for us to wake up frequently in the night to check on his wellbeing. We asked for a referral to be made to the Maudsley team, who assessed and accepted Daniel for intensive treatment.

'As a family, we received help from local services, but this was extremely limited. A psychologist working in the local CAMHS team was fabulous and later became the main local contact with the psychologist who worked with Daniel from the Maudsley Hospital team.

'The journey has been difficult for our family. Daniel's older sisters were also trying to manage their own education and social lives while living within the turmoil in our household. However, I feel we are all stronger for the experience.

'Daniel worked very hard throughout treatment and has continued to fight both BDD and OCD. We are all proud of his ability to be open and talk about his experience, particularly as Daniel's struggles had always been kept a secret from wider family and friends. We believe that his willingness to be open has helped, and continues to help, him in his recovery. His work with the charity 'Fixers' and his quest to campaign for better mental health services and treatment is admirable. He is especially passionate about campaigning for recognition of, and treatment for, BDD.

'Daniel's illness has had a significant impact on his life. With hope, compassion, and love, we support him to pursue the life he hopes to live in the future, free from BDD.'

Danny Bowman.

Dathen Bocabella

From the very beginning I was conditioned to perfectionism. Anything less was met with reprimand and ridicule. As a toddler, I'd be splattering food everywhere as I ate in my high chair. My father would shout at me for making such a mess until I was in tears. Sometimes after dinner he would forcefully trim my toenails so short that they bled. Other times he'd vigorously brush my teeth so I could hardly breathe and then scrape them with dental tools.

My petite mother spent her mornings exercising strenuously because she believed her behind looked like 'the back-end of a bus'. Once, at a Catholic funeral service, she drew attention to a young man in the ceremony by calling his severe acne 'hickies from the priest', to the raucous laughter of my cousin. Such sentiments permeated the media too; from *Law and Order* to *Harry Potter*, people with acne were mocked as though such negative perceptions were acceptable and second nature.

As the youngest child, I grew up watching my brother meticulously gelling his hair and my sister spending hours preparing in the bathroom. I saw my family kick up a major fuss over the slightest hormonal breakouts. I got the message: acne was bad and made you sub-human.

I think it is also worth mentioning that, when I was thirteen years old, my mother's cat scratched me on the cheek. It wasn't very noticeable and it didn't bother me, but my mother wouldn't let me leave for school until she'd covered it up with concealer.

Communication wasn't my family's strong point. Outward emotional displays were frowned upon, so I was groomed into being preoccupied with decency in presentation, manners, and composure. I considered things like moles to be highly indecent, despite the fact that most people had them. Some people call them beauty spots, but I had one removed when I was only fourteen years old.

When I later saw my cyst-covered, scarred and crimson face, of course all I could think was 'mangled, defective and infected'. I wasn't decent. It didn't matter that I graduated top of my class, or went to the top university, or that I was a published writer. It didn't even matter when people called me smart or cute. All I cared about was having clear skin.

I had almost completed my final year of school when my acne erupted. It was vulgar, a word even used in the medical diagnosis: 'acne vulgaris'. If I had a whitehead I had to pop it. On one occasion this led to bleeding in class. As I dabbed at my face with a tissue the teacher asked if I was all right. She thought I was crying and let me go and splash some water on my face. It was so embarrassing.

Once my exams were over I went out with my best friend to celebrate. After finishing eating my pasta, I asked him if I had any sauce around my mouth. His response was that no one would be able to notice with my acne anyway. Soon afterwards I went to the doctor and was prescribed antibiotics. They came with the added bonuses of nausea, upset stomach, and really easy sunburn.

While on antibiotics I moved from using salicylic acid washes to benzoyl peroxide cream, which was intensely irritating and drying. One friend pointed out my dry and flaky neck, while another told me my face looked plain weird and asked if I moisturised. I did, at least twice a day. During my early years at university I would slip into restrooms between classes to reapply moisturiser and lip balm so I wouldn't be peeling and to stop my lips cracking in class.

This second friend also called me 'The Joker' due to the redness of my cheeks and chin, leaving a white-ring around my mouth. It looked like the white smile of a clown's make-up. He also insulted people struggling with acne, using nonsensical lines such as, 'They should be doing Proactive commercials.' Perhaps the fact that he said such things around me meant that my own acne wasn't so noticeable at the time. His comments still affected me though, because I also had harsh thoughts about people with acne, myself most of all.

I patiently stuck with treatment and my skin cleared up. Next, I moved on to dealing with the residual scarring. Three times I subjected myself to expensive laser therapy by a dermatologist. I opted for the numbing cream, so they smeared this thick white paste all over my face, pinned my hair back in a lacy band, and sent me back to the waiting room for an hour while it took effect. There I sat among a bunch of smirking, middle-aged women.

The nurses described laser treatment like being flicked by a rubber band, but I remember it more like receiving an intense beam of sunburn directly on to my face. It causes trauma to the skin, which triggers swelling. Afterwards, they sent me on my way with a unique ice-pack. Had you seen me on the drive home, you would have witnessed someone holding a water-filled frozen condom-type thing to their very red face.

Not for a second did I think that laser was an optional aesthetic treatment. I fully believed that I needed this procedure as though it was as crucially necessary as a heart transplant. I couldn't fathom that it was possible to have a life and to be considered attractive while so scarred. I'd convinced myself that love was for flawless people, despite the fact that so many people around me were finding romance regardless of their appearance.

The laser treatment left me red and puffy-faced for the best part of a year. It also widened my pores, but the scarring did reduce over time. Each morning I'd go straight to the mirror to check (hopefully) the healing's progress. After a short time, I reached a stage of relative contentedness, then deciding against further laser sessions. However, my body image never made a full recovery. It was as if I had lost a lot of weight, but still thought of myself as overweight.

I was still scarred but moved on, immersing myself in my studies by day, working casually at night, and volunteering as a writer for experience. My appearance didn't inhibit my life, but occasionally I'd glimpse my harshly lit reflection in a train window, rear-view car mirror, or in gym mirrors, and I'd feel emotionally crushed for a second before letting it go.

To keep my acne at bay, I continued to apply benzoyl peroxide, religiously by now, which came with the secondary effect of bleaching my hair.

When people pointed this out, I began to put blonde tips through it and to cut it shorter so it wasn't so obvious. There were times when I went on salad and water diets to maintain my clear skin. I exercised excessively and lifted weights at the gym to compensate.

I began to develop coping methods to mask my insecurities. I hid behind my fringe while wearing hoodies, dark sunglasses, and scarves. When I later grew my facial hair to avoid shaving irritation, and define my jawbone, it also ended up becoming a sort of skin camouflage that I couldn't go out without. Often, I still kept to the shadows or turned away from people, which led to some really rude moments that I deeply regret to this day. My bizarre behaviour was much more noticeable than my skin.

I wasn't living; I was just getting by with the naïve hope that my time would come eventually. I saw relationships as something in my distant future, but it was difficult not to develop feelings. There were people who made me feel as though I could be genuinely attractive, but I stubbornly didn't believe them. My natural response was to pine over how I'd never be good enough and that nobody would like me up close anyway. Instead of pursuing these opportunities for romantic relationships, my response was to try to become more attractive while keeping people at arm's length.

I got expensive hairstyles and purchased flashy new clothes to stand out. More of my time became consumed by checking myself in mirrors. I got more attention, but I feared it only brought the focus back to my skin, making me even more anxious. I passively sought affection, but I never just tried actively asking people out myself. I thought they would make the move if they found me attractive.

I'd crossed the line between presenting myself nicely and becoming completely appearance-obsessed. My obsession seemed to rub off on those I spent time with, so I wasn't great company. The most unattractive thing about me had become my personality. I was shallow, aloof, and came across as disinterested in anything but myself. I'd become even less approachable and less sociable than before.

No matter how hard I tried, however, I couldn't convince myself that I would ever be good enough for people who were interested back when I was just plain ol' me. All of my effort seemed for naught. My desired future wasn't getting any closer and I wasn't enjoying daily life, so I despaired. It wasn't really how I looked that held me back though; it was my anxiety about how I perceived my appearance and myself.

I'd been slowly reducing my use of benzoyl peroxide so that the skin dryness didn't inhibit me so much, but this led to my acne relapsing. It wasn't anywhere near as severe as in the past but, because I'd become so invested in my appearance, I completely broke down. I'd managed to get by under the assumption that acne was merely a passing phase, but learning that it was a chronic skin disease to be continuously managed hit me hard. There seemed to be no end in sight as all the years of laser treatment and healing began to be undone.

By this stage I couldn't work or study, as all of my focus went into getting through the class or work-shift without having a complete breakdown. It was all I could do to keep back the tears as I struggled my way through the task at hand. I couldn't be seen with my skin in such a state. I had to get away from the world, and so I withdrew to my house.

Time passed slowly as I waited for my skin to get better. I filled the time with film, novels, games, and sometimes writing, but I compulsively had to pause to check my skin. I didn't truly enjoy anything because I measured its merits by how much it took my mind off what I looked like.

My life was a fine line between avoiding mirrors while hiding in darkness and scrutinising myself in harsh light, often smashing the mirror in frustration. I was getting cysts and scars again which would fade but never fully disappear. Scars fading is like halving a number continuously: it gets smaller but never reaches zero.

I'd long been devoid of any friends or social life as I inevitably realised that my low self-esteem made me cling to people who were harsh to me, simply because I didn't think I could do any better and didn't want to be lonely. I deserved more supportive people in my life, but I made the mistake of withdrawing from my family completely and, thus, fulfilled the very fear I wanted to avoid.

The state of my skin had become a barrier. I blamed it for my loneliness when, in truth, I imposed the isolation upon myself. I was always shy and anxious, but my skin brought out the worst in my insecurities and became the scapegoat for all of my problems. I thought that if my skin cleared up I would be able to do anything. The more I viewed my skin as a barrier to getting on with life the more I became singularly attached to scrutinising my appearance as I waited for it to improve.

The closer I analysed my skin, the more I found to dislike. My whole mood became entangled with my skin and so corresponded with minor fluctuations that other people simply didn't see. Multiple dermatologists, doctors, and even family said that my skin looked good, but I didn't believe them for a second. I thought that they weren't looking closely enough or that they didn't have high enough standards.

Something I've since learnt is that everyone looks porous, spotty, and marked up close. There isn't a person in history that could have passed the scrutiny of the up-close, magnified, high-definition, no make-up test that I subjected myself to every morning and evening, yet people still manage to function. I figured that if someone is close enough to notice, they should either learn to respect my space or to be grateful for the intimacy.

My whole sense of self-worth was based upon these unrealistic physical standards that no human being could achieve. Such was my perfectionist mind frame: I had to be better than was possible. I lost sight of being human, which commonly involves having spots, scars, and marks. Everyone goes red and flushes sometimes, which I hated in myself, but some people even use make-up to achieve that very blushed look permanently.

At the time I hadn't grasped any of this. If I left the house it was at night and I totally avoided people. I didn't want to go back to harsh acne treatments, or hiding with hoodies or scarves as I once had, so instead I hid away completely. If I had an appointment I couldn't get out of, I told whatever lie I could think of and said whatever they wanted to hear to get out of there as quickly as possible.

Home wasn't a comfortable place either, though. It became a prison of constant self-loathing. It wasn't like a paid vacation. I didn't have any money put aside for bills or costly therapy, let alone to enjoy myself, not that I could have done so in that mind-set. When I reached out for government welfare assistance I was rejected, which only worsened my mental state further.

I needed stability in order to be able to focus on getting better, but it was like getting a repetitive ultimatum: work or starve. For a long time, it seemed that my life would go one of two ways. Either I would starve on the street or end my life before it came to that. For the moment though, what little I ate led me to gaining weight because I was so reclusively inactive, which made me feel even worse.

For the most part, my hatred was directed internally at my own skin, but I envied others. I envied the fact that people drank alcohol, ate junk food, didn't exercise, smoked, took drugs, slept with their make-up on, never wore sun protection and weren't as cleanly as me, but still somehow managed to have clear skin. I was jealous that people considered it normal not to be waking up tight, dry, and flaky with new cysts every day.

While most people paid little attention to their skin and remained clear, my sole focus was fighting my acne and still it was a losing battle. It threw me into despair seeing others happy and functional when I wasn't. I couldn't stand how people who had never had cystic acne simply didn't understand, but I also hated how people with acne weren't affected by it like I was. Spite consumed me. I convinced myself that the world would be better off without people with acne like me, or that at least we should have the decency to not show ourselves in public. I held these terrible thoughts as core beliefs, which led me down the path of contemplating suicide.

I was angered by being alive and broke down at making the most insignificant decisions or merely getting dressed. I spent nights sobbing while I shook. I drove around at high speeds with my eyes closed. At times I clutched knives, smashed glass, pondered purchasing rope, thought of carbon monoxide poisoning, or punched the fridge. When misery overwhelmed me, the sheer desire to end my suffering was almost enough to make me do anything in that moment. Taking my own life was not something I could do, though, in despair, I put some family members in very unfair situations, pleading for their help to end my life. That failing, I wished only that I would fall asleep and never wake up again.

Whatever happened with my skin, I felt I could do nothing but endure it. There was no way out. This inevitably led me to a choice: either I could bemoan my existence and guarantee my misery, or I could embrace living and maybe some things might even go my way. If I truly had nothing to live for, I had nothing to lose by trying to live. I decided that I might as well give life a try. I found this decision extremely liberating. I'd already lived through rock bottom. What did I have to lose now?

The first step on my journey back to the world was being prescribed what is considered the last resort medication for acne. I was given lots of warnings about this drug worsening depression, but in my case that wasn't accurate. Isotretinoin led to a stabilised improvement in my skin that also greatly improved my mental health. It was, nevertheless, a two-edged sword due to some of the side effects I experienced, including dryness, flushing, rashes, and intense sun sensitivity. These by-products of treatment can sometimes be as frustrating as the acne itself, but finding an equilibrium between acne and treatment allowed me to move forwards.

I wasn't constantly clear though and so I wasn't completely satisfied. This led me to taking a different approach: treating my attitude, my obsessive preoccupation and unattainable standards. That is, to treat body dysmorphic disorder. For years my goal had been to have skin that I wasn't ashamed of, but now I just didn't want to be ashamed of my skin.

While I was researching online one night, I discovered BDD and instantly found it was something I identified with. It took me three years, since the time acne first inhibited my life, for me to consider a mental approach instead of dermatological one. From there it took two more years and more than five failed attempts to find the assistance I sought.

Doctors were so ignorant about what BDD was. Initially, I was diagnosed as anxious and depressed, with obsessive compulsive tendencies. When I mentioned BDD, they told me to 'keep it simple'. They thought BDD involved pure delusions and did not understand the aspect of exaggeration of existing flaws. Some doctors told me that my skin looked pretty good so it couldn't be the cause of my distress. A psychologist dismissed BDD as 'rare', while a subsequent psychiatrist told me not to use 'big terms'. It was so frustrating how completely misunderstood BDD was that I gave up trying to seek help for it for over a year.

Eventually I found and contacted a BDD specialist directly to discuss anti-depressants. I'd once heard a story about a veterinarian prescribing anti-depressants to a pet bird who wasn't eating. It seemed absurd. Clearly, the bird was depressed because it wasn't meant to live in a cage. I feared drugs because I didn't want to become complacent in my cage like the medicated bird. I wanted to fly. I thought I could if I just beat acne, but BDD makes things far more complicated than this.

With resignation, I decided to give medication a try. It was a major step for me as someone who didn't smoke, drink alcohol, or take drugs, not even caffeine and pain relief. Acne treatment was the only medication I'd ever taken. My prescribing doctor used a fitting analogy: anti-depressants are like giving your car premium fuel, but you still have to drive. With fluvoxamine, I find it so much easier to drive (as though I now had power steering), but I had to persist to find what worked for me. My initial experiences included venlafaxine and escitalopram, which led to me losing my appetite and going days with barely any sleep. Once I got beyond the initial drowsiness of fluvoxamine, I found my despair receding. I've regained my ability to focus and enjoy my hobbies. It was like being reunited with the fun, humorous, and sarcastic parts of myself that had been long lost to hopelessness.

While taking fluvoxamine, I can observe thoughts about my skin coming and going more naturally without me obsessing about them all at once. I can get on with my day, make decisions, and focus on the job at hand. Gradually I've been able to get back out socially. The more I socialise, the more I notice that the things I hate about myself are often things that other people have, yet they remain attractive as people regardless.

Even before I had acne, my expectations were utterly unrealistic. It's no wonder that I was single, but I was no hypocrite. I applied these unattainably high standards to myself and came up short. It was why I loathed myself. Withdrawing to hide my skin seemed to be the only rational response. I thought, 'Who wouldn't hide with skin like this?' All it takes is a walk among people to see many people with skin issues still going about their lives. There really wasn't anything rational about isolating myself into misery.

I also gave cognitive–behavioural therapy (CBT) and acceptance and commitment therapy (ACT) a try, but at first I found them to be a combination of mere common sense and lofty ideologies that simply weren't helpful in the grips of despair. My heart was often not committed to them because I was dragged along to sessions by concerned family members. The psychologists I saw for therapy suggested going out and getting a coffee or wearing make-up as ways to combat my suicidal desires. These consultations just left me in tears, feeling all the more helpless and hopeless.

Big steps for me in therapy were knowing what I wanted to achieve, finding someone to help me in that direction, and attending sessions of my own volition. Self-motivation was crucial because psychologists aren't hand-holders. Going along with the gold-standard textbook method was useless. However, by customising some techniques, I've been able to apply them to my life.

One particularly useful book was *The Happiness Trap*, by Russ Harris. Its methods have been helpful to me in terms of in distancing myself from harsh thoughts. It has also helped me to embrace the concept of the 'observing self' and, thus, to be more present and engaged in each moment. Through this I've rediscovered my hobbies, including hiking, writing, and music, and discovered a new hobby in photography, which have all been great outlets for venting emotions.

Just as I was starting to get back on my feet there was an incident where a member of my family was hospitalised. It gave me the opportunity I'd been needing to reconnect with my family, including my niece and nephew, whom I hadn't seen for two years. I feared the innocent honesty of children, and so expected them to say something like 'What's wrong with your face?' Instead my nephew simply asked, 'Why are you always hiding?' He had noticed my absence but not my skin. He simply missed playing with his uncle.

It was such a positive boost to reconcile with my family, and I also moved back into the family home. I was treated as though no time had passed at all. I thought what I had been going through was obvious; 'Just look at me,' I thought. People didn't understand how I was so much more bothered by my skin now than when it was much worse five years previously. Having BDD as a way to explain my struggle made it easier for people to support and understand me, as much as they could.

Getting involved with my family again made me part of something bigger than myself. Simple things like grocery shopping, a chat, or driving someone to work intertwined my life with theirs, making me feel accepted and valued beyond mere appearance. I was no longer isolated with my uncontested self-judgements. As I became less self-absorbed, I also reconnected with my personal beliefs. I'd become so entangled with waiting for when my skin was magically perfect that I'd stopped viewing life as a continuous journey of ups and downs. I thought life was pure joy or complete despair when, in reality, it's a balance of tribulation and triumph. Remembering this has helped me to achieve some perspective and satisfaction day by day, instead of just despairing while I wait for things to get better.

I've learnt that sometimes terrible occurrences can have great outcomes. Thanks to my battle with my skin I don't take happiness for granted when it comes. I've become less shallow towards others and more compassionate about the struggles people experience. I might not be able to control the circumstances of my life, but I can control whether they hold me down or help me to grow. I can choose how to respond.

One particular morning, there was a bunch of spots on my forehead that were bothering me. As I was pulling out of the driveway I stopped and gave in to the urge to assess how bad they really looked. I told myself that whatever I saw was the 'gospel truth'. I had to just accept it and get on with my day. When I looked in the car's rear-view mirror, what I saw was my mouth on my forehead, just above the bridge of my nose. I had to smile. It was a trick of the light reflecting between the mirror, the tinted windows and my sunglasses. Gradually, I have learnt to place less importance on what I see reflected back at me. Besides, who can trust something that's back-to-front anyway?

My battle with acne and treating it is ongoing, but I'm coming to invest less time, effort, money, and attention in it. My mood is less swayed by the minor fluctuations in my skin and I am no longer so compelled to check mirrors. I've become increasingly content with my daily interests and family life. I can't change what's happened or is happening with my skin, like that bird can't escape its cage, so I try to accept that, focusing on my other goals and making the most of my circumstances. I'm working on my dream of writing a novel, and that gives me a reason to get up every day.

Sure, there are still times when I think, 'I don't have BDD, I'm just mangled,' but even if that is true, it doesn't matter. What matters is how believing that thought, 'I'm mangled', used to consume my life and have a negative impact on my ability to function. Whether I want to call it BDD or not, my appearance preoccupation and unrealistic standards have been greatly reduced. Maybe one day soon I'll overcome them entirely.

Me (Dathen) at seventeen, unfazed by my skin.

Me at twenty-three, consumed with worry about my skin.

Self-portrait, me at twenty-three.

Dominic Edwards

I don't want to over-elaborate on the formation of BDD and the suffering I went through but, rather, talk about my route to recovery. This book aims to give hope to those of us unfortunate enough to suffer from BDD, as well as to their families and friends who so often live through the experience with them. I hope my story will highlight how I continue to control and manage my BDD rather than let it rule my life, as it once did.

At the age of fourteen, with all of the normal pressures of a very uncomfortable time for many, a simple worry about my appearance became a preoccupation and later a full-blown obsession. I wanted to eradicate this perceived defect and entered into a destructive quest that overshadowed every other responsibility I had at the time.

In my case, the initial obsession focused on my legs, a reasonably unusual manifestation even in male BDD terms. To correct the perceived problem, I formulated various plans of action. Rigorous daily exercise, the use of creams accompanied by obsessional touching and various other checking behaviours (looking at magazines, mirrors, videos) in order to compare myself to others and to ascertain if my routine improved my perceived defect. This also led to situational avoidance in order to keep what I considered a deformity unknown to others. I would avoid swimming, changing rooms, and anywhere with lots of mirrors. There were so many restrictive rules and obstacles that day-to-day living became a hugely stressful and exhausting task.

The main issue here is that I believed my problem to be real. This involved shame, secrecy, and embarrassment. I believed that I, alone, had to try to fix my perceived physical problem. This equated to years of ingraining these behaviours and beliefs and enduring the severe distress they brought. This vicious and lonely circle began to destroy my life and was equally damaging to those closest to me. My family and friends had no idea what the problem was, let alone any tools to help me.

This really underlines the need for wider recognition of BDD, akin to other mental health disorders. This will allow for a better chance of early intervention and possible recovery before the disorder takes a really firm hold. This, unfortunately, is not yet the case. Hence the reason, as I understand it, that this book has been put together.

Five years after the manifestation of the disorder, albeit an unknown and not personally accepted one by me, a breakthrough was made. I was lucky enough to have a very concerned family surrounding me, who, as I am sure many of you can empathise with, were at the end of their tether with worry. After endless searching and piecing together of my behaviours and emotional state, my dad called me into his office. He had found a description of a little known disorder online that he read out to me. The description could have been me. It was a word-for-word account of everything I was experiencing. Relief is not a strong enough word to describe the colossal weight lifted from my parent's shoulders and mine. After so long in the dark about my problem, I now felt that maybe, just maybe, there could be a way out. I also began to consider the possibility that my perception of my legs was not as accurate as I thought it was.

This signalled a massive turning point in my journey and the beginning of a very long and bumpy road to where I am today. I was eighteen years old at the time. This, again, really underlines the need for wide recognition and societal familiarity with BDD. The relief I got from learning about BDD put the cogs in motion to get professional help. This was not without its issues. None of the doctors I spoke to was familiar with BDD. Sadly, therefore, the referral I received led me to therapy that was not suitable for BDD. In fact, the disorder itself was not even diagnosed by the practitioner; I found treatment soothing – but largely ineffective.

Another problem here was that I found disclosure of my thoughts to be incredibly difficult, particularly after finding out they could be imagined and not actually real. There was a stigma attached to the notion that I might be mentally ill. I felt I could not trust myself, as I was delusional. This was a secondary challenge to that initial relief and something that would seem to need addressing early on.

That being said, I felt significantly better and more hopeful. This, unfortunately, proved to be a downfall when, under pressure from peers, I decided to move to Bristol for my first year of university. An unthinkable act a few months earlier and, in retrospect, an ill-judged decision. I found, as I am sure many fellow suffers do, stressful and alien situations increase anxiety enormously and, in particular, in environments where you are exposed to new people. All of the protective familiar structures that had 'kept me safe' before were compromised.

This was incredibly distressing. I spent an inordinate amount of time finding new running routes that avoided busy areas, finding out which mirrors were flattering and which not, and where to buy the creams I felt I needed. It was an exhausting task.

This has been one of the main and most destructive issues I have had with BDD. The time and effort put into these time-consuming behaviours never made me feel better for more than a few hours at best. The vicious circle continued and actually got far worse, despite my acknowledgement of it doing so. I must iterate that a lack of a support network here was instrumental in my decline back into the grips of the disorder. It is often a lonely disorder, even with support around you. When alone, it can become particularly desperate.

Unfortunately, I found that alcohol was a 'quick fix' of sorts that relieved the constant and crippling anxiety. This was not in short supply at university. Over indulgence in alcohol, added into the mix of BDD, only served to weaken me further. Of course, trying your best to look after yourself is an important part of recovery. Anything that weakens your resilience is detrimental to the process. I found there was no quick fix, but, rather, a project full of many small goals to overcome. I was amazed at how effective this way of thinking was, which I will elaborate later in my story.

After a rather exhausting first year of university I returned home in a terrible state and decided that I needed help quickly. I was finally put in touch with the Mausdsley Hospital, which has a specialist BDD department. This was where I was diagnosed and my treatment was planned.

SSRI anti-depressants were prescribed in order to stop the obsessional thinking and the behaviours that accompanied it, in conjunction with an intensive course of CBT. This involved, essentially, facing my worst fears and reducing the safety behaviours that I believed kept me safe and reduced my anxiety. For example, I was challenged not to exercise for one day a week, not to apply cream for a day, or to go into a public changing room once a week, or to try on new clothes and so on.

These types of exposure techniques meant that I had to break down the ingrained belief system I had so carefully crafted. The idea is that once you face reality and realise that you can live with that reality, however traumatic it might initially seem, you can dramatically improve your condition despite the initial trauma.

Another technique, which I am not sure is still in use, was to photograph my perceived defects and list what I thought about them before sending them around for judgement by other random people in the hospital. This was my worst nightmare, I can tell you, yet a necessary one perhaps. The results did not confirm my worst fears of having a terrible defect but, rather, showed me that the opposite was the case. This provided considerable relief for a while but the BDD devil on my shoulder tried to tell me that there must be some mistake. This really emphasises the need to constantly, I would say religiously, work against that devil. I realise how hard this is but it really gave me the best chance of a recovery.

This is not to say that I have not had lapses, especially at times of stress, which are inevitable in life. As they say though, practice makes perfect. Constantly doing small things that challenged my belief system became easier and easier over time. Never easy, but easier. Then, eventually, larger tasks could be attempted and so it goes on. In fact, I started doing more adventurous things than I did prior to my illness. I think it must be added that my reaction to the medication was successful, which helped me greatly with the exposure techniques and learning to rationalise my thought processes more effectively.

Having got so much better with treatment, I could enjoy things I had not entertained for years: spontaneously going out, social activities, and relationships. It was heaven at first. I had a really good time. Two years into recovery, however, I realised that my carefree attitude and lifestyle, which was in part a rebellion against the disorder, had put me in a wholly different situation. I had accrued a huge student debt, had failed many of my exams (simply because I was enjoying other things so much) and in general had lost control of my purpose, which was getting a degree and a job which, in turn, would stabilise my life further. One could say I had entered a state of mania.

I had been on the medication for too long and had become somewhat dependent on it. This had to be addressed. SSRIs were only a stepping stone and a temporary measure to allow me to get back on track, which they did. They should have been decreased and ceased much earlier. This is something that will, of course, vary between people and their unique physiologies.

I was able to get myself back on track when I returned home to London. I gradually came off the medication under supervision from my parents and trips to and from the doctors to see how I was progressing. At this point, it was deemed necessary to get a job or something to keep me occupied. Focusing on something concrete gave structure to my day and limited time for old fears to enter into my mind-set. This really consolidated my recovery.

I actually took up a wine and spirits course and found a job in a fine wine shop. This was a an interest I had found while working in an off-licence at university, again probably initially a bad call, all things considered, but it served me well at this particular time. I kept focused on studying the subject and taking opportunities to carry on doing things that I had previously found so hard, such as public wine tastings, talking to people, and teaching them about wine.

Despite my anxiety levels rising slightly while coming off the medication, I still managed to hold things together and carry on the positive recovery, largely due to my schedule. The possibility of the old perpetual thought cycle was constantly interrupted and eventually, again, vague background noise.

An important element to my recovery over the past few years since my return from university has been, without a doubt, keeping myself occupied and engaged in other things. Despite the stressful nature of starting new things in new places with new people and new risks, which we all face, BDD or not, these were key to my continued recovery. I think that the time lost to BDD while sufferers are distracted and disabled by their symptoms is one of the most devastating effects of the disorder. Coming out of the haze and realising what you have missed out on can be overwhelmingly distressing, to the point of lapsing into a state of further depression.

I have come to view BDD, in a way, as an opportunity in my life; I may even feel better than I would have done had I never experienced it. This way of thinking has helped me to stop the negative thoughts, which has, nevertheless, required a lot of practice. The rewards have certainly been worth it.

In conclusion, I feel that I am very lucky to be where I am today. The real key to my recovery has been the outside help I have received from professionals in the field. Their endeavours have led to effective treatment of the BDD. Both they and my family have played an integral role in assisting me through the lowest points of recovery and also in enjoying the highest. That being said, not all of us have that luxury, and what does someone that does not have it do? That's why the work being done by the BDD Foundation is so vital. The access to support groups and accessibility to educational information and treatment of the disorder can provide a lifeline and knowledge about BDD, not just for sufferers and their loved ones, but also wider society. There is still a lack of understanding not only about BDD, but mental health in general. I plan to fight for this recognition and to do all that is within my power to help others in their own personal battle against this incredibly destructive disorder. I am currently working as a specialist mental health support worker in Lambeth, where I support people with serious and enduring mental health problems, including BDD and OCD. I can safely say that I now feel I have come full circle and stand in good stead for the fight ahead. I am now thirty-one years old and enjoying life once more.

E's Story, from the Perspective of her Mother

My daughter, E, the youngest of three girls (by four and seven years, respectively), was brought up in what is commonly referred to as an 'intact family'. She was a sensitive child who did not like to draw attention to herself.

She was anxious and clingy at nursery school, but much happier at primary school with her two older sisters. She came across as very gentle as a child. She was very good-natured and caring, and very well liked by children and staff. She was well behaved and self-effacing in class. Perhaps that is why nobody at primary or secondary school picked up on the fact that she was dyslexic. Her undiagnosed dyslexia might have been one of the reasons for her increasing anxiety.

I was staggered to learn that E was unhappy with her appearance at secondary school. At primary school she had shown no interest in her appearance. She didn't talk about herself, and neither did she show any precocious interest in make-up.

E began to become withdrawn in year eight, and by year nine she was obviously deeply unhappy. She was mixing with the wrong crowd, staying out late, avoiding her homework, tearful, tired, and pale. At that time she was also developing from a pretty child to a beautiful young woman and was attracting the attention of many boys. She was on the receiving end of both positive and spiteful comments from girls. This made her feel very self-conscious about her appearance.

Outside of school, E was additionally in an environment where much attention was placed on the body. She was figure skating regularly and surrounded by people who obsessed about their appearance and weight. I knew for certain that she was seriously ill when, at the start of year nine, she refused to go out because of a 'spot' on her face, which was not something anyone would have noticed *at all*!

I remember E's descent into serious illness very clearly, although I would rather not if I am entirely honest. There were times when E was so ill that she couldn't face being seen by anyone, including her own mother. She was unable to leave her room and missed the best part of a year of school. Her mood was frighteningly low; as we know, BDD has one of the highest suicide rates of any psychiatric illness. The suffering caused by BDD can be extreme and certainly was in my daughter's case.

E's GP referred her to the NHS's Child and Adolescent Mental Health Service (CAMHS), who, despite her rapid *daily* deterioration, which I relayed to them over the phone, refused to assess her earlier than the allotted time originally given. She had to wait a good few months after being assessed and referred for CBT 'for general anxiety' for any treatment at all to be implemented.

I was told that my daughter could only be seen if she were a priority case. I asked what denoted a priority case and was told that a young person was only deemed to be a priority if he or she was self-harming. I asked for CAMHS's definition of self-harm; I was told it meant cutting or taking an overdose. I said that what my daughter was doing to herself constituted self-harm in my opinion, for example, banging her head against the wall, slapping her face, tearing her hair out, and other things which I can no longer even bear to think about. Whatever I said, it made no difference. CAMHS refused to see her until their given time, which was months into the future.

I now know that I should have taken my daughter to A&E or phoned the emergency services. I wonder if this might have prevented the illness from becoming as embedded and entrenched as it did. I suppose I did what I thought was the next best thing at the time. I rang the NSPCC, on the grounds that my daughter was suffering from extreme cruelty, though this cruelty was tragically being perpetrated by her very own hands. The NSPCC directed me to the local Director of Children's Services, who asked me to speak to the CAMHS commissioner. The CAMHS commissioner was interested; she said that ours was the second complaint in the area and asked for my permission to name my daughter. When my daughter's CAMHS psychiatrist found out, she admonished me for lodging a complaint. So, reporting the problem to the NSPCC, the Head of Children's Services, and the CAMHS commissioner just made things worse. All I wanted was immediate care for my child, who was extremely ill at the time.

At that point, we did not yet understand that E had BDD. We had never heard of such a condition, although I understood from E's bizarre behaviour and obsessive comments that her view of reality at that time did not match anyone else's by any criteria. I started researching her many symptoms on the internet and came across BDD. E was overwhelmed by the knowledge that there were other people who also suffered as she did (she still, thankfully, had moments of insight). Even so, the wait for CBT through CAMHS drove her to utter despair. She simply couldn't wait that long, but CAMHS refused to listen. During this dark time, E refused to leave the house. When, on one occasion, she did manage to get out, she then wouldn't leave the car. When she eventually entered the CAMHS building, she locked herself in the toilet. CAMHS refused to acknowledge that E had BDD and she fell into utter despair.

It was E, ultimately, who helped herself. She asked me to go to our GP and to ask the GP to ring her at home. I then heard E trying to explain her treatment at the hands of CAMHS: their condescension, their dismissive attitude, their refusal to listen. She made it very clear on the phone that day that she was a danger to herself. She explained that she was trying to do everything to help herself, but had the impression that no one else was trying to help her. She begged for help, explaining that she couldn't go on . . .

Our GP contacted CAMHS. The very next day the CAMHS psychiatrist rang me to say that she was getting the paperwork ready to refer E to an assessment at Birmingham Children's Hospital. Even so, that entailed a further wait – a few more weeks – but, by then, we'd bought the book, *Overcoming Body Image Problems Including Body Dysmorphic Disorder*, by David Veale, Rob Willson, and Alex Clarke, wherein we found the email address of a leading BDD specialist. We sent him a list of E's symptoms and set up an appointment. While awaiting this appointment, E was indeed diagnosed with severe BDD at Birmingham Children's Hospital. She was eventually treated at the Priory Hospital in London for 'severe, refractory BDD'.

My daughter is a lovely person. She is a young woman with many talents. She was overlooked in an alarming way, both in terms of her abilities and her difficulties. While in hospital receiving treatment for BDD (CBT, ERP, and fluoxetine), she was taught to draw by a fellow patient who unlocked an ability within E that she never even knew she had.

Five years on from this initial treatment, E is on the road to recovery and is studying psychology at university. She wants to become a clinical psychologist so that she can improve the lives of young people who suffer from mental illness. She still takes fluoxetine and would like to reduce her dose. It's a gradual process

Encouraging words and advice for parents, relatives, and partners of loved ones with BDD

- Once your loved one with BDD starts to receive BDD-focused help, trust that he or she will get better. It may take a long time, and there may be relapses, but my daughter is proof that is possible to make great progress. The brain is a very powerful tool; repeated practice *of the right kind* leads to good habits, but habits take time to embed. Embrace the medication if it's helping your loved one to engage with the therapy. Depending on the extent of the BDD, your loved one may need to take medication for some time. You might not like this, but perhaps need to remember that it's helping someone who is recovering from a mental illness. (You wouldn't, after all, spurn medication if your loved one had cancer, would you?)
- Be firm with your loved one in relation to practising response and exposure therapy, and do not feed the safety behaviours to avoid tantrums. You may have to experience verbal abuse, but it won't last for long if your loved one is getting treatment. Trust that things will get better.
- Seek counselling yourself. This is very important. As someone close to a person with BDD, you need help so that you know not only how best to handle your loved one (e.g., how to encourage and empower him/her, as well as how not to forever patronise or forever treat

him/her as an ill person), but also so that you don't blame yourself for your loved one's illness. Counselling can also help you to acquire skills and tools to keep your own anxiety at bay if you see your loved one's anxiety on the rise. It may allow you to reflect on your own situation and see whether or not you might need to make changes in your immediate environment, changes which may be of benefit to your loved one experiencing BDD.
- Look after your own physical health. Get sufficient sleep, eat healthy food, and take exercise to help you keep your own stress levels down.
- Consider getting a pet. They are very good for the soul. They are something for a person struggling with their mental health to love, to calm them down, to comfort them, to give them something to care for, and to give them a different point of view. Our cat, Tom, rescued E on one occasion, persuading her to get down from the roof when she was beside herself with distress.
- Remember that your loved one is not the sum total of BDD. Do whatever you can to distract and engage him/her in the wider world: for example, watch films (especially comedy); chat about the world – politics, society, different places and people; play games (Scrabble, Monopoly . . .). Model an interest in the world yourself. Let your loved one see you doing things which engage you, for example, playing an instrument, learning a language, reading, cooking, sewing, gardening. The latter can even be done without going outside the house; it's wonderfully uplifting to see cause and effect, to see green things growing and thriving.

Photo of E.   Self-portrait by E.

Ellen

I am a sixty-five-year-old woman, and have experienced BDD for almost as long as I can remember, albeit expressed in different manifestations.

I was born in 1950, into a middle-class family in the North of England. I was a much wanted child, as my mother had suffered two previous miscarriages before I was born, and had medical intervention when she became pregnant with me to complete the pregnancy. This situation was repeated with my sister, who was born two years and ten months after me.

My father was a pharmacist who had his own little shop. My mother was a shorthand-typist who became a full-time mother/housewife after I was born, as was expected in those days. Initially, I believe that we had a happy and secure childhood, with material needs being met and a feeling of love and care prevailing. With the benefit of much hindsight and reflection, however, I would say that the family expectations were around pride in the family, appropriate behaviour, and achievement. Some of these expectations were around appearance.

My happiest memories are of playing with friends, especially out of doors, picnics, and escaping into reading. The most difficult were around expectations of achievement, especially around passing the 11+ exam; I was an ordinary, middle-of-the-class child, with no guarantees of passing the exam. Most of my parents' friends' children were at private school, but this was outside of my parents' financial ability, so grammar school was seen as essential for both educational and status reasons.

In addition, my father suffered a serious coronary thrombosis when I was eight years old (he was already forty-three when I was born). He wasn't expected to live. He did, but with impaired health, and my mother had to go out to work as a result of this. My maternal grandmother, of whom I was very fond, came to live with us at this time to be there for my sister and me when both parents were at work. I was always worried that my father would suffer another heart attack, and I knew how difficult my mother found being back at work. In addition, there was a lot of tension between my father and grandmother. None of these issues was ever spoken about openly.

One of the things that stays with me clearly, nearly sixty years on, is the memory of going to Butlin's on holiday, following my father's illness, so I must have been just nine years old. I loved Butlin's – the swimming pool, playgrounds, chalets – it was a child's dream. My sister and I and two other little girls we were with were entered into a children's beauty contest. My sister and the other two girls were all chosen to go forward to the next stage, but I was eliminated. I think that was the beginning of my feelings of inadequacy related to how I looked. I was desolate, hurt, and became convinced there was something terribly wrong with me. This was compounded by me being told (teasing, you could call it) that I was a 'little fatty', many times in my childhood, mainly by my father, although there was certainly a wider family dynamic about weight.

I am aware that such matters wouldn't necessarily have affected other children so much, but something in me made me believe that I was somehow terribly inadequate and ugly, which caused me to try to compensate for my perceived faults, and started me on a lifelong journey which has had many twists and turns, and has brought me to where I am today.

A friend recently asked to see some photos of me as a little girl, and, when we were looking at them, I could only see a bonny, healthy, smiling, boisterous child, full of energy, excitement, and joy, and I wondered how it could have ever happened that I took the path I did.

I was reasonably happy at primary school, but always had anxieties about how well I was doing and what people thought of me. My mother would come up to school periodically to speak to the teachers about my progress, so I knew it was important. I was always the smallest and youngest (August birthday) in my class. I fitted in well with others, had friends, and have no memories of being bullied at all.

I was the last on the list to pass the 11+ exam, so knew I'd just scraped into grammar school and felt inadequate because of this. I was very unhappy with my appearance, feeling short, dumpy, and frumpy. When I was thirteen, I began to develop what was later diagnosed as anorexia nervosa. I lost a lot of weight, spent a lot of time exercising (I was on the school hockey team and a very good swimmer) and studied intensively in order to get good O-level results. I studied science, even though I found it extremely difficult, because my father wanted me to be a chemist like him. Without realising it, I distanced myself from my peers, and had no social life at all. Studying, exercising, and not eating became my life.

This persisted for several years. I got good O Levels, the best A Levels in the school, and a place at university. I was there for ten weeks, but had to leave as my weight had dropped to sixty-two pounds (I am 4 ft 11 inches tall), and I was unable to function at all.

After a diagnosis and mental health support, I began to recover, and after a year, was able to take up a job as a lab assistant at a chemical company on Teesside. Moving away was good for me, and I ended up with a new circle of friends, and a social life. I was aware that, at under 5ft, and weighing about seven stone, I was viewed as being attractive (a 1960s 'Dolly Bird'), but found this difficult to come to terms with and tried to hide away as much as I could. Looking back, I think I believed that a perfect appearance would be the only thing that would make me acceptable to people, especially men, and I felt the only thing going for me was to try to be as petite and cute as possible. It never entered my mind that I could actually be an architect of my own life, rather than purely an object of attraction for others.

I got married at the age of twenty-one. My husband and I had a son and a daughter and were married for twenty-three years, after which I initiated a divorce.

At this time, in my forties, my concerns about my appearance seemed to change from that of my size to my facial features. I would catch a glimpse of myself in a mirror and feel horrified at what I perceived as an old, wrinkled woman looking back at me. I became obsessed with avoiding mirrors and would go to the disabled toilet at work, as it was the only one where the lights could be switched off and I couldn't see myself. I stared to cover up the mirrors at home, and avoided going to places with lots of mirrors, such as shopping centres, as much as I could. I would put on make-up with just enough light coming in so that I could see my face but not enough to show the lines and marks I knew were there. I refused to go away to places where I wouldn't be able to do this, and would get very upset when asked why. I wanted to visit my sister in Canada but couldn't bring myself to do it as her house has floor-to-ceiling mirrors in many places.

In short, I tried to hide away for much of the time. I managed to do things, such as work (I worked on a women's health project), sing in a choir, and go out with friends, as long as I could avoid seeing myself at all. I had a series of short-term relationships with men, none of which worked out; I now recognise that my search for approval was the cause of this. My relationships with female friends, however, have been positive and supportive.

I think I just accepted that this was how things were and got on with life as best I could. It wasn't until my daughter said to me one day, a year or two ago, that she thought I might have BDD, that I heard the term for the first time and tried to find out what it was. I immediately recognised myself in the description of the symptoms. I have never spoken to a doctor or therapist about this, though I have seen both at times when I have felt depressed and anxious.

When I look back on my life, I now see that the seeds of need for approval, my lack of autonomy, and my desire to be what I thought others wanted me to be led to a form of self-hate and internal anxiety, despair, depression, and a search for security in behaviours which have been both damaging and exhausting.

The most helpful insights into who I am and what I have experienced have come from reading Susie Orbach's book *Hunger Strike*, which helped me immensely to understand anorexia. *Overcoming Body Image Problems Including BDD*, by David Veale, Rob Willson, and Alex Clarke then helped me to understand BDD. I can see how I, as a sensitive and anxious child/young woman, stepped on to the path of self-doubt and social paralysis.

I think that recovery begins when a person, by whatever means, begins to recognise that their reality is not objective but, rather, a product of distorted, incorrect, perhaps damaged thinking, for whatever reason. I suppose the entry point for this could be via therapists or the medical profession, but also perhaps through a particular life experience which calls everything into question. I think, too, that the individual needs to be at a point at which he or she wants to change. Familiarity, however painful and distressing, nevertheless can bring its own comfort, safety, and identity.

For me, the journey of recovery has been through reading and support to help me to change my habitual destructive thought patterns. I have had mental health interventions over the years as an adult – though, on reflection, very few – but these have been for anxiety and depression. There has never been, from me, any indication to any member of the medical profession about my fears, anxieties, and behaviours around my appearance. I think I must have normalised this for myself, and accepted that this was how one behaved, even though, deep down, I must have known how ridiculous it was. I was also completely ignorant, until my daughter named it, of BDD. Once I realised what it was, I felt too ashamed initially to talk about it with friends or therapists, only my daughter because she was clearly aware of it, and she was always entirely empathetic and supportive.

I read the series of *'Overcoming . . .'* books, and saw myself so clearly in so many of them, especially those looking at OCD (what a revelation that was!), health anxiety, depression, anxiety, and self-esteem. I recognised the underlying themes in them, which I understood as being that what I had perceived as objective reality was nothing but my habitual self-destructive, self-defeating, self-hating way of seeing myself and the world. I found it tremendously comforting that so many people, it seemed, knew what was going on. I felt I was no longer alone with these things. I also began to understand the saying, 'We don't see the world as it is – we see it as we are'. I read up on recent research about how the brain works and learnt that the brain is very capable of change and is not 'set in stone', as perhaps was once thought, which is a tremendously exciting notion to me.

I have read very widely over the years and have always had a great hunger to understand both myself and the world I live in. I then felt that what I had understood in terms of theory now needed, somehow, to be put into practice if my life was going to be lived differently, which I so wanted it to be. There are so often catalysts in our lives, even if we don't recognise them as such at the time. In my case, it was being confined to my home for a few weeks with severe back pain, clearly not something I would have chosen. Yet, this led me to start seeing an acupuncturist and to reading *The Mind–Body Prescription*, by Dr John Sarno. At that point, I knew everything was going to change – and it did. I decided to share my BDD with some of my closest friends. This was a very hard thing to do, as I felt so ashamed. Yet I was amazed at the reactions, mainly that of a forty-four-year-old friend, whom I had always seen as extremely attractive and outgoing, breaking down in tears and confessing to feeling exactly as I'd been describing myself. We both opened up to each other about our fears around our appearance, and about the effect it has had on our relationships throughout life. It made me more determined than ever to make changes.

I decided to try to do some things differently, and started to act 'as if', even if I felt bad about how I was looking. I made myself look as good as I could, and then carried on doing things in a positive way. I forced myself to engage in things I was afraid of, most of which turned out well. I got some nice clothes, especially things I wouldn't normally wear, and starting putting on different things each day. I stopped hiding from mirrors (that has been the hardest – I still squint when unexpectedly confronted with a reflective surface!). I have allowed a friend to take some photos of me, which I haven't for years. I have decided to be in a relationship with a man who, it seems, really cares for me.

I think my experiences around recovery, as a sixty-five-year-old, will, of course, be very different from that of a younger person. The world is a very different place now, with openness about issues, and new treatments available. The medical profession is now more aware of what were once hidden conditions, and there are more self-help books and other services available. I feel, in many ways, that I very much went it alone, with books as my support. I think for all of us though, we ultimately seek an understanding of the world, and what is going on for us, with a view to changing, and being able to step into the world to share our talents, abilities, enthusiasm, vitality, and love, instead of hiding away, full of fear, shame, and anxiety. Fear is such an exhausting way to live – I feel as though I've been fighting myself all my life. What has helped me along the road has been kindness, empathy, and understanding, but also the knowledge that what I thought was real actually wasn't. I now recognise that I can, and will, create a much better reality with determination and support.

As for me, well, I'm enjoying having a relationship with someone who thinks I am marvellous! I continue to work part-time supporting disabled people at home. I joined the University of the Third Age and play in their ukulele group, and have presented the topic of Ada Lovelace to the history group. I joined the art group and have learnt so much on a subject about which I knew nothing. The U3A has asked me to be on their 'ideas group', which I am thrilled about. I have joined a new choir, and am taking on a dog-share with a friend. My hopes for the future are to keep on keeping on, and be in the world, giving it everything I've got. I truly intend to.

I am proud that, despite having to deal with these major issues, I have survived and done many positive things. I have brought up my two children, who are doing well as adults; I obtained an Open University degree in social science (which I loved doing) when I was forty years old; I have many friends who love and care about me; I have supported myself financially since my divorce, having worked in Community Health and Domestic Violence support; I have a sweet little home which I love; I am interested in many things – history, geography and geology, psychology, and do a lot of walking in the countryside.

I wish I had had asked for help a long time ago, but am glad that I have come to terms with how I look enough to engage with the world in a positive way. I think that acknowledgement and treatment are now much more open and available than when I was younger, which is a marvellous thing. I do feel that the world in which we currently live has such a huge and all-encompassing emphasis on unobtainable physical perfection that so many people feel inadequate, and I see BDD as an extreme manifestation of perhaps a near-universal sense of imperfection. I hope that the more people recognise this, the more things will change.

Fiona

As a child growing up I had a very secure, comfortable upbringing. I was surrounded by a large family and lots of laughter. Fun and mayhem were always at the top of the agenda. I was a bubbly, outgoing child. As adolescence approached I became more conscious of how I looked and realised that I was a little plumper than other people, not on a huge scale, but I noticed it. I never struggled with friendships or popularity and enjoyed most of school. Facial hair was a big issue in my teenage years and became a massive confidence barrier for me. It also became the focus of taunts and bullying, especially from males and, in addition to this, they would mention my weight. This started to make me very conscious of my face and body image and I immediately felt that I needed to start improving, grooming and changing my appearance.

With my self-confidence already crushed without even knowing it, I started to look at magazines. I was met with flawless images and perfect skin, which looked altogether too shiny and perfect. At this point I was also beginning to scrutinise and find fault with the complexion of my skin. Little did I know that this would turn into a daily obsession, which would control my every move, thought, posture, glimpse, breath, and confidence and consume every single ounce of my life, day in and day out. As I started the never-ending obsession with my skin, I would find faults. I now know that these faults were never really there, yet I did end up with acne due to the stress of the imaginary flaws, so the obsession and stress of it all actually created the visible spots, thereby making me more self-conscious. When the pimples came up they became so severe at times that my face would swell up and I would spend hours covering them up and researching the best concealer. I spent hundreds of pounds on attempting to hide and alleviate my stress-related acne. I would avoid social situations if I felt that my skin was bad or if I had put any weight on. Bright lights were also avoided at all costs. Some days I would dread going out of the house and I came to hate the summertime, as my make-up would have to be reapplied because of the heat. Even if I managed to leave the house, I would still be very tense and perpetually conscious of people criticising my looks.

I would jump out of bed in the morning and run to the mirror to see how my skin looked, hoping it had cleared up. To make it look and feel better and to receive some relief, I would pop all of the spots, so skin picking also became an issue. Looking in the mirror to reassess and discover new flaws or to pick at current pimples was a consistency throughout the day, every day. My body was constantly tense at an extreme level. I woke up with headaches due to worrying and dreaming about my skin and would grind my teeth severely through the night. My life felt like a living hell and, on occasions, I would say to myself that it would be so much easier if I didn't wake up one morning. I wanted to live, but didn't know what was wrong with me. I wanted to enjoy my life but no longer knew how to do that.

I became scared of getting into a relationship because I thought any potential partner would just think that I was hairy, spotty, fat, and ugly. Sadly, some people did actually say these things. I looked for love in the wrong kind of places and from the wrong kind of people. I yearned for reassurance and approval from others and was desperate for them to think that I was beautiful enough, that I looked all right. Alcohol and marijuana abuse became a very close companion in my life to relax me and escape the pain of BDD. I would also purchase many clothes and lots of make-up in order to make myself feel better, but it was always a very short-term fix.

I would feel the bumps on my face continuously throughout the day and my skin would often feel as though it was crawling. I would also feel tingling sensations over my face, later learning that these were anxiety symptoms. I would compare myself to what I classed as beautiful people constantly throughout the day.

I somehow managed life day by day. I met my now husband and had a baby boy very quickly after we got married, which was a true joy and significant turning point in my life. During my pregnancy I hoped and prayed that my child would never have confidence issues like I had. This prompted me to start researching BDD, in order to have enough knowledge to promote a better a life for my family. I started to work on self-development and began praying (I am born-again Christian) and combined this with researching how the mind works. I also went along to some self-help for anxiety workshops and body confidence issues. This is when I found out about BDD after speaking with a lady at church who was a clinical psychologist. I started research immediately and this was my breakthrough! As soon as I understood my condition and understood what my mind was doing to me (which was, ultimately, telling me lies) I started my road to recovery.

A pushing tenacity of faith, love, motivation, and perseverance got me to where I am today. I had five sessions of CBT and it changed my thinking; I simply started to look at my skin and face differently. This also prompted me to get some suitable skincare, which cleared my skin up in a week. At this point, my mind was clear enough to enable me to see solutions and act upon them. I am now happily married. I still have a bit of facial hair now and again and the odd spot but you will also see me in the supermarket with no make-up and my hair scraped up, something I could have never ever done before. It sounds very simple, although the road has been tough, long, and I have had to climb some very high mountains, to say the least. Yet I climbed that mountain and set my flag at the top. I am now a student on an access course in Health and Wellbeing with the aim of starting a psychology degree in 2017 and with the hope of progressing to studying neuroscience. I want to understand more about the brain in BDD sufferers so that I can help people in the future with this condition. What I can say for certain is, there is hope. You *can* recover. I, having worked through recovery, am now bubblier than ever! I started to live again and will live life to the max. You are good just as you are and I hope that one day you will discover the truth of that.

Fiona.

Frances Roberts: A Mother's Perspective

From soon after her twelfth birthday Jenny seemed to go gradually downhill, through depression, eating issues, and dark thoughts for just over two years until Christmas Eve of 2014. We spent this particular Christmas Eve in A&E, deciding whether Jenny should be admitted to a psychiatric ward or if we could try to keep her safe at home. We went home and Jenny was given a diagnosis of BDD in early 2015. It can be the most cruel, intense, and almost unbearable disorder. Watching a child really struggle with inner voices telling her that she's ugly, repulsive, not good enough, while seeing 'craters' (teenage acne) in her face so that she can't go out of her room, let alone the house or to school, day in, day out, is unbelievably hard. It's also extremely frustrating, as the reality is *so* distorted and you feel utterly helpless. The sheer unpredictability, as well as the dramatic ups and downs, is totally draining.

At times we have not been allowed into Jenny's room. When she was very ill I would still sit on the floor just outside of her door in order to be nearby. I'd stroke the door to say goodnight which she knew was my way of telling her that I loved her. More recently, as she has started to recover, I sometimes ignore the usual 'don't come in' and do so, not looking at her but quietly sitting on her bed briefly, as I think pushing that boundary just a bit has helped her not to retreat as much. It's obviously much easier to stay under the duvet but not helpful in longer term.

Any support you can give through the utterly illogical agony of BDD helps, but I've learnt you need to look after yourself too, as giving support alongside your own worry can be so draining. Guilt doesn't help. I've gone over and over what we might have done differently, but I really don't think BDD can be easily explained. Jenny's psychiatrist said how porous she is to others and I remember how very deeply she could be affected by others' actions and words when very young. The cruelty of BDD in teens is that it hits just when the young person is trying to work out who they are. Besides the comments of others, to the internal voices about appearance are added other negative ones about parents/home and schoolwork, and self-harming and other destructive behaviour can seem like a way to cope. It can become a negative vortex, sometimes exacerbated by online images and posts. But Jenny has turned a corner, and the insight and empathy – which she previously had in spades – are gradually returning.

In the early days a 'traffic light' system suggested by CAMHS, whose support we have been very fortunate to have, was invaluable. We'd ask Jenny what colour she was when words were impossible but distress intense: green = you can be downstairs for 10–15 minutes; orange = be nearby and speak every five minutes; red = just stay in the room, no need to say anything, just be there. When you are being pushed away by your child and the utter misery about appearance leads to verbal (and even physical) attack, don't give up! One mum said to me, 'When teenagers are at their most vile they need you the most.' This seems to be even more the case with children and teens with BDD. I felt it was worth writing a note and pushing it under the door and remembering that the really horrible behaviours are a sort of release and reflection of the torment inside, rather than things to be taken personally. I've written long notes as well as simple messages: that we all love her, that she is beautiful, that her brain is distorting what her eyes see, and that she needs to get out. From what Jenny says now, at least a part of those messages was received even if there was no reaction at the time. It's difficult to say the right thing. Rather than offering any solutions, just saying to teenagers with BDD that you can see how very real and hard it is for them really seems to help, as does keeping them focused on just one seemingly small goal which is potentially achievable at the time.

A family with a child with BDD is on a very different path to a child without such an affliction. This might sound obvious but I've often had to remind myself of this in order to quietly put the 'successes' of other people's children to one side, and rejoice in our own successes. In early 2015, an A* was being out of A&E for a week or two. Later in the year it became a day when our daughter got herself out of the house and to school by herself. Another parent of a child with BDD said he simply parked ambition and extended the timescale he had in mind for recovery. BDD is not quickly 'fixed'. Meanwhile, even the smallest steps you are taking with your child towards recovery are worth celebrating. Each and every one is an achievement. For much of 2015, getting Jenny out of her bedroom was the single aim. Nine hours spent getting ready on one occasion for a party – a huge achievement at the time as she *got* out – has now given way to an hour or two, tussling with the mirror and make-up. School is harder, as Jenny perceives the light as harsher and she is not just with friends alone. It has helped me to realise that my daughter *wants* to get out. BDD is a genuinely massive daily struggle. I have sat with the car key in my pocket ready and wanting to drive Jenny to school for hours, but over all this time I know Jenny would have rid herself of BDD (she would prefer it to be called 'appearance issues') in a flash if she could have done.

Mindfulness has helped me a great deal. I love gardening and photography and when stuck at home I have sometimes gone to the back garden and taken time to look at plants really close up and decide on a plant or two to photograph, taking time to get the angle and light as best I could. I've made myself focus and have felt my heartbeat calming down as I do this – and just enjoyed the sight and later, the photos. *Anything* that helps you or your child get through a hard day or moment is worth doing.

I think there's no point in regretting what has passed (tempting though that can be), or agonising about the future. Jenny wrote a long, insightful, and thoughtful letter to me for Christmas 2015, acknowledging my love and support and how much it has helped. I know other children with BDD have appreciated the supportive role of their parents and others around them *once* they start to recover. Until then, it can seem very bleak and there are twists and turns along a very bumpy path with many downs along the way. But the blackness does lift. Chinks of light return. Each and every glimmer until then is worth celebrating. And you're definitely not alone.

Photograph taken by Frances.

Hannah Lewis

Do you know what you look like?

I don't, and I never have.

I have an idea, of course, but then it's hard to distinguish which parts of my body image are factual, and which have been created by my 'Witch'. That's what I call the Body Dysmorphic voice in my head, because she is a nasty piece of work. She says the most evil and cruel things to me, and the most annoying part is that she has said these things to me so many times, and for so long, that I have been believing them for years now.

I was always different. Or, at least, I've always felt different. For as long as I can remember I was the tallest in my class, I stuck out like a sore thumb and I was also (forgive me for sounding big-headed) always at the top of my class, attaining the highest marks and winning all the prizes.

'Great', I hear you say . . .

FAUX.

I was already an outcast for my appearance; I didn't need to draw any more attention to myself. There was only one thing to do, and it took me until I got to secondary school to figure this out. I obviously had to pretend I was average in order to not be recognised.

ERROR #1 – jeopardising my education in order to 'fit in'.

Along with my early growth spurt came everyone's frenemy, puberty. Not only was I taller than everyone else, but my body was also the first to change. I was the first to encounter acne and I had child-bearing hips by the age of ten. Sure, I had boobs and all of my friends thought I was so cool for having pubic hair at the age of nine but, in reality, it wasn't so great. I wanted to remain a child like the rest of my friends. The periods were a curve ball, too: the greasy hair, the oily skin, the bloated stomach, all the while being in chronic pain. It was too much for my child's body to handle. It was around this time that my earliest memories of the cruel comments spring from. Sources varied, from the children in my class to the children in the years below me, to whom I'd never even spoken, staring in disbelief and exclaiming, 'You're nine, but you have teenage spots!' Shocking really. It was around this time that I recall the whole class having a photo taken to put up on the achievement wall. Wow, this was traumatic. I remember seeing my photo on the wall and breaking down in tears. I think it was at this moment that I realised how ugly I was. The thought of being exposed like that made me shudder. The teacher found me in such a state that I had to have the photo taken again. It wasn't great but it was an improvement. I felt I looked less like a whale, and every little helps.

Soon, the obsessions and compulsions emerged. In order to appease the anxiety my preoccupation caused, I engaged in certain ritualistic behaviours that I believed would make me more acceptable to be seen in public. When I say I was preoccupied, I mean I was anxious about my appearance at obvious times: when I was getting ready; when I saw my friends and compared myself to them; when I saw an attractive person in the street; when I saw someone on television or in a magazine; whenever I saw a mirror or reflective surface; whenever I was in a crowded public space. But then it got worse, and these thoughts began to invade my mind at any given opportunity. My concentration would be on a task for a maximum of two minutes before my mind strayed back to listing all of the reasons why I should loathe myself.

I would spend hours each morning doing my hair, make-up, and choosing what to wear. If anything was slightly wrong, I'd crumble. This routine, this rigmarole, was to follow me for the next decade. These compulsions included dermatillomania (compulsive skin picking), excessive use of make-up as a form of camouflage, wearing make-up constantly (even in bed), constantly wearing a scarf in order to hide parts of my body, and sitting in certain positions while in public so people were unable to see my profile.

Of course, this was exhausting (to put it lightly). Although I didn't realise it at the time, these behaviours worsened my anxiety and depression, and if I wasn't able to complete them to what I considered an acceptable standard, they would lead to avoidance behaviour. These compulsive rituals regularly, and perhaps unsurprisingly, got mistaken for vanity. If only people had realised that what I was trying to do was to make myself 'un-ugly'; I felt so selfish for inflicting my horrid aesthetic on unassuming passers-by. Mirrors were my enemy, as indeed they still are in many ways.

It was around this time that my incessant desire for cosmetic surgery emerged. In class, we had to write about what we would do if we won the lottery. All I could think about was cosmetic surgery or, as I called it, 'self-correction'. From the age of nine, I wanted a cosmetic procedure to rid myself of my awful skin. I also wanted my ears pinned back, a nose job, longer hair, liposuction, my teeth fixed, my forehead reduced, my legs shortened, and even an eyelift to make my eyes look bigger. This all took place in my nine-year-old brain. The thought of all that 'self-correction' still appeals to me to this day, but I now know that it won't make the BDD go away, as the problems that actually need fixing reside in a place much deeper than my perceived love handles and sticking-out ears.

I'd say the real catalyst for my issues was the bullying that occurred in secondary school. There was one girl who really sticks in my memory, yet it's unfair to say that she was the only culpable one. I remember as clearly as anything what she wrote in a geography text book for the whole school to see . . .

'Hannah Lewis is a big, fat, lanky slag with greasy hair and a spotty face and a big nose'.

ERROR #2 – I never congratulated said girl on her original use of adjectives; bravo little one, bravo.

Lest we forget, there was the constant name calling in the street, the threats, the physical abuse . . . need I go on? Or can we all agree that it was a pretty grim time? So grim, in fact, that I incurred my first dose of agoraphobia. Wow, those pesky outdoors really got to me.

However, I soon found some wonderful people who would turn out to be my best friends, and they still are today. A couple of years in secondary school were relatively abuse-free, but the damage had already been done.

My compulsions remained, my breakdowns persisted, and the new addition of delusional thinking became a persistent presence in my life. The nature of BDD is delusional itself – it is difficult to separate reality from the falsehoods your brain tries to make you believe. I've been told that the reflection I see in the mirror is different from what other people see. I've been assured that the people I notice in public staring and laughing at me are actually not doing so at all. The most prominent delusion was probably the one where I was convinced I was too ugly, and too abnormally deformed, to have been conceived naturally. I deduced that I must have been a test-tube baby that went horribly wrong, a scientific experiment gone awry. My mum and dad must have been in on it, so I was dubious of them, which made me an awkward child at best. Fortunately, I now know that this was a delusion aroused by my BDD, and I can now comfortably say that yes, I was conceived naturally, I developed inside a womb. I am, in fact, a normal human, just like the rest of you.

College was a bit tough. I tried to start afresh and to reinvent myself (a regular occurrence), but the façade crumbled soon enough and I was once again a vulnerable, insecure wreck. I was also in my first serious relationship at this point, which really didn't help matters. The constant jealousy, the persistent thoughts that I wasn't good enough, the insecurity, the paranoia. I was a bit too young and unaware of my condition for this relationship ever to work. It was during this time that the self-harming started.

ERROR #3 – hurting yourself will make things better.

And then there was university. This is when treatment really kicked off. I believe it was at this point that I was mature enough to hold my hands up in the air and say, 'OK, I think I may have a problem.' It's a shame that it took another dose of agoraphobia, countless days of crying under my duvet and – for good measure – a good old bout of panic attacks for me to realise this. So I got help. I saw doctors, counsellors, and therapists for body dysmorphic disorder, depression and anxiety, and with the help of citalopram, my first go at an SSRI, things got a bit better. I wish my group of friends could be prescribed to everyone else having a rubbish time; they really are amazing.

The next dip was six months later. I stopped going to university altogether. The thought of entering an educational institution filled me with fear, and all the memories of school came screaming back. But then there was Christmas and Christmas was nice. Oh, and my dose of medication was increased, which was nice, too. Just after Christmas was probably my darkest time to date. I was in a constant state of depression, having a can of cider for breakfast and showering only every few days at best. Thank God for congenital anosmia, because I must have stunk.

And now I'm here, in my fourth and final year of university. After a wonderful year in Montpellier, France, as part of my degree course, I was slim, tanned, and almost fluent in French. I had been seeing an amazing therapist with whom I had a brilliant relationship , and had tried two different SSRIs since I started citalopram. I felt great. But then things caught up with me again. I returned to university in Leeds and, as usual, the trauma of what happened in school was being relived in my mind every time I set foot on the university campus. I don't know why it was so bad this time around, but for the next six months I was battling with the mental health services to get help. I couldn't leave the house or even get dressed, and I couldn't be left on my own. My boyfriend became my carer. He was like my babysitter, and even dressed me when the sensation of clothing on my skin would trigger all the distress that my body dysmorphia caused. He would order me a taxi if I had to go anywhere, and hold me while I broke down and cried when I found myself in a public place, thrown into the lion's den. Not only was I suicidal, and constantly at risk of throwing myself under a bus, taking an overdose, jumping out of the window, or drinking a bottle of bleach, but I was displaying psychotic symptoms. I had auditory and visual hallucinations and would hear voices in my ears and see people or animals in my room. I was convinced that my boyfriend, who had cared for me for the past two years and dedicated his own life to saving mine, was part of a plot to have me killed. To say that these months were frightening is an understatement. However, I switched to yet another SSRI and had some intervention from Intensive Community Services. I had home visits from mental health nurses and saw the consultant psychiatrist, who established that it was my BDD which underpinned all my other symptoms and conditions.

Nowadays, my 40 mg dosage of fluoxetine is settling, and I feel strong enough to start another journey of psychotherapy. I'm able to function better and I'm determined to finish my degree to the best of my ability, after considering dropping out on numerous occasions.

I'm now in a better headspace and can convince myself by looking at my situation objectively. I do think it's fair to say that my face isn't being pulled in different directions, because that just doesn't happen in real life – that's a delusion and I'm aware of that now.

If I had to express BDD in one short sentence, I would say it is a heightened awareness of one's physical appearance, of the volume of space it inhabits, and of the way that other people think of it. I guess an overwhelming sense of not being good enough would explain it quite well, too. Doctors and other professionals would disagree and say that it is when the patient perceives a distorted image of him or herself, but I'm not ready to believe that yet, and I probably won't be anytime soon.

I am very much aware that BDD is a lesser-known mental illness. A lot of teenagers and young adults become self-conscious due to the way the media portrays an image of perfection that we all told we must adhere to. At first, that's what I thought I was a victim of, but in fact, and as I'm sure you can see now, it was so much more than this. While being aware that my illness can be interpreted as a girl who is narcissistic and vain, the pain and constant discomfort I feel in my own body reminds me that this is not normal, that this is not an acceptable way to live, and that it is all right for me to be honest with myself and admit that I suffer with a condition. Sometimes I feel as though the real person I am supposed to be is inside this cage that is my body, scratching and screaming to get out so that I can live the life I am meant to without my looks holding me back. I like to think that everything happens for a reason, and that I have felt the amount of emotional pain I have in order to become aware of mental illnesses and improve services for people in the future. I have dedicated my research dissertation to investigating a common European mental health policy and, after I graduate, I intend to study mental health law and to go on to work in mental health policy. My motivation, whenever I feel low again, is the responsibility I feel to ensure that nobody has to go through what I have been through. I do a lot of mental health blogging, and although I am relatively young, I feel that by sharing my experiences I can raise awareness of mental illness as well as beginning to eradicate the stigma attached. I also find writing very cathartic, and when I was once really struggling with my BDD I decided to write the following letter:

Dear BDD,

There's a lot I'd like to say to you. Above all I'd like to ask why? Just out of curiosity, why did you choose to prey on the mind of a vulnerable nine-year-old, and infest her brain with wicked thoughts? Why have you made me say such evil things to myself, why does malice drip from my mind like venom?

Why have you made me feel like I'm not good enough, that I don't deserve to be here, that my presence is such an eyesore on society? Why have you told me that the only way I can rectify the selfishness of my actions is to remove myself from the planet?

Why have you conditioned my brain to think that no matter what I think, say, or do, it is all worth nothing because nobody will be able to see past my hideous exterior?

Why did you make me stay indoors for so long? Why did I have to waste so much time in my agoraphobic cocoon, missing out on everything that was going on outside?

Why do you make me feel so uncomfortable in my own skin, like a cage that is keeping me from fulfilling my full potential as a person?

Why did you make me so obsessed with my image, and provoke the ritualistic behaviours which took over my life?

Why have you made me detest and avoid mirrors and reflective surfaces, to the extent that if I catch sight of myself it can ruin my day and send me into a deep depression?

Why do you drive me into periods of catatonia, unable to move, eat or wash?

Why do you stop me from knowing what is real, and what you have fabricated in my mind? Why do you incur so much paranoia that I'm constantly on edge, unsure whether the friends, relationships and success I have in my life are a mirage, created to taunt me with the unattainable?

Why do you give me so much anxiety? And why does it make me feel sick, sweaty and shaky? Why must I have panic attacks?

BDD, you're horrible.

You're so horrible, yet you get away with it. You get away with it because you're a lesser-known mental illness, affecting a mere 2% of us or so. You get away with it because you're mistaken for vanity. You get away with it because, sadly, so many young girls and boys already have low self-esteem and body image issues that it's not considered abnormal or unhealthy to hate your own appearance. You disguise yourself as something trivial and then transform into a life-consuming mental illness, cruelly opening the door for other mental illnesses to creep in, too.

BDD, you're going to be exposed. The world will know who you are, so if you're ever spotted, you can be stopped in your tracks because the longer you linger, the harder you are to get rid of.

Everyone will know that, with the combined approach of medication and psychotherapy, there is a way to defeat you.

It is not too late for me and it's not too late for all the other young minds which you prey on.

Yours sincerely,
Hannah

I'm quite candid when it comes to my approach to recovery. I know I have a way to go, and I am very realistic whenever I have a period of being 'up' – I'm far too aware that what goes up, must come down. One of my biggest regrets is not getting treatment sooner. I went undiagnosed for about ten years, and so now I know that my recovery will take longer. My definition of recovery has also changed, as I'm now more accepting that I might never be 'cured' of this illness. However, by persevering with different medications and commitment to therapy, I know that there is a better life waiting for me. I'm saying my mental illness is more like a bad smell that you can't really get rid of, but I can control it and take preventative measures so that it doesn't bother me as it has done in the past.

It does get better, and if it doesn't, please just remember that it *can*. Your life is actually very precious, despite what you may think.

Hannah Lewis.

INTERLUDE INTRODUCTION

We were humbled to receive a contribution for this book from a man, John, who had lost his mother-in-law, Tina, to suicide. We have included Tina's journey with BDD in this volume to give a full and honest picture of the seriousness of BDD as a condition, imploring the reader to seek help or to prompt their loved ones to seek help at the earliest opportunity. As these stories attest to, BDD absolutely can be overcome. Yet, BDD also claims many lives. Our hearts go out to John and his family and to anyone who has lost a family member to BDD.

Interlude: Tina's Story, by John Martin

It would be our last Christmas together. At the time, I even said it was the best Christmas. We sat around a table as a family with no thought of the horror that awaited our beloved Tina. We ate food and drank until we could just burst. Then we washed it down with left-overs.

I start our story at Christmas for two reasons. The first reason is the fact that Tina (my mother-in-law) loved this season. My partner Nikki, her daughter, would always travel to a Christmas market and spend a fortune on trinkets and other gifts that would grace our table on that special day.

Laughter was never far away when the family was together. We counted ourselves fortunate, I suppose, that we all shared the same sense of humour. Tina would normally lead the charge as we pulled the crackers during our final, happy gathering.

Maybe there were other good days after that. But Christmas is a memory I keep in my thoughts, like an island of peace, when the dark times close in around me to drown the light of happiness.

The second reason I begin here is because I know the family, like me, will take comfort from it. The actual time that Tina became ill was in the February following that magical day. The initial comment that made her daughter Nikki suspicious was quite innocent at the time. They were both in the car one day, on the way to work, and Tina mentioned quite casually, 'Does your face burn?'

'No Mum; nothing.'

They spoke about this very briefly, but Nikki returned home concerned. She had every right to be. Tina had done this before, seventeen years ago to be precise. This was before my time with the family I might add. Tina believed something was wrong. After various visits to specialists and a trip to the USA, she was diagnosed with mild rosacea. The effects were varied. But she was adamant that she saw spots and pimples and open pores on her nose. So began her first experience of BDD.

I had not heard of body dysmorphic disorder before. It's not something you see in the media or hear in general conversation. The first time Tina became mentally unwell, no one had diagnosed this disorder. She was given drugs to help with the depression, which was caused by the things she thought she could see. No one else could see the things she could. Her face and nose looked fine to us. But what she saw was a monster. She even said as much to me many years later. Eventually, she made her first attempt on her life.

Back then the family was in turmoil. Tina's depression was making the household a hard place to live in. Her husband tried everything in his power to help his desperate wife. He even arranged for Tina to see a specialist doctor in America. Alas, nothing worked for her. She still could see the things that were not there. Her first attempt on her life took the form of an overdose. One day she took a whole packet of painkillers. Fortunately, she did not succeed that first time, as she woke her husband up in the middle of the night and told him what she had done. I am glad she did, because it meant that I had the pleasure of meeting her and enjoying some amazing times together with her.

After her first suicide attempt, it seemed as if she would be lost to the family, after so much effort trying to fight her turmoil. Then, as suddenly as it came, just as suddenly did she stop mentioning her perceived appearance flaws. Life gradually became normal again. It would be seventeen years later that she would fall into the clutches of this terrible disorder once again.

Just as before, it was her nose that was the fixation of her torment. The BDD escalated much more rapidly than the first time. Tina looked into plastic surgery, drugs, and ointments. However hard the family and Tina tried, nothing could take her sorrow from her. Nothing could be said to alleviate her pain.

The monster that only she could see was back to haunt her every waking hour. We told her to try her hardest not to think about it, and not to talk about it. This was impossible; she could think of nothing else. After a month or so, she started seeing open pores, as large as craters, she would say. She started to see bags and folds under her eyes and spots and dots across her face. Always her face. She kept a small mirror by her side the whole day. She felt she needed to see the changes developing.

Of course, in truth, nothing had changed to our eyes. We told her so as often as we could. Her husband, Russell, would have moved heaven and earth to make her feel better. Yet he was powerless to convince her she was beautiful. She was, I would like to say, a strikingly good-looking woman. Throughout the happy years I always noted how immaculately dressed she was. Even if you visited the house in the early hours of morning, she would greet you looking fantastic.

Tina was also a shopaholic. It always amused the family to see mountains of clothes in her wardrobe with the labels still attached to them. Like her own persona, her house was the best turned out of anyone I know. Her house was like something out of a Next catalogue. It was her pride that ensured no one could say anything derogatory about her or her home. In addition to that, she also made sure that we were all dressed properly if we went out together. It was a brave person who crossed her, so legendary was her wrath.

It is only now that the family and I have time to reflect. For someone as proud as she was about appearance to get BDD must have been soul-destroying for her. I don't know if this personality trait and her eventual fall to the disorder are linked. But it is a curious notion to me.

And so, once again, the family would have to witness Tina's relapse into depression, obsession, and misery. It moved so rapidly. Her son, Sam, was just a boy when she initially became ill. Now he was a man and would sit by her side, as all of the family did, stroking her hand. He told her that she was beautiful, that we could not see the marks and swellings that she did.

One evening we were all gathered around at Sam's place for tea. We tried to pretend that everything was fine. We tried to be normal. So much effort went into leading the conversation away from Tina's problem. She just sat quietly in the corner. You could see that she was just waiting to talk about her face. In the end we did, and, like every other time, we would go over it again and again, to no avail. Sam's wife tried to mention that if it was rosacea, then she should seek a second opinion. So Russell took her to see a skin specialist. Later, we would learn from others that most people suffering with BDD will look to cosmetic surgery, for their face especially. The skin specialist told Tina and Russell that if it was rosacea, it was a very mild form. They then offered her a treatment of laser surgery to take away a layer of skin from her nose.

As seems to be the case with so many other sufferers of BDD, surgery was a failure. It failed because there was nothing to take away in the first place. Tina was booked in for three treatments with the laser. She had one treatment and deemed the rest to be pointless.

It was after this treatment that Tina attempted to take her life for the second time. The frustration that had boiled within her led her to cut her arm to shreds with a craft knife. Once she had done the deed, she had the sense to phone Russell, who came home as fast as physically possible. When he arrived there was blood everywhere. She had even tried to clean some up herself. When he got her to the hospital, they patched her up with stitches and tried to piece together her lacerated arm. When I saw what she had done to herself, knowing how much she hated imperfection, I feared that she would hate her appearance even more.

But when we asked how she felt about it, she didn't care. 'That's all right' she said. 'It's just my face I am worried about. I just need to get that sorted.' She had even told the doctors at Accident and Emergency the same story. They were a bit surprised when they asked the woman with a horrendous cut on her arm how it was to then be told, 'It's bad, what can you do about my face?'

Shortly after this step backwards, Tina looked into plastic surgery. As I mentioned before, Russell would do anything for his wife. Fortunately, the surgeon they met was one of the good people in life. I will not mention his name, but when this book is published I will give him a copy as a token of our gratitude. The consultation was a short one. He examined Tina's face and nose in a professional manner. He asked many questions before coming to the conclusion that there was nothing he could do for her. He went on to say that there were a few mild marks on her face, but nothing any normal person would not have. We all have tiny imperfections, of course. It's what makes us each uniquely us. The difference for someone suffering with BDD is how they handle and cope with these normal imperfections. For you and me, we might see a small pimple and never think twice about. But for Tina and others with BDD, that pimple or mark can seem as large as a crater, and a hideous one at that.

This consultant needs to be applauded for recognising that Tina's problem was a mental one. She had the scars on her arm to prove it. But she hid them from him under a long-sleeved top. Not once did she mention the attempt on her life. It was Russell in the end who pointed this out to the consultant. He knew what she really suffered with at that point. He did not charge them for the consultation. Another thanks the family owe to that man.

With that avenue explored, a recommendation was made to see a psychiatrist via Tina's GP. Things, I must say, were very bad by this point. Waiting for someone to see her was tortuous for us all. Especially Russell, who took the time off work to stay by her side and offer any comfort he could. We all tried to spend time with her. We tried yet again to tell her that there was nothing to see.

I remember a heart-to-heart we personally had. I tried to get her to put her face out of her mind. I challenged her to break away from the endless looks into the mirror. When we had finished talking, we were both in tears, holding each other for the coming battle. Unfortunately, her victory only lasted the night. The next day she and Russell were cast back into the hell they had both become trapped in.

Tina was eventually seen by a psychiatrist, who gave her some advice but mainly took notes and suggested that if she ever felt suicidal again, she was to admit herself to the mental health unit at our local hospital.

Day after agonising day her mental health deteriorated, much to the frustration and anguish of us all. My son, Thomas, was Tina's only grandchild at the time. He had always been a joy to her. She would watch him play and take pleasure from his antics. But even Thomas could not bring a smile to her face any longer. One day her bags were packed and she told her husband that she had to go to the mental health unit. It was all becoming too much for her. At this point, I would like to say what a terrible environment the mental health unit was for someone suffering with BDD. I did not want to make this story a rant or to blame anybody, but once Tina had been admitted to this ward, her condition went from bad to worse.

Just imagine it. Her worst nightmare was people seeing her face. She thought they could see how ugly she thought she was. For someone like that to be left in a room all day with strangers with all kinds of mental conditions must have seemed like torture. She was seen sporadically by a staff member. More notes were taken and more medication was given. No communication or diagnoses was given until near the very end of her stay. Throughout this time the family carried a tremendous burden.

We were told that Tina's assessment would have to wait until somebody came back from holiday. Eventually, a lady came to the home and spoke with Tina. She took notes and, thankfully, had empathy for Tina and the family's situation. She offered what help she could, and recommended treatments for Tina that might or might not have helped her, if she had held on. We then saw the first spark of hope, as the lady from the hospital indicated that Tina could very well have a condition called BDD.

It was a relief to think that we might be moving towards an actual treatment for Tina. To finally break the chains, which were shackling her to the depths of misery. The relief, sadly, was temporary. On and on we waited for her assessment to be completed by the board at the hospital. Russell received very little help and support. He was verging on breaking down himself. Tina was changing rapidly now. She researched the internet for any cosmetic solution she could find. However, the search for her miracle cure was only limited to her face. Not for her mental health. She had stopped wearing make-up shortly after her relapse, thinking that this would increase her skin problem further. She had also stopped eating and would not drink water from plastic bottles, just in case she aggravated her rosacea further. Her physical health, therefore, also began to rapidly deteriorate.

Tina lost weight dramatically, and her skin did change in the last few months. It had become pale from staying indoors, out of the sun. She stayed indoors because she did not want anyone but close family to see her. She also believed that the sun would make her skin worse.

Still we waited for some intervention from the NHS. I am sorry to keep having a pop at them. I am sure they have wonderful staff among their ranks. We even met some of them. But the management involved in the treatment of mental health is unbelievably slow; too slow to save our loved one.

Which brings me to the end of our story. The hardest part to write.

To watch this once happy family become crushed by mental illness has been a terrible thing to witness. We used to see something about mental health on the television and say, 'Oh my goodness, isn't that terrible.' And then we would change the channel and forget about it.

There was no changing the channel for us, though. No way to put our heads above water and take a breath of fresh, normal air.

Finally, the first meeting came through with the nice lady from the hospital. Russell and Tina sat down with her and hoped that something could be done. Tina asked if she would ever have to return to the mental health unit again. She was still fearful of that place. The lady told her compassionately that she would not, unless, of course, she had the intention of committing suicide. She told Tina that harming herself was the last thing she wanted to do. In fact, the meeting was so positive, Russell phoned us to tell how well it had gone. It was the first time in a long while that we dared to hope, dared to imagine, an end to Tina's mental health deteriorating. In that meeting, Tina finally seemed to come around to the idea that her problem could be to do with her mind and not her appearance. Yet it now seems that she might have been just saying what they wanted her say.

Shortly after that day, Nikki received a phone call from her brother, Sam. Like a Shakespearian tragedy, the play we were all in had come to its conclusion. This was the third attempt to take her life. To our everlasting sorrow, it was her last attempt.

Nikki received the call from Sam after work, on the 2nd of June. I had dropped Nikki off to prepare dinner while I went to collect young Thomas from my sister's house. It was just a normal sunny evening. Sure, we had the worry of Tina's condition in our minds. In truth, we believed that the previous attempts to kill herself were just cries for help. I will never forget, for as long as I live, returning home to Nikki that afternoon. As the sun set over the farm where we live I saw the love of my life crying like I had never seen her cry before. At first I thought she had hurt herself cooking. I remember making sure that Thomas was strapped safely into his child seat. I remember rushing to her side screaming, 'What's happened, what have you done?'

She replied, barely able to conceive speech, 'My mum just hanged herself.'

You sometimes imagine how you will receive news like that, when a loved one has been killed so suddenly. I would like to say that I had the strength of character to hold Nikki straight away and tell her it was all going to be all right. But the news was so shocking; I just fell to my knees and dramatically shouted 'Why?' at the sky and broke down. Fortunately, I regained my feet and pulled her in tightly. I said very little to her. We didn't have to say anything really. Then she left me with Thomas at the house and made the long journey to her parents' place. The house was only twenty minutes away. But she told me later that it had felt like hours. She did not know what to expect when she arrived there.

I won't go into too much detail as I wrap up our story. I will just say that Russell is the strongest person I know for enduring and going through what happened. He called Sam and other close family members. We are blessed with a good family. In our darkest hour it is our family we often turn to first. Everyone played their part on that day. Our darkest day.

At the funeral, the crematorium was bursting at the seams, so great was the number of friends and family who came to pay their respects. Tina was such a character, so well thought of.

We raised a sum of money for the BDD Foundation that day, and tried to raise awareness about BDD in the process. Ever since then, the family and I do what little we can to help the cause. If we can stop this happening to another family, we will surely try.

If someone with BDD can gain some awareness and understanding from this book, I know it would give our family a small comfort at least.

We now approach our first Christmas without our beloved Tina. I am sure there will be some tears that day. But we will remember our last Christmas together – that perfect day of laughter and joy.

Helen Jackson

It's 3 a.m. and I'm still awake, but this is not unusual these days. In fact, it has become the norm to be sitting up in bed, laptop resting on my knees, searching cosmetic websites and forums until the early hours. This manic phase has lasted longer than usual, though.

Sometimes it seems as though it's not even me sitting there. Instead, I am perched high above my bed and, with over-tired but sleepless eyes, surveying this poor, pathetic figure who is gradually slipping further and further into an endless frenzy of desperation, flicking from page to page, twenty or more tabs open, grasping for knowledge, for solutions, answers, remedies, that will make it all better, make it all go away, make these anxious feelings dissipate.

It is difficult to know what started this episode. I can't think of anything particular, but after a week of more than the normal amount of mirror gazing, tweaking, poking, and restlessness, one night I reach what I believe to be a conclusion: of course, it has been staring me right in the face so to speak – it's my forehead; too small, too flat, not feminine enough. How had I not noticed this before, when all this time I thought it was my nose, which seems overly small now, after a botched nose job and a subsequent revision, but … maybe if I had a rounded forehead, it would give some definition to my profile, then, with the lip lift I am planning, I might look halfway decent.

It is 4 a.m. I must sleep but cannot, not until I've done a bit more research on plastic surgery such as forehead contouring and cheek reshaping. I want them to shave the bone to a more desirable shape.

I wonder if this could be the answer to all of my problems.

I have an appointment for a lip lift consultation in London next week, and wonder if I can ask about the 'feminisation' surgery at the same time. Yet, I also know that I must take care not to worry the surgeon by bringing up too many issues. He might suspect BDD. I have become the master of subterfuge with surgeons. I will tread carefully at my consultation, choose my questions diligently, and judge whether or not we have a rapport, and whether it is safe, therefore, to bring up the other issues.

It is 5 a.m. and my anxiety is temporarily quietened. I feel comforted by the fact that it is possible to change my flaws. I want to be normal so that I can just get on with enjoying my life, my adorable son, my thriving business, my partner, and my precious little dog. I don't want to have to worry about my appearance any more. I know, somewhere deep down, that this is flawed thinking, but it consumes and soothes me and I fall into a deep sleep, at last.

The next day I think back over the conclusions I made yesterday and now realise how ridiculous my thoughts were, that I was seriously considering shaving my cheekbones and having forehead implants. Had it really come to this? After all, haven't I, at one time or another, obsessed about each and every part of my body and sought remedies through exercise, surgeries, and cosmetics? BDD can be like that; it bypasses common sense and trundles on regardless.

During the day, while browsing the web, I come across an article that causes me to pause. For once, my internet research has come up with something worthwhile and constructive: the Body Dysmorphic Disorder Foundation.

I knew I had BDD from reading the odd articles here and there. I knew enough to know that it was something that wasn't universally understood by the medical world. I knew that it was often dismissed as vanity. This made seeking any kind of help too embarrassing and intimidating. But here was an organisation taking this condition seriously, with interesting articles that I could not only relate to but also actually show to the select friends to whom I had tried to explain my experiences. And so I decided to add my own article.

It was not a success story that I contributed but, rather, a continuing saga of self-realisation, learning, and optimism. Reflecting on my journey has helped me to make sense of certain events. For example, many years ago I was a film student in London. I won an award to make an animated film for the Arts Council and Channel Four. My storyboard was a film about a man who was being haunted by a ghostlike form which appeared during times of gaiety, threatening his hedonistic existence, filling him with a sense of guilt and forcing him, reluctantly, to contemplate and re-address his pleasure-seeking way of life. It was to be dark, menacing, yet humorous, in the style of some of the Eastern European animators I loved, a sort of Kafkaesque nightmare. The Arts Council loved it and I was all set to start production. Then, suddenly, I decided to scrap the idea and changed the story altogether. I ended up making a film about a woman instead, a woman who lives alone and is preparing for a date. Her date is coming to pick her up and she is busying herself with getting ready. She stares into the mirror in quiet contemplation and, after a while, picks up some scissors and snips her nose, first a tiny bit, then more. After this, she turns her attention to the rest of her body, snipping here, snipping there until, eventually, she starts snipping herself apart in a manic frenzy, until she is completely gone.

I didn't know what I was writing or why. It made no sense to me, and neither did it make sense to my disgruntled sponsors, or, indeed, the people who came to see it. To be honest, I felt rather embarrassed about it. I cringed at the private viewing, hid away when it was aired on Channel Four and, to this day, do not even have a copy of it. At the showing, the producer, who I had been working with quite closely during the making of the film, came up to me and said, 'You are very brave to have made this film.' What did he mean? I forgot those words for a very long time, decades in fact.

Three years after the film was released, life imitated art and I underwent the first of many plastic surgeries; rhinoplasty, which is something I have regretted ever since. Had I had the insight back then, as a young animator, I might have stopped and analysed my film and my intentions more closely and seen the warning signals. But no one knew of BDD back then.

And so on I bumbled through life, seeking surgery to plaster over the cracks of further surgeries and telling no one, not even close friends, of my deepest, darkest thoughts. Because I am outwardly happy and eternally optimistic despite my demons, friends and family do not suspect my inner turmoil. I make them laugh. I am the joker, I make fun of my insecurities and they join in the laughter. If, in a more sombre moment, I open up about my BDD they are surprised. Of course, they haven't heard of it. When I try to explain, they say they would have never thought I worried about my appearance. They say that I seem so confident. That doesn't help.

And so I have kept my demons to myself and continued my struggle in silence.

Many years after the animated film episode, I spotted the producer one day while walking in London. I wanted to stop him and chat about the old times. He had been a very lovely, kind person to me and I had fond memories of him. But as I approached him I remembered the words he had said about being brave to have made such a film. I didn't speak to him. I couldn't. I had a botched nose job, surely he would notice. He had understood me more than I understood myself and I now felt ashamed and convinced that if he saw me he would think I was just a vain, shallow, messed-up person, not worthy of the money and faith the Arts Council had invested in me.

It took my discovery of the BDD Foundation to even dare to delve into my past and confront memories that have since helped me come to an understanding about myself, which now seems so glaringly obvious. I have had years of regret about that episode of my life but the growing understanding of this condition has helped me to put a lot of ghosts to rest. I don't feel regret any more. With hindsight, I can see that I had problems, indeed still have them, but knowing that BDD is recognised and that there is information out there to help seek the right kind of support is half the battle.

I wish I could meet the producer again and I now wish I stopped him in the street that day. Sadly, he has since died. That's BDD. It can rob us of opportunities and stop us from doing things because of nagging insecurities and negative thoughts. I will not allow it to rule my life any longer. I have a beautiful son; one would think that would put everything into perspective and make the BDD problems dissolve into insignificance but, still, there is undoubtedly tough work ahead. Armed with research and self-help, however, I believe many positive changes can be made.

I want to educate my friends, not to keep BDD as my little secret any more. I believe with research and a readiness to talk openly we may all help BDD sufferers to cope with this debilitating condition. Onwards and upwards!

Joanna

My view of my childhood is very mixed. Since going on my BDD journey, I have come to realise that the idyllic childhood I thought I had contained darker undertones. My memories of my mother are few and fragmented before the age of twelve. She is a sad, mostly absent figure. Always late for things, always in the kitchen. Never smiling. My memories of my father are wonderful up until that age. It is as if he shone during my early childhood. He was my ultimate hero, a climber, hiker, adventurer. I loved going on those adventures with him, climbing mountains and experiencing life. But he became angry and frustrated as I got older. He demanded perfection; nothing was ever good enough. As a head teacher, he was used to children obeying him. So there was no tolerance of rebellion, self-expression, choosing a way other than his own. It is only with hindsight that I see all of this. At the time I felt so lucky to have two wonderful, beautiful, amazing parents and would have said that I had the perfect childhood.

Criticism was prevalent. I took it because I felt I could deal with it and defend my two younger siblings from it. I became a shield, a buffer between my dad and my mum and siblings. I thought I was the strongest because I was the oldest and I hated to see my dad shout at the little ones. It broke my heart. I also believed that I could defuse his anger at my mum's increasing reluctance to follow his lead. I felt tension and I felt pressure to relieve it. I seemed to be the only one who could.

Looking back, the reason for my dad's change was possibly the sudden death of his father when I was about seven years old. It was unexpected and brutal. My granddad had been in hospital with stomach ulcers. Just a few days after being discharged and given the all clear, an ulcer burst and he died. I think I was there at the time but my memory is very hazy related to this period. I now realise that the change in my dad had nothing to do with me, although as a child I took on my parents' unhappiness and tried to solve it. I thought I could do this, thought that my existence was enough to heal them. I didn't realise that it was their problem, not mine. My failure to make my parents happy left me feeling helpless, ineffective, not good enough, and unlovable. A defective child. A bad child. *The* bad one.

This paved the way for my future role as the family scapegoat. A role I willingly embraced, having such low self-esteem and feeling as though the family unhappiness was my fault. I took it on. It made everyone else feel better. I thought I could handle the criticism, shame, self-loathing, disgust, and neglect. I thought I had to take it. It felt like the only option. This mission really took hold in my teens and continued within my family throughout my life.

When I was seventeen, the truth came out. My dad had been having affairs. My mum had an affair when I was very little (two years old) and my dad left us for another woman and became a father to her children. It felt like a huge relief at the time and was the beginning of a very long process of self-examination, healing, and ultimately, recovery.

School was a horrific experience for me. I have no positive memories, only fear, panic, anxiety, self-loathing, and shame. I was bullied by peers and teachers, as I was an obvious target. I was so self-conscious and willing to put myself down for them. They had a field day. I didn't skive off school, I hid. I was still trying to please my family and get good grades, yet it was an awful struggle. I reported the bullying and nothing was done. For three years it went on and on and I gradually just accepted it as a result of my defectiveness and hideousness. I was told how ugly and stupid I was. I believed it. I wore glasses. Then I got bigger, thicker ones. I had train-track braces. A mouth full of metal. I was skinny, flat-chested, pale and shy. In the 1980s, the ideal body type was supermodel style, with curves, big hair, and a tan. I was ahead of my time; heroin chic wasn't due for another ten years. I was the antithesis of the ideal 1980s woman. I was a geek before being a geek was cool. I hated myself.

I first noticed that I was unhappy with myself when I was six or seven years old. Someone told me I was nothing to look at, and then I was told I had chubby legs and looked like my dad. I took this to be a very negative comment because my father, of course, was a male and I was supposed to be female. I was constantly having my hair cut short, despite repeatedly objecting. I wanted long plaits but was told that my hair was too thick and unmanageable and I just gave up bothering as I wasn't listened to. I wanted to be a beautiful princess and felt the opposite. I wore hand-me-down clothes, mainly trousers and boy's stuff, and felt anything but pretty.

However, this really took hold when I was thirteen. My circle of friends turned on me and began to criticise me in some very personal ways that cut incredibly deep. I had trusted them; I cared for them. I desperately wanted them to like me and took on board everything they said. I remember at the height of it all I was so convinced of my hideousness that I couldn't even walk across the school playground in case someone saw me and said something critical. I began to think I walked funny, which made me unable to walk properly. I thought I was doomed to be ugly for life and felt sorry for people having to put up with looking at me every day at school. I thought the boys were right not to fancy me or ask me out.

I became periodically obsessed with the ugliness of different features of my face: my nose at one time. I felt it was big and pointy, like a witch's nose, so I used big glasses to cover it up. In fact, the glasses were so big and heavy that they hurt my ears and the bridge of my nose and were always slipping down my face. This became a point of hilarity for the bullies who mimicked me by pretending to push glasses up their noses to each other.

My eyes were another focus of my BDD. I hated my eyes. Everyone said I had my dad's eyes; he was a man and I wanted to be a woman. I wanted eyes like my mum's. I felt my eyes were too small, that my eyelashes were short and fair and couldn't be seen. I had no encouragement to wear make-up, as my mum believed in 'going natural'. The bullies took advantage in every way they could.

The deterioration of my sight had a massive impact on me. At about the age of seven, I began to struggle to see the whiteboards at school and this caused a great deal of anxiety as I couldn't get the correct answers to maths problems; I couldn't see the workings on the board, and strained harder and harder to keep up. Eventually, I was tested and told I was short-sighted and given glasses to wear all the time for distance and schoolwork. My eyes rapidly deteriorated with the glasses, I needed thicker and thicker lenses over a short space of time until they finally settled down at about the age of eleven. However, I had been very sporty and the glasses put a stop to all that. I couldn't play for the netball team, swimming was impossible, gymnastics was out of reach (glasses and gymnastics do not mix), so I became withdrawn, introverted, and physically frustrated.

It ruined the years of my blooming into adulthood, aged thirteen to eighteen. I was not 'sweet sixteen'. I was miserable. I couldn't look in a mirror. I hated everything I saw. My appearance in photos at that time shows a bundle of clothes. I wore huge coats, jumpers, baggy things to hide my shape. I hoped to hide myself. I wanted to become invisible so that no one would bother me. I wanted just to be left alone. I was fine at home, in my room, with no one looking at me and forming opinions, some of which they might express, usually negatively. I didn't socialise except with my family, preferring to hang out with my younger siblings and their friends who were too small to have critical opinions about me.

Back then nobody had cosmetic surgery and nose jobs, although I wanted desperately to fix my nose and have bigger boobs. I had a sporty body. I wanted to be a bombshell. I hid my flaws from others by turning one way, the best side for my nose so it didn't appear so large. I hated my legs and thought they were fat, so wore huge Doc Marten boots to make them appear thinner. I wore baggy clothes to hide my shape and covered up wherever possible. On a holiday in Cornwall, I felt so exposed and self-conscious on the beach. I never wore a bikini (it wasn't even suggested although mum wore one, but I felt inferior in beauty to her) and have a photo of me in an unflattering black one-piece costume. Even so, it felt quite liberating to wear even that.

I had no social life, or very little. I hated going to clubs, I disliked pubs. Later on, when I did begin to socialise, I had to drink in order to feel in any way comfortable and to get rid of the awful feeling of exposure and self-consciousness. Drinking became a seemingly effective way to numb the anxiety and pain and I have used it throughout my life to self-medicate, only realising that this was a problem for me later in life. My small frame cannot take much alcohol. I 'switch off' after just a glass of wine and, although I continue to function, have no awareness and no memory of what I am doing. It is as though I have left the building and someone else has taken over for a while. My drinking really took hold at university, but was manageable. Then I went through an abusive relationship and, after leaving it, the blackouts began.

There really wasn't any help around at the time. It is only now that I even know I had BDD. There were no books about it. The internet didn't exist (I am forty-three), so I was really left to manage this on my own. I do remember finding self-help books at the library and just collapsing into floods of tears after reading a chapter on how to love yourself. I knew I had a problem by then, but I didn't know what it was or how to deal with it. I just knew I didn't want to feel this way any more. This realisation came when I was about eighteen. I got contact lenses and life opened up again. I was able to swim and do sports. It felt great and when I looked around, I saw that the bullies had flaws too, but didn't seem to care. It made me question why I felt so inadequate and unacceptable when their flaws were more pronounced and they seemed fine with that.

I had no formal diagnosis of BDD. My mum didn't believe in doctors, so I hardly ever went. The only person who addressed it was a naturopathic doctor I was taken to at the age of seventeen. He suggested that I practise yoga, write a daily diary, splash my eyes with cold water, and cut out wheat as I had a gluten intolerance. This changed my life. I started to do yoga and immediately felt the benefits. Yoga is amazing because it reconnects you to your body. I was so disconnected from my actual body, the image in my mind was so distorted, and deep down I knew this but couldn't get past it. I didn't trust myself enough to know what was real any more. Yoga helped me to start to see the true me. I began yoga at the age of seventeen and have never stopped. I truly believe that yoga has healed me and has been the greatest thing to ever happen in my life. That is why I now teach it and created YOCD classes (Yoga for Obsessive Compulsive Disorder) to help others like myself with BDD, OCD, and anxiety to reconnect with their bodies and to heal.

This transformation at the age of seventeen was the start of a long process of healing. It was helped by my leaving home for university. I spent three years far away from my family and home town, leaving behind my overwhelmingly negative image of myself and starting again where no one knew me. It was fantastic! I pushed myself to confront my fears, I studied English, drama, and dance, I put myself on stage and performed to people, I explored the capabilities of my body and I continued to do yoga. I began to heal and found courage, strength, determination, and beauty. I had a relationship. I had friends. It was the beginning of a rollercoaster ride to recovery.

After university I returned home and everything disintegrated again. Home wasn't good for me. I easily slipped back into the scapegoat role. I left as soon as possible and moved in with my boyfriend. My twenties were really a time of self-discovery, trials, and tests of courage and self-belief. I experienced two abusive relationships (one of which was a marriage) and struggled to find my vocation. I went back to university and completed a Master's degree in Medieval English, achieving my goals for my academic career. It wasn't enough. I began to work, starting at the bottom as an admin assistant and eventually working my way up to a job as Olympic Project Manager, working on the London 2012 Olympic bid! The role was fantastic, exciting, exhilarating, challenging, and perfect for me. Another form of healing. However, this success and new-found confidence wasn't appreciated by those around me, my old life and world as the scapegoat and 'wrong' one. My husband divorced me. My family hardly acknowledged my achievements. I was still looking for approval. But this time things were different. I had money, a job, the internet, a life. I decided to confront myself and accept things as they were. I bought myself an apartment. I decided not to get into another relationship. I read every self-help book I could find and realised, finally, at the age of thirty-three, that I liked myself! As if by magic, the love of my life appeared on the scene. We got married, had two children and I trained as a yoga teacher, setting up my own business, Jojoba Yoga, in 2010.

It hasn't all been plain sailing. After the birth of my son, I had a relapse. It was a traumatic birth and he was in intensive care for the first week after delivery. I had no family support and experienced difficulty bonding with him as a baby. I became anxious and developed obsessive behaviours based around my son, such as constant tidying and cleaning. Then the compulsive thinking set in. I became pregnant again very quickly and the same thing happened after the birth of my daughter. I now know I had maternal OCD, but at the time I thought I was going insane. The thoughts were awful, terrifying. I felt that I couldn't be near my children as babies at times because I was a danger to them. The thinking is so awful and painful. I thought that I was hideous again. I became reclusive and this led to suicidal thoughts. My husband encouraged me to seek help and I went through a course of medication and counselling. It helped. As I began to recover, I started practising yoga again and reconnecting with my body.

The OCD went. But the BDD remained. I began skin picking, on the shoulders, neck, the chin, mainly around the face. It is a compulsive behaviour and a desire to do something soothing but constructive, clearing flaws from the skin, smoothing it all out.

I never told anyone other than my family (even then I tried to hide it from them) as I didn't want to draw further attention to myself. I already felt as though people recoiled in disgust when they saw me and I just couldn't handle seeing their reactions. I hid from sight at any opportunity, even though I wanted to participate in life. I felt that life didn't want me, others didn't want me around, I caused pain and suffering by my presence and that it was better for me to stay out of sight.

I ran the OCD/BDD support group for my local area and found great comfort in the group, talking about similar issues and experiences. I now offer online support and yoga for OCD and BDD as a way of further helping others and continuing my own journey of self-healing and recovery. I also read books by Louise Hay on positive affirmations and listened to tapes of them. These helped to morph the subconscious negative chatter into positive thoughts that support me instead of battering me down. I really recommend doing this, as the internal chatter is so very painful and destructive. Turning this around can make such a difference.

I view BDD as an addictive behaviour. I deal with it in the same way as I dealt with the alcohol addiction. The more I feed it, the worse it becomes and the only way to manage it for me has been complete abstinence. I have to be tough with this and draw strict boundaries with behaviour and tolerance of others. The tendency is for me to slip back into old habitual modes of thinking and behaving, especially if I am feeling low, so I manage my diet (no gluten, vegan, and no alcohol) and my environment. This becomes more intense if I have been working hard and don't have the energy to manage myself. Self-neglect is part of my BDD and I have to look after myself and be careful at these times. Life happens, things go wrong, and it can trigger a spiralling down into negativity and BDD/OCD. I know the steps I need to take in order not to let this happen.

Generally, I like my appearance now. I have periods when I struggle with it, but I manage it with yoga and CBT. I took some brave steps recently and put videos of myself doing yoga on YouTube and Instagram and my website. It is the first time I have able to do this and expose myself in this way. The response has been overwhelmingly positive and although a small part of me still doubts positive reactions to my appearance, I am so very grateful to the world of the internet and social media for enabling this form of self-expression, communication, and connection. It has been a part of my recent healing journey.

I am so delighted that BDD is now recognised as the debilitating, destructive, and harmful mental illness that it is. It is wonderful that it is being addressed and properly dealt with by medical professionals. I think that the yoga/physical side of the healing process is still slightly neglected, though mindfulness is accepted as helpful. I hope that yoga and the healing of physical trauma trapped in the body will also receive the recognition it deserves one day and become an accepted part of the recovery process.

My life is amazing. I am proud of everything I have achieved in my life, against all the odds! I am constantly dazzled and bewildered by all the positive, amazing things that are happening around me. I am so very grateful for my life, my health, my body. It is amazing to me that I can post something online and receive overwhelming support from people I don't even know! My own family unit is so supportive, loving and caring, and my wider yoga community and friends are also showing me that it is all right to be me. I am accepted as I am and I am able to accept myself.

I have achieved many external goals in my life and my future goals really focus on my children, and my health. I want to stay strong and healthy and I want to be able to help others like myself who are going through BDD and feel so helpless, lost, and alone. I want to become an example of hope and to show them that not only is it possible to survive this illness, it is also possible to thrive and to achieve everything you could possibly want in your life. You deserve it. You are not alone. You are lovable and are loved.

BDD sufferers and survivors/thrivers have an important message to spread out there. Part of the recovery process is helping others. They can offer so much to others in the same situation. I want to help them see this.

My final message to other BDD sufferers is never, never, never give up on yourself. You are not your thoughts, you are not your body, you are so much more than that. You deserve everything life has to offer. Stay strong. Be brave. Seek help and together we will survive, recover, and thrive. I have been there, I know how it feels and I know it is not easy to turn around, but it is possible and it is necessary. You are important. You are loveable. You matter. I have recovered, and I am here to show you that you can, too.

Joanna practising yoga.

J. W.

My story is one of extremes: great happiness and joy when I'm well, terrible sadness and fear when in the grips of BDD. I have had an obsession with my eyebrows for thirty-seven years. Over the past four years I have frequently been in a frozen state of terror, only occasionally leaving the house. I have had no work or social life. I have been unable to speak, even to my husband and son. And all because of my emotional reaction to the appearance of my eyebrows.

It started when I was fifteen. A teenage 'friend' said that I had ruined my face when I'd plucked my brows. Combined with a sensitive nature, a perfectionist father, and a family history of OCD, I have barely had an hour without thinking about them. I am otherwise completely unconcerned about my appearance.

Fortunately, I have also had very happy and successful periods in my life, of many years' duration. I had disturbing thoughts, but enjoying life took the upper hand. I achieved a BSc in geography and environmental biology, a PGCE in primary education, and an MA in development studies. I have been a primary school teacher, a lecturer in environmental politics, and have worked with young people with challenging behaviour.

I have also sustained good and loving relationships. I have a husband who has stuck with me despite his own enormous personal suffering. Living with someone with BDD is as distressing as having it. I have a wonderful son. I was almost symptom free for the first eight years of his life and the happiest I've ever been. So there is hope that it *is* possible to live a full life despite BDD. I managed this by reassuring myself that there was nothing wrong with my brows. I hardly looked at them during this time.

However, during the past four years, my concerns and preoccupations and resultant anxiety have increased and intensified. I worry and ruminate about the shape of my eyebrows: whether they are symmetrical; too gappy; falling out; going grey; not natural enough: too messy; too unattractive . . . you name it. New worries come into my head and I feel I must keep checking my eyebrows for any of these signs. At my worst, I was checking in the mirror continuously for up to sixteen hours. This went on for years.

I was convinced that people would ridicule and reject me because of them. I can no longer reassure myself that they look all right. I have tried to accept them as they are. I can't make them any better because I feel they cannot be improved.

I have seen psychiatrists, psychologists, psychotherapists, and counsellors. I have taken the recommended medication for OCD/BDD since my early twenties. I find it almost impossible to be open about it. Hence, I have chosen to remain an anonymous contributor.

When I'm well, I am funny, intelligent, fun to be with, compassionate, interested, and interesting. I'm well-travelled, love music, nature, yoga, coastal walking, volcanoes, and care passionately about social, disability and development issues. I am creative. I love my husband and son. Therefore, I have a lot to lose to this hideous illness.

I have really enjoyed travelling widely with my husband and son. From as early as six months old our son joined us in travelling the world. We've been to Grenada (in the Caribbean), Cuba (the music is amazing), Spain, France, Costa Rica (a natural tropical paradise), to Mexico three times (we love the food, colours, and friendly people), the Dominican Republic, Australia, Holland, and a road trip from Las Vegas to Denver (this was one of the best trips. The landscapes are incredible earthy colours of ochre, pink, and orange. The forms are sculptural and of epic proportions. We lived in a lovely camper van and felt immersed in the landscape).

I have sung in choirs all my life. I sing a range of styles from classical (choral works and madrigals) to blues, jazz, world and popular music. It is a real joy for me.

I have campaigned on social, environmental, and development issues. I've worked in the voluntary sector, fundraising and public speaking about child welfare. I have also felt suicidal, but would never act on it because I cling on to the hope that I can regain the life I once had. Also, I would never do this to my husband and son.

After a traumatic six months of hospitalisation and cognitive–behavioural therapy (CBT), I was admitted to a residential unit for anxiety disorders (ADRU). I was assessed by the unit manager and one of the medical doctors. Both were highly professional, gentle, and really seemed to feel my pain. They gave me hope at a very hopeless time for me. My therapist was exemplary. She was compassionate, understanding, encouraging, and clear thinking. We spent several weeks really exploring the roots of my problem. She challenged me with CBT, which had a clear rationale. She also helped me to build strength and resilience in the face of my difficulties. All of this was combined with compassionate mind training; this has an evidential base showing it to be helpful for those with anxiety disorders. All of the support staff were respectful. The other residents were encouraged to support each other. There was a full programme of interesting, stimulating, daily occupational therapy activities to support therapy. I did pottery, woodwork, textiles, jewellery making, and mosaics. These have become lasting passions.

And how is the BDD? The CBT experiments I did at ADRU demonstrated that other people either don't think there is anything wrong with my brows, don't care if there is, and certainly don't reject me because of them. The evidence showed that, in fact, people generally like me a lot! Intellectually, I recognise this. However, I still believe that my brows look unpleasant and I attach too much importance to them. I think about them all the time. I get help from my community mental health team. I also started taking olanzapine, which has been helpful.

I am now reconnecting with my non-BDD personality. I am a volunteer in arts and crafts for people with learning disabilities. I am getting fit. I have discovered ariel yoga. My husband has created a space for my creative endeavours. We are seeing friends. Our family has plans to travel again. We are doing family therapy.

I still have significant BDD symptoms, but I have progressed enough to give me hope that it can take a back seat in the future and live on my shoulder rather than engulfing my whole body.

Laura Bexson

The following is the story of my own battle with body dysmorphic disorder. A battle I continue to fight to this day and one that almost defeated me several times. It's a difficult read, but one that shows anyone suffering from this horrific mental condition that there really can be light at the end of what can seem an incredibly long, dark, and lonely tunnel. Something, I'd like to point out, that I would never have believed myself.

In the numerous therapy sessions I have had over the past nine years, I was always first asked about my childhood to see if there were any early causes of my body dysmorphic disorder. I imagine it is standard procedure to first discuss a client's childhood when helping to treat a mental health condition, along with parental relationships. However, I remember that I would often feel annoyed by this, as I had a wonderful childhood full of nothing but happy memories. I have the most incredible parents anyone could wish for.

Now, at the age of twenty-six, I can better identify both my experiences of senior school and my relationships with the opposite sex as being the causes of my BDD. Looking back, as a teenage girl I was always conscious of what I looked like and would refuse to leave the house without a full face of make-up. I would say that I worried about my appearance as much as the average teenage girl did. I was desperate to fit in at school but no matter what I did or how much make-up I wore, I never felt accepted. Those feelings have stayed with me and, to this day, I still feel aesthetically inferior.

It was not until the age of around seventeen that my 'normal' body image concerns began to spiral out of control and would signal the start of a life-changing battle with BDD. My story does have a very positive ending but I want to start by sharing just how debilitating and all-consuming this illness can be and how much damage it can do not only to the sufferer, but also to those around them.

I started seeing my ex-boyfriend when I was almost seventeen, in April 2006. During the first year of our relationship there were several occasions when he lied to me about where he had been and whom he had been with. I think this was the trigger of my BDD; the lack of trust and questions of infidelity. It caused me to develop an overall feeling of not being good enough. Mainly, I did not feel attractive enough. These feelings increased as time went on and, for some reason that I will perhaps never understand, I started to fixate on my skin, becoming obsessed with making it look 'perfect'. I remember feeling convinced that my boyfriend would leave me because I was so ugly. We ended up staying together for seven years, arguably for the wrong reasons. There were lots of good times but our entire relationship was tainted by my BDD, putting a huge amount of strain on us as a couple.

The earliest memory I have of my skin concerns is my eighteenth birthday. I had planned a trip to Alton Towers with my friends. While packing our bags for the day, all I was concerned about taking with me was my compact mirror so that I would be able to check my skin. At this point I do not recall how much I was looking in the mirror but I remember this day clearly and it being tainted by my skin concerns, acne in my case. Every time we stopped or were in a queue I would get the mirror out to check my face from all angles to see if any new spots had appeared and to check on the spots I believed were already there. If I saw any new bump or blemish, my heart would pound, my breathing rate would increase, and I would get a strange heat sensation in my chest. I now recognise this as a BDD attack. My friends kept asking why I was looking into the mirror so much but I didn't care, as long as I could satisfy the overwhelming urge to check.

From then on, the first thing I would do when I woke up each morning would be to check my skin in the mirror before school. I would also take a mirror with me to school so that I could check whenever I felt the urge to, for any angle I felt I needed to. Luckily, I managed to get through my last couple of months at school and complete my exams without my BDD causing too much interruption. It was during the summer holidays, before starting university, however, that my BDD began to take a more extreme hold on my life. I became quite reclusive and started to cancel endless social events. I became too scared to wear make-up or let anything at all touch my face for fear that it would break me out in acne. At a time when I should have been out with friends enjoying life, I was becoming completely obsessed with the condition of my skin, which, to me, was getting worse and worse each day. My perceived condition of my skin would dictate my whole day. If I had bad skin, I found it impossible to leave the house. I was due to start university in the October of 2007 and remember hoping and praying that what I was seeing would be cleared up by then. It was not.

My parents could not understand what was happening to me and struggled to cope. They watched on as their once confident daughter turned into a desperately sad recluse before their very eyes. I would get angry with them for dismissing my skin concerns and was told to 'pull myself together'. I asked myself hundreds of times, 'Why couldn't they see what I saw? Why were they lying to me?' They would try to reassure me endless times a day, saying that they couldn't see anything more than one or two spots and sometimes nothing at all. To me, I felt completely disfigured and started to style my hair so that it covered one side of my face. I would get strange looks but all I cared about was concealing my spots from the gaze of others.

My first week at university was quite possibly one of the worst of my life, culminating in my first suicide attempt. I remember sitting in one of my introductory law lectures unable to concentrate on anything but my skin. Everything else was a blur. I could hear the lecturer speaking but it may as well have been in another language. I remember my hair being over my left cheek and wearing a black hat with tears rolling down my face. It was in that moment that I decided that I simply could not live looking like the hideous monster I felt I had become. On a tearful journey home, I decided that I would put an ultimate end to feeling like this.

I returned to an empty house and found all the tablets I could, around fifty in total of various kinds, and proceeded to take them with vodka. I had done my research and found that this was supposed to speed up the process. After taking them I felt horrifically sick, but was panicking that it wasn't working quickly enough. I was worried about how long it would be before my mum came home. Desperate to end my life, I ran to get a knife out of the kitchen drawer. I made a small cut on my wrist but the pain was too much to bear and I couldn't go through with it. What else can I try? I asked myself. I ran upstairs desperately looking for something else. I found my dressing gown cord and tied it around my neck and pulled really tight but again it didn't work, though it did burst lots of blood vessels on my neck and around my eyes. I looked even more of a monster than before. Then I heard it. The key turned in the door and I knew that my mum was home. My plan would be discovered. I was shaking uncontrollably from the overdose and had been crying, so when mum looked at me, she knew something was wrong instantly. I told her that I had done something stupid and lied saying that I had only taken ten ibuprofen. I thought that if I told her how many I had really swallowed she would take me to the hospital to have my stomach pumped. I don't know why I told her at all. In hindsight I think I just desperately wanted someone to listen to me. I needed people to see that I could not go on living with what I saw in the mirror.

We went to the local walk-in centre, from where I was sent to A&E. While there, I saw a psychiatrist who let me see a dermatologist after I begged over and over again. Having lived with BDD for almost ten years, I think it was a bad idea for the doctor to let me see a dermatologist, as this only gave me the acknowledgement that I did indeed have a skin problem which clearly needed medical help. This highlights a lack of understanding in the mental health profession about BDD. For years I would use this as proof that what I was seeing must be, in fact, be real. Why else would they have let me see a dermatologist? Why else would he prescribe me antibiotics? From that point onwards, I stopped listening to anyone else around me who would try to tell me I didn't have a skin problem. I had the evidence that I needed to justify what I saw in the mirror and believe it to be an accurate reflection of what others must have seen when they looked at me.

Once back at home, I deferred my place at university. There was no way I could contemplate going back. I spent the next few months at home barely leaving the house until my parents told me that I should try to get out to work to keep me busy. They didn't understand that the idea of letting other people see my skin was completely terrifying. I started working the odd day here and there at my dad's office. Most of the time, I would sit at my desk inspecting every lump, bump, and red mark on my skin. Sometimes I would cry and had to go and calm myself down in the toilets. It was a living nightmare. I could not believe what my life had become. I was supposed to be doing my law degree and making new friends and memories. Yet, here I was barely able to leave the house more than one day a week. I also suffered crippling depression coupled with the now daily BDD attacks.

As ill as I was, a part of me refused to accept that this was my life and I started university again the following year. It was the hardest three years of my life. Nothing compared to the mental battle of having to get out of the house and be around girls of my age with what I saw as their 'perfect skin'. I would spend my time in lectures staring at other students' skin, constantly comparing mine with theirs, which only ever made me feel worse. There is nothing I wouldn't have given in order to look like any one of them. I used to fantasise about swapping bodies with them and being able to get ready for a night out with friends, to be able to put on make-up and go out and have fun.

I lived at home during my time at university. I was in no mental state to be able to handle living away from home. Who would want to live with someone who would cry for hours and hours, who was completely unable to go out and socialise? I felt like an utter freak physically. My BDD, in addition to my perceived skin blemishes, was also something I had to try to hide. University for me was about plucking up the strength to get out of the house, get through my lectures, and come home again. No parties, socials, clubs, or friends. I never went on one night out and didn't even attend my own graduation ball. That is the reality of living with BDD. It can take everything away from you and leave you feeling completely hopeless.

After graduating in July 2011, my next challenge was to find and hold down a job. My ultimate goal was to work with young offenders, but I found that this was a very competitive area to get into. I managed to get a job as a young person's support worker with children leaving the care system. I loved my job, but it involved long periods of working alone. This gave me endless hours to think about my skin. I had several BDD attacks at work and no one to turn to. At first, working seemed to help as it gave me a distraction but in the many hours I worked alone I would think of nothing but my skin. My BDD gradually got worse and worse until it reached a head in May 2013, leading me to plan my next suicide attempt.

This time I had researched exactly how many paracetamol I would need for a fatal overdose. I bought them and crushed them up. I had sent a text to work to say I couldn't come in. I wasn't bothered about following the correct protocol at that point. When they rang I simply ignored the calls and then turned off my phone. I remember feeling relieved that all my internal pain and mental torture would all be over soon. I had broken up with my boyfriend of seven years a couple of months before this and remember thinking that this would, at least, be one less person to miss me. I honestly felt, too, that my family would be better off without me as I was incredibly difficult to be around, angry one minute then crying inconsolably for hours at a time the next. Just as I was crushing the last few tablets, my dad came home from work early. He came upstairs and announced that he and my mum were taking me to the GP that evening as they just didn't know what to do any more or how to help me.

We went to the GP appointment that evening together. After my parents had explained how the situation at home had become quite desperate, the GP asked if my parents would leave us alone for a couple of minutes. Once they had left, she asked if I had made any plans to hurt myself. I don't know why, and I regretted it as soon as I opened my mouth, but I told her about the tablets. I told her that I had crushed up over one hundred paracetamol, along with some of my mum's medication, and that it was hidden in a bowl under the sink in my bathroom. She asked if she could tell my parents and I nodded. I just wanted someone to help me. I guess I didn't want to die but equally at that time, didn't want to live either. I was in a hideous, limbo-like existence. When the doctor told my parents what I had been planning to do they were understandably devastated. They said that they didn't feel they could keep me safe at home any longer. The doctor then decided to call the Crisis Team. The next day they came to see me and said that they were going to find somewhere for me to stay for a while. It turned out to be a psychiatric ward at our local hospital. I was absolutely terrified.

I remember being in my bedroom, packing my bag, not having a clue about when I would be home again. I was petrified that they would take my mirror away from me. At this time, I was looking in my mirror, which was a mirror tile I could move around to catch the harshest light, for twelve to sixteen hours a day.

BDD had completely taken over my life. My ex-boyfriend came round as I'd texted him to tell him where I was going. I just remember holding on to him tightly, apologising for everything, desperate for it all just to go away. He walked with me to the car. I got in reluctantly and my parents drove me to the hospital. I remember going on to the ward, a hot, suffocating atmosphere with that horrible hospital smell. I could not believe this was happening to me. Questions ran through my head. How had it come to this? Why couldn't I just be like other people my age? When would I be able to go home? Why did I tell the doctor about the tablets?

I was shown to my bed area, a dormitory of six beds with only a curtain for privacy. Some of the women in there were staring at the floor, one was shouting and talking to herself, and another was crying on her bed. I didn't want to be there, I wasn't like these people. To me, I just wanted my skin to clear up and then everything would be all right. I refused to accept that this was a mental condition and that what I was seeing wasn't visible to anybody else. When my parents left, I got into my uncomfortable bed and cried myself to sleep. The next day I was woken at 7 a.m. and told to take the medication given to me in a white cup, 10 mg of citalopram. I was told by the nurses that within a week I would be on 40 mg.

I felt completely numb at first. My anxiety was heightened by the fact that they had taken away my mirror and only allowed me to have it for thirty minutes twice a day. For a BDD sufferer, it can be utterly devastating to have their mirror taken away, like being unable to scratch a constant itch. I had little contact with the psychiatrist while in hospital, which turned out to be for a total of four months until I discharged myself, unable to take living in those surroundings any longer. I wasn't getting any better in hospital. I wasn't receiving any form of therapy; I was just in there to prevent me from hurting myself.

I came home in September and decided that there was only one way to get better and that was to do it myself. I continued to take my medication every day, which I think helped a great deal. I had always been very reluctant to take medication before, as I was so worried about taking anything that had the potential to make my skin worse. In hospital, I had no choice other than to take it, so, in one way, I am glad I was sent there, as I don't think I would ever have taken it properly otherwise.

Medication has definitely been the only thing that has ever worked for me. You may notice that I haven't talked about any of the therapy I have had over the years. The reason for this is that none of it worked for me. Yes, it was nice to have an outlet, a place to go away from home to be able to talk about how I was feeling for an hour a week, but nothing I was advised to do ever made me feel better or changed what I saw in the mirror. I think if I had been on medication and had therapy at the same time that might possibly have been the best treatment plan for me. Different things work for different people, I suppose. When CBT didn't work for me for the third time, I felt hopeless and resigned to the fact that nothing would ever help me to lead a normal life. Finding the right medication, however, has finally given me my life back.

Since leaving the hospital in September 2013, I have held down two jobs and am now in the process of applying to become a primary school teacher. I cannot express how different my life is now on account of finding the right medication. I would never have believed I could feel so 'normal', so good, and so interested in life again.

In the past year, I have jumped off a boat into the sea in Portugal, completed a mud run, had many nights out with friends, found my dream job, and been on some pretty good dates. These are all things I never ever thought I would be able to do. If I were to give one piece of advice to a sufferer of BDD, I would say not to give up. I know I came very close to giving up a number of times, but I am so glad I fought my way back to normality. Yes, I still think about my skin but it no longer bothers me in the extreme way it used to. Recovery is possible, no matter how bad your symptoms are.

Having BDD has ultimately made me the person I am today; a strong, resilient and appreciative person. What might seem mundane to people who haven't suffered from BDD, such as going out for a walk in the daylight hours, feels incredible to me. I am so grateful for every single day. I am so relieved not to be constantly worrying about my skin and what everyone around me is seeing and thinking any more. It is the most incredible feeling and one I would have never felt without having had BDD. I now use my mirror for no more than an hour a day, which I feel is manageable and is astounding progress.

I know that BDD can make you feel very isolated and alone. I hope that my story can offer some hope that none of us is truly alone and that there is every chance you can recover from this cruel illness.

Lauren

I first became aware that I disliked my appearance at around the age of eight. Yet, the anxiety and overwhelming fear of what other people thought about me started many years before. I was unaware at the time that my hatred for my appearance and the anxious feelings were ultimately linked. It all started after an experience at my first dance class, where my mother left me on my own. I felt scared to death and was only four years old. I remember feeling abandoned and ashamed just for being there. At the time, I could not articulate how I felt. I was just incredibly fearful of what everyone thought of me, which I assumed were negative thoughts. I imagined that the dance class was to blame for my feelings. I just wanted to run and hide. Now I know this is called anxiety, but at the time I was too young and not capable of understanding what this meant or what anxiety was. It just felt like something terrible was going to happen, as though the world was ending and there was nothing I could do about it. No matter how hard I tried, I could not avoid this feeling. These early feelings were the beginning of suffering which I have experienced on a daily basis for most of my life.

As far back as I can remember, I have always hated the way that I look. The main areas I was concerned with were my shape and weight. I have always felt fat and chubby. I felt too big for my height and disliked the overall size, shape, and colour of my legs. Furthermore, I always had scars from insect bites that I would scratch, serving only to make them even uglier than they already were. I have always wished I had thin legs. The paleness of my skin has also been a major issue. I was called 'milk bottle' as a pet name by my mum, which I hated and still do. I feel that my hair needs to be worn a certain way otherwise it makes me look strange. I believe my stomach is not flat enough, my face is funny-looking, and that I look like a man depending on whether I wear make-up or not. I feel as though my eyes are too small, my lips are too red, my toes are ugly, and I make them worse by picking them. I have scars from picking and pulling hairs from different places on my body to try to make it look nicer. Of course, this only makes things even worse.

My behaviours during the really dark times varied but mostly involved trying to avoid that feeling of high anxiety. Getting up and getting dressed would be a trauma and certain circumstances had to be put into place in order to deal with the distress I experienced. I felt that certain lighting was needed, not too light and not too dark. I believed that certain colours were necessary for my hair, clothes, and skin. I wore concealer on my lips to make them paler. I wore fake tan to cover up the colour of my skin, as the thought of my natural skin colour would make me feel sick. I associated it with being pale, which I correlated with being fat and unacceptable. My curtains would always be closed, even in the middle of the day, to the distress of my parents. Sitting in the dark somehow made it easier. I tried to avoid anything that would resemble a mirror, such as shop windows and those annoying reflective sunglasses people wear within which you can see yourself rather than them.

It used to take me more than two hours to get ready to leave the house regardless of where I was going. On good days, I would be able to leave the house with minimal fuss. On bad days, every item of clothing would be out of the wardrobe. Nothing would seem to fit right and I would feel as if I was unacceptable to be out in public. I avoided exercising because I was worried what others might think of my appearance. Sports clothes and jeans became my biggest clothing fears, along with swimming costumes and bikinis. I would run from the changing room then jump directly into the swimming pool so that I could get in before anyone else saw me wearing a swimming costume. None of these things made rational sense, but they were real feelings that were excruciatingly painful and made me feel lonely, confused, and scared.

Food and eating have been an ongoing issue since I was eleven, at which time my mum put me on a diet. I would wear oversized clothes and multiple layers to hide my hideous body. I would never wear trousers and the thought of what I looked like in them made me feel sick. Tight trousers also felt too revealing, as if I was walking around naked and somehow enticing people by displaying my body shape. I started using food as a way of controlling things and as means of distracting myself from feeling my painful feelings. I would avoid the things I loved to do, such as theatre training workshops and theatre classes at university, because the anxiety felt too strong.

The negative feelings about my appearance spilled out into other areas of my life. Everything needed to be in place. I thought if I could control things externally I would be able control the feelings I could not express or deal with internally. How wrong I was.

My childhood was difficult, to say the least. There was always a lot of sadness among the feelings of being empty and unfulfilled. I faced daily criticism from my parents throughout my life growing up and in adulthood. I was treated like a doll, as though I was not allowed to have feelings, opinions, or needs of my own. It felt as though I did not have a right to exist. I needed something from my parents that they did not have the capacity to give, which meant that my emotional needs were never fulfilled. I was always bored and had nothing to do to occupy my overactive mind. I often distracted myself with doing extra homework in an attempt to repress my anxiety. I also desperately wanted my teachers to like me and for my parents to think that I was a good person. I used to spend my holidays hiding under my bed in the dark, reading with a torch. I would pretend I was somehow in another place in some other time, where I did not have to feel like this. For a very long time I was dressed by my mother in clothes that I can only describe as making me look like a doll. For me, this reinforced the idea that I needed to try to be a 'perfect' person who did not have feelings of my own and must always do what was expected of me. Everything I wanted or chose to do was always wrong. My thoughts were not valid and how I felt was not as important as how other people felt. I was told I was selfish and needy for having thoughts and feelings and that I needed to learn to entertain myself like everybody else. I was also told to leave my parents alone unless they needed to off-load their feelings or problems. If I did not do what they wanted, I was given the silent treatment, abusive language, or criticism. Thus, I learnt to ignore, repress, and hide my own feelings and needs in an attempt to get my parents and other people to like me. This led to isolation and loneliness for many years and feeling unfulfilled and unloved for who I was. I often longed to be taken away by someone. Anyone.

My family home was very focused around endless diets and unhealthy eating habits. There was constant criticism of anyone and everyone on the television and magazines for either being too fat, too ugly, or both. No one was spared the abuse. Ultimately, this led me to develop an eating disorder alongside my BDD, which I kept hidden away from everyone. I was so desperate to be liked and accepted. I thought that the thinner I was the more attractive I would be and that I would finally be accepted and loved for who I was. I thought that being thinner would help me to feel better about myself. Sadly, this never happened.

I found myself in a dangerous situation when I was fifteen. A stranger who was twice my age raped me in the middle of the day. I made the choice to pretend that it never happened and kept it to myself. I did not feel as if I could tell my parents, or anyone for that matter. I thought I would make the situation worse if I spoke about it, as it would only confirm what they already thought of me, which was that I was ultimately a bad person. I thought my parents would assume that if I was not so needy and requiring so much attention it would not have happened. In my eyes, I felt it was my fault, so I had to deal with the consequences on my own. I kept it a secret until I was about twenty-eight years old, at which point I could not ignore it any longer. By ignoring it, I felt it would somehow go away and I could forget it ever happened. I also thought that I could erase my 'bad behaviour' and become a good person. Sadly, this only made the incident stay with me, somewhat hidden but managing to manifest in my life in other ways. For example, I would feel angry but unable to articulate these feelings. I turned that anger towards myself. Over time this became very damaging.

I also found myself becoming involved in disrespectful relationships and friendships, within which I would make all of the effort and do whatever I could in order to stop the other person rejecting me as my parents had done. I felt that I should be thankful if people actually wanted me to be around me and grateful they would spend their time with me. I completely disregarded my own needs. It was really painful because I somehow knew that this was not the way life should be, but I was not able to change this at the time.

For many obvious reasons it was very hard for me to be in relationships. It was something I really wanted but I felt as though I could not show anyone who I really was. I always ended up people-pleasing and changing myself to suit what I thought the other person wanted, regardless of whether they asked me to do so or not. I would go from being anxious and needy to avoidant and disinterested. I had been given contradictory messages growing up about love, which meant that I unconsciously re-enacted situations from my childhood in my relationships. I came to realise that the reason I was in disrespectful relationships in all areas of my life was due to my own lack of self-respect and belief in my own worth, yet I struggled to break the cycle.

School, like home, was a very difficult time for me. On the one hand, I loved being there and enjoyed studying and learning. I was a determined student and always wanted to do my best. But I was suffering a lot at the time. I faced bullying in primary school for being 'fat'. I look back now and see I was, in fact, not fat in any way, but those jibes, alongside the criticism I received at home on a daily basis, added to a negative impact on my overall body image. I now understand that these things contributed to my BDD. I was called names such as 'slag' and other hurtful things. Strangely, this is one of the contributing factors as to why I never told anyone about the sexual trauma I experienced. I am happy to say that many years later I sought therapy and am now able to share my experience with people. I now know that it was not my fault. No one has the right to rape anyone else and rape is always wrong, regardless of the circumstances. This experience contributed to my BDD in contradictory ways. I wanted to be attractive in order to be accepted, but also did not want to be attractive in case this would mean somehow 'asking for it'; I feared that I might be raped again.

I never shared my appearance concerns until a few years ago, at the age of twenty-eight. I felt as though there was something fundamentally wrong with me. I believed that if I could just sort out how I felt about how I looked then everything in my life would be all right. I thought I would then be happy. I now know that this is not true, that this problem is a recognised mental illness and is not my fault. This has been really difficult to accept, as I have always thought I did something wrong, which is why I suffered so much. When I first started talking about my BDD, people brushed it off and said things such as, 'Oh, everyone doesn't like the way they look in some way.' Yet, I knew this was something bigger. I avoided so many things because I could not face the feeling of how disgusting I looked and the shame that anyone should have to look at me. I became more aware that this was a problem after reading the book *The Broken Mirror: Understanding and Treating Body Dysmorphic Disorder*, by Katharine Phillips. I knew something was wrong, but was not sure what. I did a lot of searching on the internet and came across Katharine's book. Suddenly, everything made sense. It was a huge relief to be able identify my thoughts and feelings as part of BDD, but it scared me to death that I might have a recognised mental health disorder. I went to my doctor in 2013 and told him everything, including that I thought I might have BDD.

After one year on a waiting list, I was offered CBT therapy as part of the OCD/BDD specialist services in Sheffield. I am so grateful that I was able to access this service because it was a free service and I was not in a position to pay privately for treatment. I was also pleased to be given an experienced therapist, who was also a female, as this made all the difference in my journey to recovery. I started therapy in September 2014 and had weekly, fifty-minute sessions. I finished therapy in August 2015. Initially, I was able to keep in contact with my therapist via email and was told that I was able to contact her if need be, which made me feel less stressed and anxious about the therapy ending.

I only started telling other people about my BDD once I was referred to the BDD specialist service after talking with my doctor. Once I felt as if I was being taken seriously, I no longer felt as though I was making it up and started telling friends and family. It was more difficult to tell my family and they still do not really understand it or take it seriously. Surprisingly, the television series *Hollyoaks* was running a story at the time about one of the characters who was suffering with BDD. Good friends of mine have been really understanding and supportive. Other people have been less supportive and those are people I no longer want to be part of my life.

As well as attending therapy I reached out to people through practising Buddhism and attending local Buddhist meetings. My love of theatre and performing arts really helped me. When I am in a rehearsal room creating a show, my BDD is somehow not there. It is the one thing that is bigger than BDD in my life. The freedom I feel from my time without BDD is like seeing life in a completely different way, as though a cloud has disappeared from my mind and I can see, think, and feel clearly. It lasts for a short time, then it creeps back in. I would love to create theatre every day and say goodbye to the BDD for good.

How do I feel about my appearance now? Well, it has been an ongoing process since my treatment ended eight months ago. I still do not feel as though I am 'cured', but I feel more able to face my life without being so restricted by the need to perform certain behaviours in order to feel all right. I have spent most of my life with these issues, however, and less than a year in therapy for me did not feel long enough. I would have liked my therapy to have been a long-term thing but I guess these things cannot last forever. I also know that I need to take responsibility for my own life. One issue that came up strongly as a result of undergoing therapy was my eating disorder. This is something I am now addressing rather than simply ignoring it. I need to do this in order to truly heal all parts of myself and to be happy within my own skin.

I would like there to be much more general awareness about BDD, as so many people do not know about it. Most of the literature and websites I have found seem not to take it seriously enough. I think it is crucial for BDD to be treated seriously in order to educate others. I appreciate that certain famous people have been open about their own struggles and think that this helps younger people to feel as though they have someone to identify with. It would be great for more formal support groups to be set up. I have tried accessing Facebook groups, but felt it was not moderated properly; it ended up doing more damage than good for me. As I no longer live in the UK, it would be great to get a moderated online forum focused on positive rather than negative sharing, or even face-to-face support groups around the world.

These days my life is very different. I am a much more open and honest person in all areas of my life. I no longer feel the need to wear a mask in order to the hide parts of myself I feel are unlovable, unworthy, or not good enough. I am up front about my anxieties, thoughts, and feelings with friends, as well as to the new people I meet. This is of fundamental importance to me. Up until recently, I used to ignore how I felt and go against what I truly wanted, which only meant that the feelings came out in other destructive ways. I am now also able to face issues that come up and seek help through friends, Buddhism, and mental health professionals. I recognise when I need help and am no longer ashamed of my vulnerabilities.

In terms of the future, I am working towards making theatre my full time career. I am moving forwards day by day. As a professional theatre maker, I am determined to use my skills to create value for others around the world. I am currently studying my PhD and enjoying living in Europe. Living abroad is something I could never have done when I was suffering so much with anxiety and BDD-related issues. I can now travel to hot countries and not worry about what I will wear or feel the need to cover up in extremely hot weather. I have even worn a bikini on the beach. It was hard, but I knew it is something I needed to do. I have dreams of one day not caring about what other people think and truly being myself in all situations. I am working on it every day and am happy to say that I am nearer to my dream than ever before.

My advice to others experiencing BDD would be to seek help, even if you think your problem is not as bad as someone else's. You cannot compare your suffering to another person's. This will not go away by itself and your mental health is crucial to your overall wellbeing and enjoyment of life. Life is meant to feel as though it is worth living and you, whoever you are, deserve to live with joy. It may be difficult at first to admit that you have a problem. Sharing your worries with another person can be really tough, especially when these worries are appearance-related. I felt as though I was making a big deal out of nothing at first, but the more I shared with others and read up about BDD the easier it became. It is also important to really want to change. I got to the point where I truly did not want to continue suffering and living half a life. I was determined and committed to changing, even though it was hard. It might be hard but it will be worth it. It is also important to remember that changing the outside will never change how you feel on the inside. I really hope that my experience can help someone to reach out and to get the support they need. It just takes a little courage. If not now, when?

Lauren's boots.

Linzy

I was born in Bristol in 1988. My dad was a successful stonemason who had fallen madly in love with my beautiful but troubled mum. My dad sold his business and house and bought land in Portugal, where he built a family home. Over the next year my mum became mentally unwell and their relationship fell apart. My mum returned to England with me, her third born, and we moved to Cornwall. My memories of living with my mum are vague but I do remember us both being unhappy. She was depressed and her moods were up and down all the time. As I began to develop my own personality I began throwing tantrums with my mum. I didn't understand why she was always depressed and constantly moving me from place to place. I never had time to make friends and would constantly cry for my dad. When I turned four years old my mum decided that she could no longer look after me. I moved in with my dad; he had moved back to the UK as his dream in Portugal was over. Living with my dad was fun. He attended acting college in Cornwall and I was allowed to join in after school instead of childcare. I was looked after by his classmates and felt part of a family there. We lived in shared accommodation and the house was always busy and full of life. Looking back now, I can only imagine what went on at the parties.

My contact with my mum was limited to letters and phone calls and she became very distant. My dad said I used to cry and ask why my mum didn't want me but I was much happier living with my dad. I remember going to visit my mum and her sister when I was thirteen years old. This was the first time I had seen my mum since I was four. I was always a tiny child, petite and very skinny. I remember having a bath at my mum's flat and coming out with a towel on. She told me to drop the towel and show her my body. I remember her saying 'You have not developed at all, you look like a boy. You will never have any tits, you're so skinny.' This has stuck in my mind to this day and, although mum pretends she did not say this, I have never forgotten it. In the past five years my mum has been given a diagnosis of bipolar and now takes anti-psychotic medication. This explains a lot and although my memories of my mum's behaviour confused me over the years, I am sympathetic and understanding now that I know her diagnosis. I did not meet my mum properly until I was thirteen and by this time I was a teenager who had seen a lot of things most teenagers would not have witnessed.

Looking back now, I can see where my diagnosis of body dysmorphic disorder has grown from. Self-hatred was a part of my childhood and at its worst when I was a teenager. I was told I was undeveloped and flat-chested and, although boys liked me, I was bullied a lot and physically punched and beaten up. I had my first boyfriend when I was twelve and he wanted to have sex with me. I was not ready. Once we had broken up he told everyone in school that I was not a proper woman, that I was undeveloped, flat-chested, and too 'tight'. He continued to bully me throughout my teens and I did not complete my education as I was expelled for bad behaviour.

School was always tough. By the time I was eight and settled into my home town, Bristol, I had been to so many different schools that I was numb to being the new girl. I was always outgoing and confident but naïve compared to city kids and about the ways things were in a city. I always dressed in mismatching clothes from charity shops. I was the kid with the eccentric dad and a different way of doing things. I used to stand up to the bullies and show no fear. I made best friends quickly and had a close group of girls that I value to this day as part of my life. My dad moved us into a council house in one of the notoriously rough areas in Bristol. Despite this, I managed to get into a local grammar school. My three best friends also attended this school and I can remember my first day as though it were yesterday. I was part of a group and had the opportunity to not be the weird kid any more. It was a fresh start. We wore a uniform to school so I didn't have to worry about not being able to afford the new clothes that the other kids wore. I quickly made new friends and was very happy in my first year of secondary school. It was when the other kids started to hit puberty that my BDD began to affect me. I was not developing. I did not wear short skirts and low tops as I was still a child. My close friends began wearing bras as their bodies changed. Boys, of course, started to make it clear what their interests were.

After dating one of the older-looking boys in my year I learnt the hard way about what boys talked about. I was disengaged from school and obsessed with body image. I used to wear very gothic clothing and found friends who were also gothic/punk and generally disengaged from the norm. I used to wear padded bras with extra padding inside of them. This made me more confident and seemed to ignite more male interest. I felt so different from my old friends at school and started bunking off from lessons and taking drugs. The group I was part of was a lot older and I wanted to be like them. I was scared to go to classes and my education fell apart.

I did not tell anyone how I felt and I think that was what damaged me the most. I met an older boy called Jimmy who was the popular Goth boy of the group and everyone knew who he was. Every girl fancied him and I made it my mission to make him fall in love with me. I became more styled, like his own gothic Barbie doll, and my image was at its most extreme. I got piercings, wore leather, and listened to death metal and horror core. My plan worked; Jimmy and I adored each other. He was eighteen and I was thirteen but the age thing didn't matter . We did everything together and shared so many memories, but these memories involved class A/B drugs. I tried speed, acid, ketamine, ecstasy, cocaine, and TCB drugs at the age of thirteen. I felt part of a family and the group I was a member of was exciting and lived for the moment. I met similar girls my age who were like me, a bit lost and not part of the normal teenage life we were forced to engage with. All of us had problems that we were battling with and the answer seemed to be to get high and enjoy ourselves.

Of course, BDD was still affecting me and my perfect relationship began to fall apart. One day Jimmy asked me, 'When are you going to look more like this?' and showed me a picture of a curvaceous model. 'When are you going to start growing boobs?' I hadn't slept without a bra on since

I was thirteen and at fifteen years of age I had convinced myself that no one would notice I was flat-chested. The reality hit me that I would never be able to keep Jimmy happy having the body I did. This is when the BDD feelings really came back. Jimmy and I lasted another year and then I found out he had cheated on me with beautiful, big-breasted, curvy women. Not a little girl like me.

I still felt like a child and believed no one would ever love me without having a woman's body. In every relationship I would compare myself to ex-girlfriends of partners and became a jealous and selfish person. I would punish past partners for looking at other women. In this way they also became victims of my condition.

I spent £800 on pills that were supposed to make your breasts grow. I spent most of my time crying and drinking to cover up how I felt. I had a boob job at the age of twenty-one and would spend about two hours a week looking at pictures and profiles of women I idolised. I have always looked on my boyfriends' phones and at their internet history to see what women they look at in order to compare myself with them. I want to know what my partners' ex-girlfriends look like so that I can compare myself to them also. I have missed out on social events and kept my partners away from certain friends, as they are more attractive than I am. I have spent days crying and causing self-harm physically and mentally with the use of drugs and alcohol and I also used to cut my arms. When I was twelve I tried to overdose with paracetamol and alcohol. I wanted to be loved and it was a cry for help and attention.

My friends would tell you that I always wanted surgery and that they know some of the extent of my unhappiness. I've always tried to hide my BDD, however, as I thought other people would just think I am vain and overreacting and selfish. It's so hard to explain as you don't want to come across as completely crazy. It makes me feel weak and I don't want people to know how weak and lost I have felt over the years.

After many years and much bravery, I think speaking about my BDD honestly has helped me the most. I have told my current partner about my BDD and he understands. He knows I have bad days and is really supportive. I think there should be more awareness of BDD, as it can affect people in so many negative and destructive ways. Knowing that you're not crazy and not alone really helps. I think social media has become such a part of life now that it is hard to ignore the perfect body image. There is so much pressure to look good and it can be incredibly hard to resist this pressure.

Promotion of health and true inner happiness should be seen as more important than the perfect selfie. I, and many other women I know, spend ages getting the perfect photo to get extra likes and comments on social media sites.

My GP came to take my thoughts and behaviours seriously and diagnosed me with BDD. She referred me to a counsellor and cognitive therapist who both helped me realise and understand the condition. After a few sessions of CBT, I really started to look at how I thought and realised that my negative behaviour was caused by my negative thoughts. I was living a negative, self-fulfilling prophecy. This was not going to get any better if I didn't help myself. CBT needs to be put into practice on a day-to-day basis. I now believe that I am in control of my own thoughts. If negative thoughts and beliefs should come, I take a moment and remember the techniques I learnt in CBT.

Most people I have told about my BDD have seemed confused, as I appear to be an outgoing person and can seem very confident in how I present myself. I have never met anyone who has been diagnosed but can see traits of BDD in everyone. We all look at ourselves differently to how others see us. Once I explain how I feel, people generally seem sympathetic. Overcoming BDD has given me the confidence to be open with people about how I feel. I used to tell people some thoughts, not the extent of my feelings. I was ashamed to tell people, as I believed they would mistake my thoughts and behaviours for vanity or perceive it as me fishing for compliments, but it's actually the complete opposite.

Having good friends around has definitely helped in my recovery. Having successful plastic surgery has also helped me to feel confident and feel more comfortable with intimacy. I now go to the gym and really enjoy this. Having hobbies is a great way to take your mind away from the negative thoughts and prevent you from hiding away being miserable.

I would explain BDD as being a prisoner within your own mind. Being controlled by negative voices is a constant drain on a person's happiness. It causes anxiety, low self-esteem, and depression. It's like looking into a mirror that is distorted and having the way you look on your mind 24/7. I realised it was a mental issue and not a physical one when I started getting jealous of my friends for no reason other than their appearance. A part of me wanted to hate them. Having BDD is very lonely and trying to explain it to someone can be frustrating. I noticed when I changed the things I was worried about, like wearing a padded bra and low-cut top, I would be more confident. It seemed to me that people liked me more and that men were more attracted to me. It is only when I realised that it was my confidence they liked that I started to see it as a psychological problem. Being home alone a lot and missing out on social events due to BDD made me want to make a change, as my friends would enjoy themselves while I stayed inside, depressed and alone.

I have now managed to appreciate myself from the inside out. I have met my soul mate, who I have told about my condition, and he really understands. I think having surgery did change my life but the thoughts and behaviours are still there; I just know how to deal with them a lot better. I am having a second enlargement as I feel that my breasts are still too small. I have lost weight and they have also become smaller. I think my BDD plays a part in my reasoning for this but I am aware of this and of my negative thought processes. Surgery is not something to take lightly. It can be dangerous and is a massive decision. I am also aware that surgery is not successful for most people with BDD, as their obsession tends to shift from one part of the body to another.

I would like BDD to be more widely known and understood, especially within the education system. Mental health in general should be discussed as part of the curriculum as it affects everyone in one way or another. I think maybe having a BDD specialist within local medical centres would also help, as doctors do not seem to know how to advise everyone. I think we desperately need focus groups as a place to discuss feelings and share ideas on how to overcome this condition.

These days, I feel like a new person with the ability to control my thoughts and negative feelings. I feel proud of how far I have come and am now training to help other people. BDD has had a massive impact on my life and I used to have so many regrets that I wasted time hiding away. Yet, it has also made me grow as a person. I know I cannot get those wasted years back so I am more positive about enjoying each day. You never know what is around the corner and there is so much enjoyment to be had from life.

I am starting a degree in social policy in September and, following completion of this, I would like to go on to study cognitive–behavioural therapy. My own experiences of living with BDD have inspired me to want to help others. I use CBT in everyday life and it helps me to deal with negative thoughts and feelings. I am in a happy relationship and can finally say that I am open and accepting of my condition and so is my partner. I have plans to enjoy every day to the full and I am happy knowing that the worst of my condition is over.

I would advise other people struggling with BDD to get help. Remember that you are not alone! No one is perfect and having BDD is very lonely. Speaking about your feelings is so important and may help you to feel a lot less anxious. Everyone around you has been through struggles or is facing their own battles in life, so know that the way you feel about your appearance is understood and just one of life's possible sufferings. You might not be able to remove the thoughts of BDD completely, but you can learn coping mechanisms and come to manage them. Cognitive–behavioural therapy helped me and I still find myself using the techniques on a day-to-day basis. If you're having a bad day, know that tomorrow it will get better. Life is not a rehearsal and we only get one chance to make the most of the time we have.

Linzy.

Liz Atkin

I grew up in an unpredictable and turbulent alcoholic home where anger, violence, and fear were common denominators in everyday life. Initially, my wealthy father funded an affluent lifestyle and we lived in a large house with a swimming pool. I was shipped off to boarding school for my early years. My mum's drinking escalated dramatically and her weight dropped to around seven stone as she became more unwell. Her hair was falling out, her gums were bleeding; she had stopped eating as alcoholism took over. At this point she went to her GP, who gave her a month to live unless she stopped drinking. In desperation and at rock bottom, my mum began attending Alcoholics Anonymous in 1985. I was just eight years old. AA saved her life and she has now been sober for almost thirty years.

However, rather than her sobriety solving all of the problems at home between my parents, things worsened dramatically and they split up after rows which were more violent and frightening than ever before. My parents were not married, so dad moved out of the home he had bought us, while their disputes continued, leaving us to fend for ourselves. He withdrew me from boarding school just before my twelfth birthday and suddenly I was enrolled at a local comprehensive and was bullied owing to my posh-sounding voice. My dad employed the best lawyers to gradually claim back what was his – pieces of furniture and other items were repossessed from the house, he had the electricity gas and water supplies cancelled, and the police came in the middle of the night to take back a family car. But worst of all, after a long and complicated court case, my dad managed to evict us from the house I had grown up in and, at the age of twelve, I was homeless. For many months we lived with friends, sleeping on people's floors before being re-housed by the council. It took all my strength to support and care for my mother in such dramatic and terrifying circumstances.

I coped with unspeakable fear throughout these circumstances. As an only child I had no outlet, no one else, no other adult to support me. I was vulnerable and very frightened but I also had to be strong enough to support my mum. Mentally, I was already significantly affected and suffering more than I had language for. Fear was probably a dominant factor in my development of a chronic and uncontrollable anxiety disorder called dermatillomania, or compulsive skin picking (CSP), which was to dominate my body, thoughts, and behaviour for the best part of the next twenty years.

Compulsive skin picking is a complex physical and mental disorder that often develops in young childhood. I had no idea as a child that it was a recognised illness falling under the category of 'body focused repetitive behaviour', or that many thousands of people all over the world also experience it. Compulsive skin picking provides comfort, pleasure, or emotional release through endlessly picking at often healthy skin, but this can frequently lead to bleeding, infection, scarring, and even physical deformities, as well as significant emotional and mental distress. Skin picking was, for me, from a young age, a way to release tension in my body, to block out emotions and hit a zoned-out sense of calm. It became a private vicious circle that totally dominated my life behind closed doors. Without my mum knowing, as things got bad at home in those rows between my parents, I would be picking away at my body with tweezers and pins until I bled. My body was littered with wounds and marks beneath my clothes. Skin picking also developed into something I did subconsciously, so there were many hours each day during which I would be picking my skin. Some nights I would pick until the early hours of the morning. I got to the point when I would even pick in my sleep.

Many times I would be poised in the bathroom because this was a private space. No one knew about it. I masked and covered the illness from those closest to me, wearing clothes that concealed the parts of my body covered in scabs and scars, lying that I'd recently had chicken pox, making excuses and even using make-up on my body to mask it. I experienced intense physical anxiety, followed by guilt and shame over the things I was doing that caused harm to my own body, yet felt no control over it or any ability to stop. Frightening depressive episodes, nightmares, and hallucinations were common as the illness dominated me. I suffered in silence for a very long time. The illness was actually undiagnosed until my early thirties, by which time I'd been picking for the best part of twenty years. It was only through internet searches that I realised my painful secret had a name. I had even hidden it from various doctors and psychiatrists over the years. Finally, I got to the point of not wanting this illness controlling me or my life any more. The cycles of shame, embarrassment, and chronic anxiety were perpetual. I had no choice really but to try to help myself because it was destroying me.

The body has always been a source of fascination for me. I had studied dance and drama throughout my education and at university elected to study drama. My dream was to study performance and the body, but beneath my clothes the compulsive skin picking continued to prevail. In my early thirties, I signed up for a Masters in Dance, and it was then that I found I had to confront the illness head-on. Studying movement at this level meant I could no longer hide the picking. As part of the course, we were encouraged to study our everyday movement patterns. For the first time I looked at how this illness dominated my physicality every day. Very slowly, I began to document what the illness had done to my body. I began to recognise the illness as a unique dance, and to begin to see that I could turn my illness into something else, something creative to move me away from the harm it was doing to me. Through dance, I found that I was able to express things I didn't have language for; I channelled the specific movements of the illness across my body into something positive. I began making artwork about my skin, using film and photography. I recognised the physicality of skin picking and began to turn it into a creative practice: to use the skin as a soft canvas for imaginative transformation and, ultimately, healing. I explored the way my body moved and used body-focused repetitive behaviour as an art practice and miraculously began to get better. I now create artworks about compulsive skin picking, depression, and anxiety with textural materials such as latex, clay, and acrylic paint to transform the skin. I have exhibited my artwork in therapeutic settings and galleries all over the world, including Japan, Los Angeles, Melbourne, and London.

Anxiety is one of the most common mental illnesses but some chronic anxiety disorders, such as compulsive skin picking and trichillomania, are seldom recognised. Treatment in the UK can be very hard to access for these more specific disorders. They are, however, much more common than initially thought and I know from first-hand experience the complexity and distressing impact they can have on a person's life and on the lives of those around them. Most people with compulsive skin picking suffer in secret and silence, thus feeling totally isolated. I now aim to normalise compulsive skin picking. I'm speaking about my experience in an attempt to de-stigmatise and help others with this devastating condition who may feel that they have nowhere to turn. Skin picking dominated my thoughts, my body, and my life for many years, but there are ways to recover. CBT and medication can be prescribed through your GP. I developed an understanding of the body and use my artistic practice to keep well, and I now have some degree of control over my condition. The marks and scars will always be with me, but many are fading and I now see them as being an important part of the tapestry of my lived experience, as well as inspiration for my artwork.

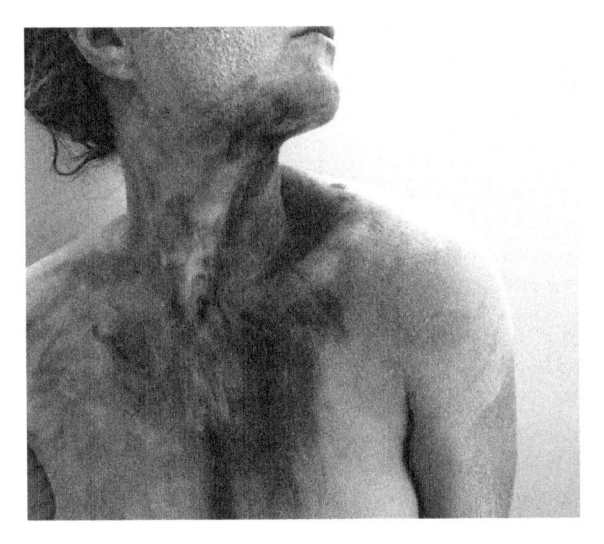

Blue – a tender re-thinking of a former site of skin picking. Here, repeated touch is illustrated with pastel dust, evoking a bruise.

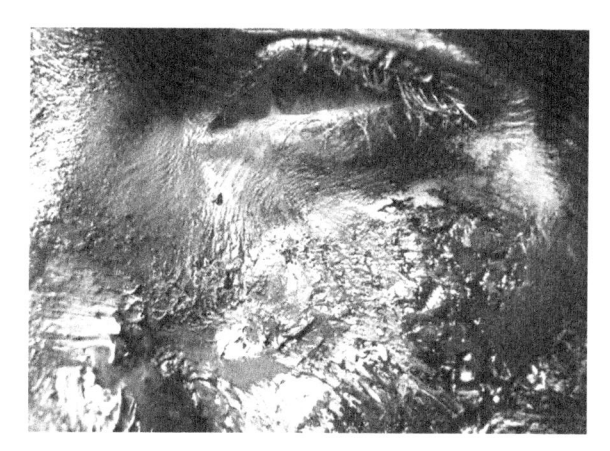

Lavish – a textural self-portrait. Formerly a site of skin picking, I re-imagined and transformed my face with thick, vivid acrylic paint. A visual representation of what my skin feels like from the inside.

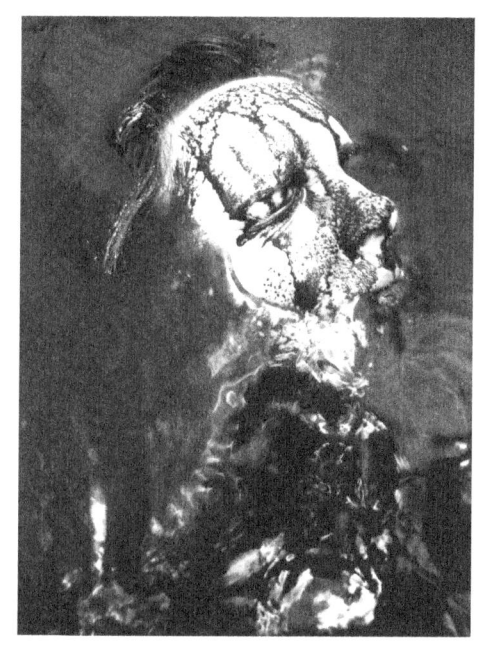

Curdled explored the overwhelming physical sensations I experienced during a ten-month period of severe depression and chronic anxiety disorder, coupled with a recurrence of skin picking. It was exhibited in a solo exhibition in 2014 for the Anxiety Festival.

L's Story, by his Mum, Emma

L was just eleven years old when our lives were turned upside down and nothing has been the same since. I still remember when life felt 'normal', but those memories are beginning to fade. For twenty-one months, my son and family have been living with BDD.

BDD totally blindsided us and appeared to have come from nowhere. Our beautiful, positive, happy, funny, and extremely popular son disappeared overnight and was replaced with a child we barely recognised. An unsatisfactory haircut triggered a profound reaction unlike anything we had ever seen. L became hysterical and described himself as fat and ugly. He explained that he had been feeling depressed for about two weeks and been hiding during school playtimes and comparing parts of his body to those of his school friends.

He quickly became obsessed with his appearance and constantly talked about it. It was exhausting and terrifying listening to him obsessively and hysterically analysing his appearance, threatening to cut off his (perceived) fat and discussing dieting and not eating. (We initially believed he was developing anorexia.) He believed that being skinny would make him happy – he wanted to look like his best friends at school, who were extremely thin and athletic.

He constantly compared himself to the boys he wanted to look like. He described in detail how he hated his hair, teeth, and the shape of his face.

L was hysterical, agitated, frightened, and at times extremely violent from the moment he woke up until bedtime. Catching his reflection in any surface induced hysteria and violent episodes. We had no choice but to remove most of our mirrors, as our house was repeatedly 'trashed' and necessitated police intervention to calm L down on a number of occasions. We were absolutely terrified and in a state of shock. Our son had drastically changed overnight and we didn't understand what was happening.

It has been the most frightening and traumatic experience my husband and I have ever lived through. I still recall the look of terror on L's face during these episodes, and I have many memories of him experiencing horrific panic attacks (he doesn't recall many of them as they were so severe), and having what we can only describe as BDD episodes. He has been so distraught by his perceived appearance, and embarrassed if he believes we have caught a glimpse of his body, that he's kicked and banged his head and body against the wall repeating, 'I am so ugly', 'I am so fat', 'I have no friends' over and over again. One of the saddest aspects of his illness is that we are unable to console him when he is feeling sad and upset; he won't let us hug him as he feels too self-conscious about his body. We feel so utterly helpless when he is at his most tormented.

His anxiety and aggression were so out of control at one point that we were scared for his safety and our own. We knew his aggressive behaviour was being fuelled by absolute fear and anxiety. He appeared to be trapped in a permanent state of fight-or-flight stress response, with 'fight' being his main coping strategy.

Within a few days, L was refusing to leave the house as he was frightened of what people would think of his appearance. He never returned to school and so was unable to make the transition to secondary school. He also began to withdraw from us, spending less and less time in our company. His bedroom became like a sanctuary to him, and he retreated into his smaller and so-perceived safer world.

He began to wear one baggy outfit day and night and refused to change into any other clothing. His camouflage quickly became dirty, smelly, and riddled with holes, but he continued to wear it for months and was too frightened to change. L could no longer shower or wash, as he couldn't face seeing his body. He also refused to wash his hair as he didn't like the way it settled after washing.

Because our lives changed so dramatically so very quickly, it has been difficult coming to terms with the tragedy of L's illness. We have been trying to cope with the sense of loss of the son we once had, while dealing with L's extreme behaviour. Having to watch our son suffer to this extent has been unbearable for us. We feel helpless, frightened, and heartbroken every second of every day.

Sometimes it's hard to talk to anyone about these worries and feelings, because people just don't understand the complexity and severity of BDD. Someone once commented, 'Isn't it just vanity?' while others have repeatedly said, 'He seems fine to me.' One (now ex) friend actually questioned his illness and implied that he/us were exaggerating it, and believes I am a negligent mother for not forcing him to attend school.

The effects on the entire family have been enormous and interfere with every aspect of our lives. I've given up work to take care of L full-time and am largely housebound because of his social phobia. It is very hard, therefore, to keep relationships going with my friends. My husband and I very rarely go out together and we no longer have family time or visit friends and family. My eldest son, Joseph, is seventeen and tries to understand L's condition, but gets frustrated by L's angry and anxious state. There are many occasions when Joseph just wants to check on his younger brother and chat with him, but L's self-conscious state fuels many verbally aggressive outbursts. BDD can be so deadly, as it doesn't just destroy the life of the sufferer; it profoundly affects the lives of those who care for the sufferer, too. As his primary carer and mother, I feel isolated, frightened, misunderstood, and judged too. Living with heartbreak and devastation can be overwhelming and it's sometimes so hard to keep motivated and positive. But we have had to stay strong for the sake of both our sons.

L has withdrawn from everything he once knew. Fear has reduced his world to sitting in his bedroom on his computer in the dark every day. He no longer eats with his family. If we try to talk to him about BDD or try to encourage him to engage in anything outside of his room, he becomes extremely agitated and verbally abusive towards us. We have learnt to withdraw at the appropriate time to avoid violent outbursts. We all miss him so much.

As parents, our minds are full of worry for L: his safety, lack of education and social development, lack of hygiene, his sedentary lifestyle, no sunlight, etc. The worry could be endless if we allowed it to take over.

One of the hardest struggles we've had is that we've had to battle the system to try to get L help with overcoming his BDD. Our local mental health service has been appalling. He was initially misdiagnosed, had no access to therapists, was left for months with no contact, received no medication reviews, and was continually blocked from accessing professionals who could help him.

Fortunately, OCD Action supplied us with information to help formulate a letter to write to our local health commissioners to request a referral, and it proved extremely helpful.

We had no choice but to contact a private BDD specialist and finally had an official diagnosis and a recommendation to get L referred for specialist treatment at the Maudsley OCD and BDD unit. We read books about BDD, which we found really helpful. Having a deep understanding of the disorder, and feeling empathy for the sufferer, is imperative in supporting and encouraging people to seek help and find the strength and courage to recover from BDD. After speaking with L's therapist and reading and researching BDD, we were relieved to find that BDD is treatable and found that the inspirational stories we read gave us hope at last.

L was prescribed SSRI medication, which helped to calm his violent episodes. With the help of private therapy, L managed to go for daily walks (most days), lengthening the walk each time. Over a period of about three months, L was managing to walk to town regularly and even sit in cafes and restaurants with me. He even began to experiment with different items of clothing and occasionally wore skinny jeans. It took a lot of bravery on his part, and a lot of motivation and support from us. Even though he was able to tolerate his anxieties during these exposures, his body image concerns were still very strong.

On the advice of L's private consultant, we asked our local service to refer L for specialist treatment at the Maudsley Hospital. We were horrified when they refused. They believed, as a local service, that they had the expertise to help L themselves, even though they have no experience of treating BDD specifically. We believe budgets and procedure were to blame for the refusal. Begrudgingly, we had no option but to end L's private treatment, as we needed to work with our local service if we were to ever get L into specialised treatment at the Maudsley.

During this period, L began to deteriorate and found leaving the house too challenging. He/we were also under pressure from our local school authority; they wanted L to attend private teaching sessions on the school premises. Despite my continued concerns that he was not ready for this, we were forced to persist and encouraged L to engage with his school. Unfortunately, he was unable to do this as the thought of his presence at school was too overwhelming and anxiety provoking for him. This pressure combined with lack of treatment for BDD led to L's relapse, six months after he was beginning to make progress.

This was the lowest point for us. We were not expecting a relapse as we naïvely assumed he would keep making progress. L quickly withdrew back into his room and refused to leave the house or spend any time with his family. His depression worsened and he was sad all of the time. We had a little thirteen-year-old boy who was dirty and smelly, sat in the dark alone all day, cried helplessly during the evenings and throughout the night, experienced horrific panic attacks and hysterical BDD episodes, and was completely isolated with no friends and no professional support or treatment being offered. Experiencing this was mentally torturous and we were terrified he might take his own life.

After continued requests, letters to our local MP, letters to our local NHS commissioners, lost referrals, and inadequate handling of L's case, our local service finally agreed to the referral. L was finally assessed by the Maudsley Hospital in November 2015. They changed his medication, addressed his insomnia, and put his name on their long waiting list for CBT treatment.

The system has exhausted us. Because of his BDD and lack of treatment, L has missed two years of education and important socialisation with his peers. He no longer has any friends and even with successful treatment, we fear L may never make the transition to secondary school.

At last, L's treatment has begun and the first session at the Maudsley Hospital was a really positive experience. We now have a new sense of hope that we've found so hard to maintain all of these months. L's new medication is beginning to take effect and he has recently occasionally accompanied me to a coffee shop and lunch. He even managed a trip to buy new clothes and is progressively attempting to wear skinny jeans again. He appears to be happier and a little more positive, and is finally at the beginning of what will be a difficult journey during which he will need to be committed, brave, and strong.

With the Maudsley Hospital now on board, we can see a glimmering light at the end of the tunnel. We know we have the strength to support L through his recovery and live in hope that he will fight to get his life back.

If you or someone you know is suffering with BDD, please remember that there is always hope. There are proven treatments available and I urge you to pursue them. Recovery is absolutely possible. My advice is to empower yourself with knowledge and to read as much as you can to understand the disorder. Be brave, find the strength, stay committed to the treatment, and believe that you can overcome BDD.

Lucy Tattersall

I can honestly say that I had a really fabulous childhood. I have wonderful parents who have been nothing but supportive of me. However, I was exposed to issues of mental health from a young age. My mum has suffered with several episodes of depression and my family have always been quite transparent about this. I was well aware, therefore, that my behaviours were unhealthy and needed addressing when I started to get ill. On reflection, I think this is what allowed me to have a relatively quick recovery, as opposed to suffering for years and years. It also meant that I didn't have any problem communicating my worries to my parents, as they were used to issues of mental health and I had no concerns about them judging me or being disappointed, which I know are common fears for mental health sufferers.

I went to a highly academic secondary school, which I loved. I think the environment I was placed in (one in which everyone had to strive to do the best and where getting anything below an 'A' was deemed a failure), however, has really shaped my character. For a long time, I have constantly put pressure on myself to be 'perfect'. In many ways, I think this somehow extended beyond my studies to my appearance. I suppose being a perfectionist also includes wanting to look perfect, which is perhaps an underlying factor in my BDD.

In early 2015, while studying in my final year at university, I was diagnosed with depression and body dysmorphic tendencies. In the months before my diagnosis, I had become extremely stressed with the pressure of my final year, and slowly became fixated on my appearance. I became obsessed with what I looked like to others, convincing myself that the reflection I saw in the mirror was not what everyone else could see.

This obsession started with constantly checking my appearance in the mirror or in the camera of my phone. It then moved on to obsessively picturing and videoing myself for hours on end. My BDD mind was desperate to discover what my 'true appearance' really looked like, and videoing myself in my bedroom was the way in which I believed I could begin to understand what I looked like. I would then analyse these videos for endless hours, pausing the film and looking at every angle of my face and body. I was horrified by what I saw in these photos and videos. In my mind, I was ugly. I was repulsive. In particular, I became obsessed with the right profile of my face. In my opinion, I had the ugliest profile in the world. I convinced myself that everyone else was more attractive. I became scared of rejection. I truly came to believe that I would never be able to get married or have a family of my own, which were goals I was desperate to achieve in my life. I firmly believed that no one would ever want to love or marry me because I had the ugliest profile in the world.

With my dissertation deadline approaching in the New Year, I began to realise that spending three to four hours a day videoing myself and attempting to analyse these videos was both unsustainable and unhealthy. As a hardworking and fairly academic individual, I became frustrated at myself about my obsession and preoccupation with my appearance to the extent that I could barely concentrate on my university work for more than five minutes at a time.

In the awful cycle that so commonly characterises mental illness, my negative thoughts had a knock-on and unhealthy effect. My thought cycle manifested itself along these lines: 'You're so ugly and you have the worst profile in the world. You may be ugly, but at least you are quite clever. But now you can't even focus on your university work and therefore you are useless, ugly, and no longer clever. If you aren't clever or attractive, then what is the point of living?' I had fallen into an awful state of mind, composed cyclically of suicidal thoughts. My BDD and depressed mind could not escape these. I never attempted to commit suicide but the thoughts continued very strongly for quite some time.

I knew I would never kill myself. I once wrote a suicide note to everyone I cared about and loved. While writing this note, I knew it would never be read but it was a therapeutic way for me to realise how many people I care about and would be hurt if I ever did kill myself. I remember getting my dressing gown cord and tying a noose and placing it over my head in front of the mirror to see what I would look like if I hung myself. After a few seconds I broke down in tears and removed the dressing gown cord, knowing that suicide would never be a choice I could make, because even in my darkest moment I knew I could get better and fight the negative thoughts.

In the New Year, I told my parents about my terrible obsessions and negative thoughts. A few members of my family had a history of mental health issues, and so my parents, while extremely concerned, were not judgemental but listened, understood, and told me that I needed to take action. This was the first step of my recovery: acknowledging that I couldn't do this on my own. I needed support in the form of medical professionals but also from my family and friends.

I saw a psychiatrist, who diagnosed me with depression and body dysmorphic tendencies. I was immediately put on 20 mg of escitalopram which I am still on today, and undertook several CBT sessions, which helped me to challenge my negative thoughts and promote more logical and healthier thought processes. I ended up taking a five-week break from university and spending time at home, where the combination of the medication, CBT, and the support from my family and friends resulted in my BDD thoughts and depression slowly diminishing.

Specific CBT exercises that really helped me included the following.

- My therapist and I created a graph called the 'Hierarchy of Attractiveness'. It entailed putting people I thought were beautiful at the top and less attractive at the bottom. This might sound very judgemental, but this graph was used for me to think about where I am realistically on this hierarchy.
- The main focus throughout my CBT was exposing my BDD thoughts and learning to argue with them. When BDD thoughts came into my brain, I could draw upon alternative thoughts to counter the negative thoughts. This took a lot of practice, patience, and time to master.

- My therapist also engaged with my negative behaviours. We deliberately took photos of my profile to help him to understand my reaction, and we then developed better ways of dealing with the thoughts these images provoked.

BDD will remain a part of my life and has by no means gone away. I still think about my profile daily, but instead of it being an obsessive thought, it is now just a passing thought. CBT has helped me to understand that there is a difference between my BDD-mind and Lucy's mind. Lucy's mind will always win. I returned to university after five weeks of recovery and graduated in June 2015 with first class honours. I am now pursuing a Master's.

During my darkest moments, I often felt as though I had lost myself. The Lucy I knew and used to be had gone. However, I can now say that I was not lost, but had merely misplaced myself. I have found myself again and am truly content with my life and with what my future holds. BDD and depression were the worst part of my life so far, but I wouldn't change my experience; as a result of these illnesses I have become a more confident, compassionate, and happy individual. I guess every experience, no matter how painful, ultimately makes us who we are.

Lucy Tattersall.

Margaret

I'm sixty-two years of age and have been suffering (and I really have been suffering) from BDD almost all of my life. I remember being about five years old, living with my parents and two brothers in a little two-bedroom terrace. My dad worked nights and my mum worked part-time jobs. We were quite poor really and didn't have much but I was happy in my own way with my own thoughts, safe in my little bubble.

My dad was a staunch Catholic and my earliest memories are of going to church with my dad and my brothers.

I was always a little shy and nervous but bright and intelligent. School was sometimes a bit scary but I quite liked it and was doing well. My body image wasn't too good but I didn't hate my looks. My right breast was larger than my left and the girls at school used to ask me to stand up so they could look at me. This was quite upsetting. I think this is when the BDD really started.

At about the age of six I was abused by my older cousin; I never told anyone. He didn't really hurt me; we were just touching each other. I didn't like it and didn't understand what was happening. I don't know if this had any effect on me, but it stays in my mind these many years later. I thought that if I told anyone at the time it would cause me so much trouble. I thought my dad would be really upset and that my mother would make a huge drama of it all.

My mother had mental health issues; she was always worrying about what other people thought, was always fighting and arguing with my dad, and was constantly saying to us children, 'I'm leaving now, I may see you in town sometime.' I used to cry and my brothers, who are four and five years older than me, used to tell me that she wouldn't leave. I would hear the door shutting then my mother coming back in saying, 'I've forgotten something.' I think she was trying to get some sort of a reaction. It happened many times, yet each time I thought she'd gone and was simply heartbroken. My brothers must have been really used to it.

My mother wasn't emotionally stable and had three children under the age of five to see to. My dad was working nights for the money. My mother used to lose her temper with my brothers and hit them. I think that they were scared of her. My mother was ill in her mind and couldn't help it. I know she loved us as much as she could. We were always fed and she used to make my clothes. She was always critical of me though and used to run me down in front of my friends, saying I couldn't do this and I couldn't do that, which was really upsetting. Once she asked a friend of mine to come out with us on a Sunday and I didn't want her to come (I was about seven years old). I think because she'd asked her, my mother didn't want to let her down so she took my friend out instead of me and I was made to stay at home. This stays in my mind – it really hurt. I felt I didn't matter as much as my friend. My auntie felt sorry for me and took me to the shops for some sweets. This perhaps gives you an insight into my mother's behaviour throughout my childhood. Other people's feelings always came first.

My brothers also had issues as adults but are clever and found good jobs. They have struggled with problems with relationships though. All of us had our confidence eroded as children. Our Catholic upbringing also caused a lot of fear: missing Mass was a mortal sin. I could never understand that.

One memory is walking home from school and suddenly becoming conscious of 'me'. Who am I? What am I? This feeling was so unexpected and uncomfortable. Now I feel as if things have reverted to that point in time and I am always in that uncomfortable world. For a few seconds now and then I have peace in my mind.

When I was nine years old we had to move to a bigger house, which was upsetting in itself, but we had to go. I understand that. I moved schools and the new school was an old building, unlike my other school, which was nice. The headmistress and nuns made my life hell. They were always picking on me and when I started suffering from migraines they wouldn't let me go home (I was once sick all over the girl in front of me due to a migraine, which was really embarrassing). I was called in front of my teacher every Monday for not going to 9 o'clock Mass. (I used to go later with my dad and brother but that was wrong in her eyes.)

I can't understand why my mum and dad didn't go and speak to my teacher, to tell her to stop treating me in these unkind ways. She blamed me for anything she could. My head used to shake so much it's a wonder it didn't come off. I was a nervous wreck. Another teacher used to say that I wasn't good at drawing. I knew this – but was good at other things. She once accused me of copying even though it was my friend who copied me. I didn't tell and my friend didn't own up. Next thing I knew I was being slapped across the face in front of the whole class with, 'And don't look at me like that!' I didn't even know what was wrong with the expression on my face. Again, no repercussions for the teacher. Perhaps I never told, I can't remember, but I think I would have done. I find it hard to imagine that my dad would have let things go.

I was bullied from the first day at school – it began with a boy kicking me under the desk. At my junior school a boy told me to bring him things from home (I never stayed at school for dinner). Through all this time I still had my difficult thoughts. Things then seemed to get even worse when I met Mary.

One of the nuns at my school said no child of mine would go to a 'Protestant school'. We weren't *her* children. I told my mother and I think she was so afraid of what the nun would say that she made me go to the Catholic school. This school had a rough girl there and my mother said that's why she didn't send me there (but by doing this she put me in the way of bullies who picked on me, kicked me, and called me names). I was good at rounders and one of those girls was on my team. We got talking, she was all right and the bullying stopped. I was always thought to be stuck-up and soft. I would like to think that this girl told the other girls that I was all right, but I don't know. But going back to Mary, I was always in the top class, good at English, etc. Mary was in the bottom class and hated school. I can't remember how we first got talking but we lived near each other and started hanging out together. At first we were good friends but as time went on (I can only think that she was jealous of me in some way) Mary would say things like someone was looking at me or laughing at me. She used to say that I was boring and that nobody liked me.

This went on for a while. Then some girls who knew us began to say that Mary was lovely and I was horrible. Sometimes people would mention my nose, which I've always hated (too big), my eyes (too small), and my lips (too thin). In time I started to believe these things, having nothing to fall back on. I believed I was ugly.

On the other hand, I was always popular with lads from a young age. When playing kiss-catch in the street it was me they chased (how innocent) and bought things for.

One day in class I can still remember how the thoughts started. I was sitting in a lesson and had a thought that everyone was looking at me. I stepped out of my safe world into the world I inhabit now: a frightening, lonely place where I feel like an alien, different from other people. It was like a light switching on that hasn't been turned off since. From that day onwards all I could think about was being watched and being ugly. I couldn't study any more, couldn't concentrate. I even lost pleasure in reading, which I loved. I couldn't really learn any more. So I went from being quite clever and capable at the age of twelve to losing the ability to be 'me'. I left school at fifteen, even though I could have stayed on, and went to work in a mail order firm. I thought everyone was looking at me, thinking I was ugly. If someone looked at me, a man maybe, I assumed it was because he thought I was ugly. But if he didn't look it at me it was because I was ugly, I reasoned, so I couldn't win either way.

This BDD has robbed me of my ability to love. How can you love someone when you hate yourself so much? From crying on the doorstep when my dad left, thinking he was my world, to hurting people and not thinking of anyone but myself.

Every day I was scared. My mind now tells me that I was *not* ugly when I was younger (and tells me that I am ugly now because I am older). When I was younger I was never short of attention and had lots of boyfriends but hated – and still do – my looks, thinking that I looked odd. Of course, people picked up on this. People used to say when I was younger, 'What's wrong with Margaret? She looks nice and yet she doesn't think so.'

Compliments went through like holes in Swiss cheese; I didn't believe them. Yet insults stuck; I believed them to be true. I found it very stressful to hide my uneven breasts. I side-stepped men whom I should have slept with, who actually cared for me. Even though I fancied them, as soon as I knew they liked me I thought there was something wrong with them. I became obsessed with one man at the age of twenty. I let him use me and even had an abortion when I became pregnant with his child. I once took an overdose, a cry for help, but was saved.

I had a few jobs and got attention from men wherever I worked. My legs used to get lots of compliments. I always thought God had given me lovely legs to make up for my breasts. I met my husband at work. I shouldn't have got married really. I'm too selfish, though I'd give anything not to be. I slept with the man I was obsessed with three weeks before our wedding. I found out that I was pregnant. I was pleased at first but suddenly realised the ramifications of this baby not being my husband's.

I woke up one morning and told my husband what I'd done. Long story short, I ended up having a nervous breakdown. My husband was very angry and wanted me to get rid of the baby. I was about three months pregnant when I started bleeding and was told I'd had an incomplete miscarriage.

I took an overdose again. If my husband had not come home when he did I would probably have died. I wrote suicide notes, looked at wedding photos, couldn't live with my guilt any longer, and felt very strongly that I was doing everyone a favour and that they'd be better off without me. People often think that suicide is selfish, but it seemed to be the opposite in my mind.

After I took the overdose, I was in hospital for a month, still wanting to die. I was put on an anti-depressant and woke up one morning feeling wonderful. My husband is a good man and a really good dad, but from the day we married he hasn't kissed me. Before we married sex was good, we kissed a lot. But afterwards I had to nearly beg for sex and he used to come out with evasive comments and put me off. The sad thing is that I was really beginning to relax and enjoy sex with someone who loved me.

This made me feel uglier as it seemed that my husband didn't want me sexually. So, feeling very frustrated, I took things out on my two sons, hitting them and feeling angry with them.

A woman who worked with my husband made a friend of me to get to him. I got really close to her and told her all of my worries and what happened just after we got married. After years of friendship I found out that they had been having an affair. It hurt to think that my husband would be intimate with her and not with me. I nearly caught them and he still denied it. They said it was finished and three years down the line I found out it was still going on, even though she wasn't in my life then. With hindsight, lots of things were odd but I didn't see it at the time. I trusted her I suppose.

I don't blame my husband. I was never there for him really. He must have felt lonely too. Emotionally, I couldn't relate to him properly.

I ended up in hospital again with the stress. I couldn't believe a 'friend' could be so cruel.

I now believe that the things that have happened in my life were caused by how I think, including my thoughts that I am ugly. Things in my life could have been so different if I did not have such low self-esteem.

I wonder how different my life would have been if I didn't have BDD. I've seen all the medical professionals over the years and had my share of anti-depressants. I told my doctor thirty years ago that I felt ugly. I have also seen counsellors and had CBT. One of my problems is that I drink to feel better, so any tablets don't have the best effect. It's a vicious circle.

I think I got BDD because I was never made to feel good about myself as a child. I was sensitive too, and at a vulnerable age – twelve - when I met Mary, although she didn't mean to do me any harm. Fear of other people, that's what BDD amounts to in many ways.

I worry so much about my sons, one of whom is seriously ill, and about what is going to happen in the future. At the moment I am going back on anti-depressants because I blame myself for my son's multiple sclerosis. I worry over my husband as he gets older, too. I'm scared of dying but scared of living but don't want to leave my family and friends.

I wish there was a tablet to help with my thoughts. I sometimes think it's too late for me now, though I must carry on being here. I can't think of a worse mental illness than BDD. Things are a bit better these days than they used to be, and my friends help me and have always been there for me.

I couldn't have managed without my friends. I don't know how I've got friends, I feel so false. But I love people in the best way I can. That's all I can think of to write now but I hope my story helps in some way. It's good to know I am not on my own in this lonely world.

If you suffer from BDD I really do recommend that you get help quickly. Anti-depressants and CBT help, but don't drink alcohol! It's the worst thing to do. I will carry on living as best I can. Please find the courage to tell trusted people, to explain what you are experiencing to doctors. People told me that I am not ugly but it didn't sink in. People might find it difficult to understand what you are talking about but don't give up trying to explain how you feel to the people you trust. I wish I could have, just once, seen myself as other people saw me.

Megan Butcher

Growing up was difficult for me. My family life was incredibly chaotic and in many ways my mental health issues have tied into that. I spent a significant number of years feeling depressed and anxious due to my family and even went as far as to attempt suicide at the age of twelve. I was diagnosed with BDD at the age of fifteen after many years of battling with various mental health problems such as depression and an eating disorder. I had a real hatred for the way I looked. At the time of my diagnosis I was hardly leaving the house at all, except to go to school, and even that was an issue as the slightest perceived flaw in my appearance would leave me tail-spinning into a total meltdown and I would be unable to leave the house due to my perceived 'ugliness'. Days would be spent either staring at my reflection for hours on end or being preoccupied with my appearance. There were even a couple of years where I refused to wear short sleeved tops and always had my arms covered because I saw them as fat and disgusting.

In many ways I felt trapped. Trapped in a body that I saw as too ugly to be loved in any way and trapped by these feelings I couldn't control. While my close family would constantly shower me with support and reassurance about how pretty I looked, it felt as though they were seeing a completely different person standing in front of them compared with how I really felt. CBT and counselling helped to some extent and I gradually began to go out more over the space of a couple of years, with fewer hours spent focusing on my flaws. First, I would either go out at night or to the cinema, where it would be dark and fewer people would see me, and then I gradually found the courage to leave the house slightly more in the day.

Looking back on those dark days aged fifteen and sixteen, I see now not only how truly unhappy I was but also how much I have achieved and accomplished since then. In the years since my diagnosis of BDD I have completed my GCSEs and A Levels and am now studying at university, which is something I would have never imagined would be possible during those difficult times. Things are still tough for me and I wonder if I will have to deal with BDD for the rest of my life. I imagine there will be good and bad days. But I also know that this diagnosis does not have to be the end of the world, even though it might feel like it at times. I see now not only how much support my maternal grandparents have given me, which I knew already, but also how hard it must have been for them to try to stay upbeat when I was struggling so much. In many ways I know I wouldn't be in the place I am today without them.

When I think of the future now, I feel so much more positive than I did at the time of my diagnosis, when everything seemed so bleak and hopeless. In the short term, I look forward to moving in with my boyfriend, who has also been incredibly supportive with not only my BBD but also my other mental health difficulties and unstable family. I am also excited about starting my second year of university in September. I see myself not only succeeding at university and having a career where I can support those going through difficulties, but I also see myself settling down and having what I hope will be a calm and stable family life, something I didn't have growing up.

For all of those many people out there suffering with BDD, which I believe is a much greater number than those who have been professionally diagnosed, I hope my story shows just how much can be accomplished even when dealing with mental health struggles. While some people may be lucky and get rid of their BDD with CBT and other therapies or medications, there are others who will not be fully cured. This shouldn't be seen as the end of the world though, as with the right support mental health problems such as BDD do not have to control your life, even though this may seem untrue while in the grips of this disorder. I have prepared myself that I might suffer with BDD for the rest of my life, but I also know I'm in such a better place now, at the age of just twenty, and hope to continue to improve, enjoy life, and to flourish.

Megan Butcher.

Minnie Iris

I was born in Northern India and remember feeling like an outsider from a very early age, perhaps as early as three or four. At school I was so shy that I would rarely speak.

We had mental illness in the family. My uncle had been diagnosed with psychosis and several other members suffered from severe depression, especially my grandfather, who, unfortunately, took his own life when I was five years old. This incident went on to change the course of things for me dramatically. In 1973, after sorting out my grandfather's affairs, my father decided to take the family and immigrate to England for a fresh start. I couldn't speak any English, only Hindi, and remember the dramatic change vividly; an altered landscape where everything seemed strange and foreign.

I was still incredibly shy and struggled at my new English school. This is when the bullying began. Children were quite physical with me, scratching and hitting out. I remember sitting in a circle in the classroom once and a little boy whispered in my ear, 'You're so ugly, no one will ever marry you.' There were no other Asian children at the school so maybe this is how he saw me; as strange looking. Nevertheless, those words seemed to ring true and they became deeply imprinted into my being.

My parents had a circle of friends who had also emigrated from India, some of whom were related to us. We would see them on a regular basis and I would often be left alone with them in what became abusive environments. These experiences further taught me to hate myself, to be ashamed of my body and to feel afraid, as I never knew when something bad was going to happen.

My parents had been struggling to find their feet in the new country and their marriage eventually began to fall apart. My father was often violent towards my mother. My brother and I witnessed these incidents and were frequently caught in the crossfire. I was about six years old and began to see it as my role to protect my mother and to keep her safe.

The following year I started primary school. These kids did not treat me in the same unkind ways and I remember those years as being full of joy. Although I loved this school, I had started engaging in rituals and safety behaviours by this time. One of the things I used to do was to put an almond nut, wrapped in a piece of tissue, into my coat pocket whenever I left the house. I believed this would ensure that my mother would come to no harm. Sometimes a voice in my head would say that if I didn't run down the stairs quickly enough, my mother would die. So I would race down them, nearly injuring myself. I realise now that these rituals were a way of managing my anxiety and some way of gaining a sense of control over experiences that were often frightening.

At secondary school I was put into a remedial class from the age of eleven to sixteen. My brain had been so overwhelmed by this time that it affected the way I could process information.

We lived in quite a rough area, which at the time was a stronghold of the National Front. It was the early 1980s and the height of the skinhead era. As a young person I watched television with bands like Madness sporting their look with shaved heads, Doc Marten boots and braces. I also remember Farrah Fawcett in *Charlie's Angels* with her golden hair. I began to understand that my appearance was far removed from the cultural 'ideal'. It was also around this time that I was assailed with racist bullying both inside and outside of school. Receiving those messages just reinforced my belief that I was ugly, not good enough, and not equal to other people. I remember someone drawing a poster of my face and putting it up at school; it read, 'If you see this girl, she is a witch.' I came across it and realised, in shock, that it was me. This was devastating at the time.

I had inherited a prominent hooked nose from my grandfather, which I now realise was nothing more than a normal variation. Unfortunately, because my nose stood out, it gave the bullies something else to latch on to. I had various humiliating experiences, such as when they would walk past me and chant, 'Witch, with a big long nose.' Again, these experiences became deeply imprinted into my being.

All the groundwork had been laid for the BDD to develop and to start rising to the surface. I began to become obsessed with the size and shape of my nose and the lines around my neck. I would spend hours in front of the mirror inspecting them, feeling afraid and very anxious. The negative belief system was now fully embedded, too. I soon began to believe that I must always do whatever I could to improve my appearance and to try to be perfect in order to be safe. It felt as if my life depended on it.

One evening I watched a film called *Roxanne*, starring Steve Martin and Daryl Hanna. In the film, Steve Martin's character has a really large, oversized, nose and he uses make-up to make it appear smaller. The next day I got some brown eye shadow and used it to shade in the areas of my nose that I perceived to be the most prominent. This then became a mask/ritual that I became very dependent on and continued to engage in until I was well into my teens.

Although I had not considered cosmetic surgery, my mother suggested that this could be an option. We looked into it and found that, for legal reasons, I had to be eighteen years old before any surgeon could legally operate on me. So, on my eighteenth birthday the surgery went ahead. There was a sense of relief afterwards for a while but I found that the feelings of being 'ugly' soon returned. The obsessive focus on my appearance, which had been gaining ground over the years, became even more intense and started to switch to other parts of my body. I would still clearly hear the voice of the bullies; 'you're ugly', 'you're worthless', 'you're disgusting', 'go home'.

By the time I was twenty years old, following the nose operation, I had lost quite a bit of weight. Externally, I had started going out, socialising, and getting a considerable amount of positive attention. I felt really confused by this though, as I still felt ugly and worthless inside. The compliments didn't seem to make any difference and just served to bring my attention back to my appearance. My entire identity and how I defined myself rested solely on my physical appearance now. All of my focus went into keeping myself as slim as possible, covering up any perceived imperfections and spending a lot of time looking at clothes, make-up, etc.

During the following years I met someone and got married. I completed a degree in Fine Art at Central St Martin's college of Art and Design. I worked in various jobs. To the outside eye, everything appeared to be normal but no one knew about the obsessive thought patterns and behaviours which kept me locked inside the disorder.

Things finally came to a head when my mother died suddenly in 2005. Apart from feeling a huge sense of loss and sadness, I found it very stressful to sort out her affairs and, as a consequence, started to lose my hair. My hair was something I had seen as an important part of my identity and self-worth. As the weeks and months went by, I would spend hours in front of the mirror checking to see how much hair I had lost. I would compare my hair to other people's all the time – on the train or just while walking about. Overwhelming feelings of fear and anxiety were with me for what seemed like every second of every day. The question I would ask myself was, 'How can I go on if my hair keeps falling out?'

For the next few years I somehow managed the distress. I tried various treatments for my hair loss, including seeing a dermatologist, a Chinese herbalist, a homeopath, and going to specialist hair clinics. I ended up parting with a lot of money.

Things had been building for some time. By this point, when I looked into the mirror, I would be completely horrified by my own reflection. My circumstances had become so distressing that the only way I could see any way out of them was to take my own life. I had heard of BDD by then but only had a vague idea about it. In desperation I decided to do some internet research and found various bits of information online, including a documentary. Watching this was a real eye-opener for me as I was able to identify with so many patterns of the disorder.

A few days after this I went to see my GP. Luckily, she had heard of BDD. I explained that I was in a lot of distress and was in danger of taking my own life. She was very understanding and made a referral for me to have treatment with the NHS. Because I was suicidal I was made a priority case and only had to wait four weeks for my treatment to start. I was extremely lucky and I will always be very grateful for this.

The treatment began and through gaining understanding about BDD, using mindfulness techniques to separate myself from my thoughts and going through the exposure exercises, things slowly started to change. I began to realise that I was suffering from a severe physiological disorder. Yes, my hair had been thinning, but only I could see this; it wasn't apparent to other people and it didn't mean that my life would be over if it didn't look perfect.

During the following months I worked very hard on the CBT homework and my therapist was pleased with how well I was engaging with the treatment. The safety behaviours and rituals became less and less frequent and the levels of distress started to decrease. I also attended a support group for people with BDD at the Priory Hospital in North London. The support group was a great help. I was able to relate to others and realised that I was not alone. Gradually, I started to gain compassion for myself as I was able to see the typical patterns of the disorder. Over the following few years I continued on my recovery journey, occasionally having relapses. I learnt, however, that these were times for learning and an intrinsic part of the recovery process.

Eventually, I started to co-facilitate the BDD support groups. This helped me to slowly build up my confidence as a person and later I became a trustee with the BDD Foundation. This added another valuable dimension to my life and gave me a sense of purpose. My involvement with the charity somehow gave my myriad experiences, stemming from my childhood, a meaning.

A year ago I went back into treatment. Even though I had a good amount of recovery from the first round of CBT, I felt that things had plateaued and I wanted to see if I could push my recovery further. This time we worked on changing some of my core beliefs. We also did some memory re-scripting work, which involved working through some specific events from the past that still had a hold over me. I found this work really powerful and, by combining it with changing my core beliefs, I was finally able to put the abuse and the voices of the bullies far behind me. I was able to see that there was nothing wrong with me at all; the abuse was about the people who carried it out. Unfortunately, I had been put into the wrong environments, which, at the time, I had no control over.

These days, at the age of forty-eight, I see myself as a whole human being with many different facets. I no longer solely define myself by my appearance. I can appreciate all the other qualities I have, be they warmth, kindness, a sense of fun, or depth of character. I am coming to see myself as a worthwhile and loveable person who has a lot to offer the world. My life is full of socialising, travelling, being creative, rewarding work, and adventure. I am still on a journey of personal growth and self-discovery. Occasionally I'll get some of the BDD thoughts coming up, but now I'm able to say, 'All right, that's the BDD doing its thing.' I know now that the thoughts have no relevance to my life or to reality.

Living with BDD
Artwork by Minnie Iris

BDD falling away

Minnie Iris.

N: A Mother's Story

My son has got BDD but my son is not BDD. This is a mother's story.

I am writing this anonymously because my son would be very upset if he read it. He would say that he has not got BDD but I know that he has. He would say that he has got a physical problem and that is partially true, but it is not the whole truth. Sadly, I cannot persuade him to see things from a broader perspective.

My son was born with a birth defect. It wasn't anything very obvious and the doctors said he wouldn't even notice it when he grew up. There was no suggestion that there was any treatment available and this was before the days of the internet, so I took the doctor's word for it. What else was I to do?

I was delighted with my baby. I had always been a career girl and many people thought that I was not the maternal type. I was ready for motherhood, however, and to me my son was absolutely perfect. My side of the family had a long history of having girls so a boy was completely unexpected and a tremendous gift. I threw myself passionately into parenting. My baby grew and the defect became less noticeable. For long periods of time I forgot about it completely.

BDD arrived in our family like a particularly vicious, stabbing bolt of lightning or, at least, it certainly seemed that way. I can no longer watch programmes like *One Born Every Minute* on the television because what was once a happy event for me has become tinged with sadness. I was so happy when my son was born but he later became so unhappy with himself. I would ask myself time and again, 'Is it my fault?' The guilt was enormous and relentless. Did it have anything to do with something I did while he was in my womb? Why had I just accepted what that doctor had told me? Should I have done more? I have been told by an eminent surgeon that there was nothing I should have or could have done, but nothing will remove that little voice of guilt. I feel that my son blames me. He wonders why we didn't fix him when he was a baby.

Since BDD infiltrated our family, I have looked back many times and asked myself, 'When did my son stop being the happy boy he was as a young child?' These musings come when I see a little boy in an advert or in the park when I walk the dog. As a young boy, up until the age of fourteen, my son was a happy lad. He had plenty of friends at nursery and primary school. He enjoyed family activities, outings, holidays, and playing sports in the garden with his father. He was loving and affectionate. When I look back now, however, I can see that there were some signs of things to come even in these early days. My son had a tendency to be obsessive with things that he particularly liked. This usually involved the collection of various items. He would put together vast quantities of something and know every fact about them. We used to marvel at his encyclopaedic knowledge. Eventually the fad would die out and another one would come along.

My son also seemed to lack imagination. He never played imaginative games and just wasn't interested in them. I noticed this contrast particularly when a sibling arrived who loved creating imaginary scenarios, dressing-up, drawing and painting. I have read somewhere that people with BDD do not see whole faces or bodies very well. They are not good at seeing the whole picture and focus on very specific elements.

I became aware that my son had an anxious personality when he was about six years old. This didn't really surprise me. I had a very anxious side until early middle age, by which point I think I had had enough life experience to stop catastrophising about everything. My son's anxious side came out in myriad ways; when he was little, he showed his anxiety freely and I felt that I was able to respond. By the time he was a teenager, however, he withdrew from sharing his emotions in the same way. I was not foolish enough to think that he had grown out of it, but he began to internalise his feelings, as so many teenagers do.

The transition to secondary school was negotiated, I thought, reasonably well, considering that my son was the only child from his primary school to go to his particular secondary school. He seemed to make friends fairly easily. He was not gregarious but there appeared to be other boys to socialise with and he never complained about bullying and never refused to attend school. He has since said that he was bullied about his appearance but has also said that no one ever pointed out his birth defect to him, so it was difficult to know what to make of it.

At around the age of fourteen my son's mood seemed to change considerably. Initially, I thought it was just normal teenage angst and probably some of it was. He didn't make much of his appearance and didn't seem overly worried about it. He did seem angry, however, and withdrew into online gaming. There was the usual teenage friction at home and we were concerned about the lack of actual physical relationships with peers. Throughout this time, he continued to work hard at school. On the whole, we thought he must be doing all right.

When my son was fifteen, he mentioned his birth defect to me for the first time. This was like a dagger through my heart, although I have no idea why I was so foolish as to believe that he would never notice it. My husband and I dealt with it calmly, and we hoped that my son would just forget about it. I cried to my mother on the phone, fearful at what this turn of events might mean.

At the age of sixteen, my son went to Sixth Form College. Again, another transition, another new school. He was beginning to ask for reassurance about his appearance more often but continued to go off confidently each day to school. He made friends but his work ethic slipped. University plans were being mentioned but my son seemed strangely apathetic. I began to wonder whether everything really was all right after all.

Later on in the year, I took my son along to his chosen university. I knew that he was worrying about his appearance more but he made a good start to his first academic year. There were plenty of friends and lots of socialising. He was getting out and about a lot. We were pleased, but texts regarding his appearance were increasing and he asked if he could find out more about his defect. He wanted to know if anything could be done to amend it. I arranged a visit to an esteemed plastic surgeon. If I am honest,

I now wish that I hadn't done so, but I did what I felt was right at the time. The surgeon's comments were not entirely helpful. He told us that an operation could be done but that my son would have to see a psychiatrist first. I think the surgeon had guessed what was going on and, for that at least, I will be forever grateful.

The psychiatrist confirmed that my son was indeed suffering from BDD. My son was devastated. I was more practical, instantly looking into what could be done. I arranged CBT but my son did not engage with the therapist. At this point, we were getting texts night and day. Some sought reassurance, some asked for specifics about his defect and general appearance, some made accusations. There was anger in every word and each of our replies were analysed minutely by him. The anxiety at this time would sometimes keep me awake all night. My son was miserable. I had read about the high risk of suicide in people with BDD. I had a constant sense of imminent danger and did not know what to do for the best.

On one occasion, my son made a flying visit home. He thought that he was going mad. After five days he went back to university. Somehow, he limped to the end of term. We tried to persuade him to get help but he was only interested in getting plastic surgery. I ended up in tears at the receptionist's desk at the GP surgery. I couldn't face being on my own at home with my son as he was so angry and even got to the point of verbally, and sometimes physically, pushing me around. He is taller and stronger than I am. I was afraid that he would hurt me. The doctor prescribed SSRIs, which seemed to make my son a little better. We breathed a sigh of relief and took him to the railway station for the return journey to university. My husband and I then took a short, much-needed break by the coast. Just ten hours later a text expressing hopelessness arrived. We couldn't reach him and called the university. Fear of suicide is a terrible thing. Feeling suicidal, of course, is worse. Somehow, the end of the first year arrived. We were happy to have him home but he was still so angry with us, still so depressed and hopelessly obsessed with his appearance. The safety behaviours were still evident, which took the form of continuous mirror-checking, and constant texting to seek reassurance about his appearance. We were living under the same roof, yet all forms of verbal conversation were rejected. We went on holiday and my son sadly stayed home. He wrecked the house, not accidentally, not carelessly, but deliberately. I was angry but didn't share with him the full extent of my anger as I didn't want to make things any worse.

We wanted my son to have therapy and asked him to visit the doctor again. He reluctantly agreed but is certainly no fool. My son is highly intelligent and, despite me priming the surgery, he hoodwinked the doctor and returned home with an anti-depressant. Again he took it short term and, just as his depression was improving, he stopped taking it again. At this point I was receiving counselling myself, which I desperately needed.

My son persuaded us to fund a minor operation to amend his birth defect. He entered the clinic with optimism. The surgeon did his best but my son was not pleased with the outcome, as is so often the case with people who suffer from BDD.

These days things are so much better than they were then. My son is away again, living his life. Happiness is all we want for him. I know that the BDD has not gone away and there are good days and bad days, but at least my son is getting out and about and living his life. I mention therapy and re-visiting the doctor as often as I dare to but am always rebuked. Yet, I will keep mentioning it. In the meantime, I am living my life too.

Things that have been good:

- Private medical insurers: they had a crisis line and listened to me howl my way through my story, later providing support and encouragement. They authorised and paid for CBT without argument and helped me to find an appropriate therapist.
- The GP surgery: they listened to me and did what they could to help.
- Counselling: when you can't help someone else I believe the next best thing to do is to help yourself. It may the only thing you can control.
- Dog walking: exercise and space to clear your head helps.

Things that have been unhelpful:

- Plastic surgery: I would not advise that you go there with BDD.
- Local mental health services: I found these to be too slow and unresponsive. I rang their crisis line in desperation one day and was told that they would only help if my son had actually swallowed a bottle of pills.

At the start of this, I said it was a mother's story, but it is also a father's story and a sibling's story. As a family we have been tested beyond our limits but are still holding hands in a circle around my son and will continue to do so until he is ready to step outside of his BDD. I have to believe that day will come. My son is clever, friendly, determined, stubborn, kind, caring, generous, and handsome. I adore him. My son has BDD but my son is not BDD.

Peter's Story: Supporting a Child with BDD

Peter had a happy childhood. He was a bright, cheerful, and energetic boy with whom we and his siblings had a strong and loving relationship. At school he was confident and happy and had a wide group of friends. He fully participated in school life and was doing well academically. Peter enjoyed attending clubs and pursuing his interests. As parents, we never had any worries regarding our son and had no knowledge that he had any worries until, over a very short period of time, he changed almost beyond recognition.

Our experience with BDD started some five years ago. When Peter reached early adolescence, he suddenly changed. He completely withdrew from what we considered to be 'normal' behaviour. He started to find it very difficult to attend school or any social activities and at home gradually withdrew from his family. We contacted our GP, who referred him to CAMHS. This all happened so unexpectedly. As parents, our lack of understanding, and not knowing what was affecting Peter in such a massive way, caused us much anxiety.

The following four years are difficult to summarise. Life changed for our family. Peter was diagnosed with BDD only nine months ago and during the intervening years his illness developed over time. We supported him as best we could with advice and help from CAHMS, who initially diagnosed him with social anxiety. We had to change our lives and one of us had to stop working to care for him. To say that there were lots of ups and downs is an understatement and it is hard to describe the emotions that we experienced as parents, suddenly having to cope with Peter's withdrawal from life and having to deal with his high levels of distress and anxiety, as well as keeping things as normal as possible for the rest of our family. At times it felt like a bereavement, as though we had lost our son, and we felt much frustration at not being able to help him. Through difficult times we were always driven to keep going by our desire to support Peter as best we could.

Peter withdrew from school and his friends. School created huge amounts of worry and anxiety for him. It took him hours to get ready, hours to get through the school door and, when he did attend, he found it difficult to cope. He couldn't concentrate on schoolwork and it felt as though he used every ounce of energy to just get there and then couldn't do anything else. As we were initially told that Peter suffered from social anxiety, we focused all of our efforts on trying, with the support of his school, to help him to continue to attend mainstream school. Over time, school gradually ground to a halt, as did our son's ability to see any of his friends or to have a social life of any description.

Peter then, sadly, withdrew from family life. We were no longer able to go out as a family. At times he would not allow us or his siblings to be in the same room as him. He didn't want any of us to see him and hid in pyjamas, duvets, anything he could conceal himself under. He didn't want to attend family events or family holidays and often found it too difficult to join in with celebrations such as birthdays and Christmas. Peter wanted to disappear and couldn't let even his closest family see him. It was very difficult to see this self-inflicted isolation and so hard to understand why our lovely son needed to do this.

We started to understand that all of Peter's behaviours seemed to be related to how he felt about his appearance. Our son became very preoccupied with certain parts of his body. Over time, this seemed to move from one area to another, with different areas causing different levels of anxiety at different times. At home he was prepared to take what we considered to be quite drastic measures to try to change his appearance and to 'fix' what he perceived to be the problem. His behaviours became obsessional. We learnt that his thoughts, too, were obsessional.

Slowly, over a period of time, Peter became able to explain to us how he was feeling. We started to hear about his self-loathing and about how he felt disgusting and that he didn't think people should see him. He described how his constant thoughts were exhausting, so much so that at times he felt he couldn't do it any more and that no one truly understood. We heard how he constantly felt judged and how he tried to change the way he looked, believing that this would make him feel better, but it never did. Deep down, as parents, we knew this was something more than just social anxiety.

It took many attempts with professionals to get a proper understanding of Peter's condition. When BDD was finally diagnosed, we felt relieved. This enabled us to start another journey of understanding and learning. It also enabled us to explain the condition to our son, who instantly felt that the symptoms of BDD seemed to describe him. This helped him to feel understood and to realise that he is not the only person who feels the way he does. Peter is now receiving medication and CBT specifically aimed at BDD and, while he still believes his BDD thoughts, he is starting to manage things better and, very slowly, is taking small steps forward. It feels as if our son's personality is starting to return and his mood has lifted. We see a determined, funny, loving, and courageous child. We don't know how long this improvement will last or where it will take him, and we are starting to understand that his condition might always be part of his life, but we know we will never give up trying to help him to make the most of his life.

So, what advice would we give to other parents in a similar situation?

- Be patient, loving and understanding.
- Sometimes it is necessary to give tough love.
- Don't blame yourselves.
- Be honest with your child.
- Make time to listen and to talk.
- Give your child time to take steps at his/her own pace.
- Treat BDD as a bully that your child doesn't want in his/her life.
- Don't give up on getting the right treatment and medication, and remember that you know your child better than anyone.
- Celebrate successes, however small!

It may be a very long road and one that will test you and your family emotionally in a way that others will never really understand. But always remember that your child is still there, even though he or she might be hiding behind the BDD, and is desperate for your support and understanding of his/her condition. Our experience has taught us that with lots of love, patience, and flexibility you can start to help to improve your child's and your family's enjoyment of life. With this focus, you will undoubtedly have the best chance of coping with, and perhaps even beating, BDD.

Rachel Trewartha

So, my parents thought it was funny and harmless to make fun of my nose; 'pig nose' and 'ski-slope nose' were their favourites. When I started to develop breasts around the age of nine years old, this was another source of amusement and mickey taking. I still remember being 'puff panned' up to the ceiling while a song called 'Ghostbusters' by Ray Junior Parker was playing. They shouted out 'Rachel Busters' instead.

My mum was very critical of my weight the older I got. I recall being eleven and watching the film *Dirty Dancing*. My mum commented how nice it must be to be so slim. There were many of these instances. I don't think my parents thought anything of it; to them it was just a bit of fun, a joke – but for me it was the start of feeling uncomfortable and highly aware of my flaws.

Around this time my parents started having really bad arguments and I saw mum attack dad on a few occasions, one time throwing a knife at him. I had always been a daddy's girl and was petrified of mum, so when dad left home to live with a woman he had been having an affair with, my world fell apart. A cycle of him leaving and coming back began, as he couldn't decide whom he wanted to be with. Eventually, they divorced when I was eleven years old, only to get back together a year or so later.

Around this time my one and only real friend, Helen, moved to Australia. This further destroyed me. As a result of all this abandonment, I became withdrawn and started to feel depressed. I began exhibiting symptoms of OCD. Hand washing, tidying, order, and repetition were the driving forces. I felt compelled, as these things were all I had control of in my life.

I became pretty much a recluse for the next few years, going to school (which I hated with a passion) and living in my bedroom was my life. I spent a lot of time crying and wishing I was dead; I felt worthless, fat, ugly, and as though I had nothing to offer the world.

School was a scary, lonely time for me and also a place where I felt incredibly self-conscious about my breasts, which continued to grow and grow. Because of their size, I got a lot of unwanted attention and spent a lot of time with my arms crossed and my coat on (even on the hottest days). I skipped high school regularly, as I hated it and didn't feel as if I fitted in. I left school just before my sixteenth birthday with no passes in my GCSEs; I wasn't interested in trying my best, I just felt relieved to be leaving school.

A few months later, I started work as a packer in a factory. This was the first of many factory jobs, which were highly monotonous and not what I wanted to do with my life. Yet, I had no confidence to go to college and my one desired career of becoming a writer, which I had talked about to my parents, was met with, 'You have to be really good to make money as a writer.' So my poetry, stories, and artwork were my way of escaping to a different place in the confines of my bedroom.

When I was sixteen, I started my first course of anti-depressants, prescribed by one of the first psychiatrists I saw. Over the next few years I would try various medications, see different psychiatrists, and have some counselling in a bid to win my battle with severe depression, OCD, and social anxiety. There were also a couple of times I attempted suicide via overdose.

At the age of twenty, I finally left home, something I had wanted to do for years to escape mum. I was also referred for art psychotherapy by my GP around this time. Bill was (and still is) a pivotal person in my life. I learnt so much from him about why I was suffering with my mental health. I continued to see him one a week for a year and in that time I felt unbelievably better, the change was so noticeable. However, the feelings about my appearance continued and resulted in me discontinuing with my therapy because it was now summertime and the clinic I attended had two routes to it, which both meant walking past a pub. I could not face walking past all the people sitting outside enjoying a drink because I was convinced they were all staring at me, laughing at hideous, fat, ugly Rachel.

I found summertime extremely difficult for many years, not just because there were more people about, but trying to cover up my body on hot days was uncomfortable and depressing. I would be applying make-up in an attempt to try and look slightly more acceptable for society. But the sun reflected and magnified every hair, spot, and flaw a hundred times worse when I was looking in the mirror. I would literally get 'lost in the mirror'; I couldn't stop looking at that hideous person and all of her flaws. There were many days when I would end up staying in. I would go to the shop when it was darker or if it was raining, as I knew people wouldn't notice me as much. I requested a nose job, breast reduction, tummy tuck, laser treatment for facial hair, and surgery on my acne-pitted skin through my GP but was turned down every time.

My social life was very sporadic. If I managed to go out, I would get drunk and sleep around. I thought it meant I was desirable if someone wanted to have sex with me, but this was short-lived, as I knew men didn't need to fancy you to have sex with you. Mum would call me a slag for sleeping around. I cancelled nights out as I just felt too ugly to be out in society.

At the age of twenty-seven, I had my first relationship since the age of thirteen. I had just slept around since then as I didn't know how to have a trusting, loving relationship. I was scared of commitment and, to be honest, wasn't really attracting the right kind of men anyway. The relationship was extremely dysfunctional, as we both had mental health issues and I was massively insecure and jealous of my partner having any kind of interaction with other women. I ended up being very controlling, going through his phone, making him delete any women's numbers, accusing him of looking at other women, sleeping with other women, etc. In our many arguments I became physically abusive as well as verbally abusive. Nine months into the relationship I became pregnant and, nine months later, gave birth (via emergency C-section) to our daughter. The relationship ended for good when my daughter was three years old.

A year later, I fell into another relationship with a man I barely knew, who was homeless with a chronic alcohol addiction. Again, the insecurity of him looking at other women, whether it was on television, in magazines, or on the street was there. I just couldn't get over the thought of him comparing me to them. I believed that he was only with me because I was a safe bet as no one else would want me. I soon realised that he was the most controlling one out of the two of us. He was accusing me of cheating and, six months in, the physical abuse started. This time, he was attacking me. This relationship caused me so much stress, pain, and fear. The police, social services, and the courts were all involved. In the end, I had to make a choice between him and my daughter. The two-year relationship ended. Looking back on that period of my life is very hard, as I feel a lot of guilt about what I put my daughter through and actually can't believe that was my life. But at the same time I learnt some valuable lessons.

At the age of thirty-five I accessed art psychotherapy again. Initially, this was individual therapy, just me and the therapist, Bill. A few months in, Bill suggested I joined one of his groups as he thought group therapy would really benefit me. So I agreed to give it a try ... as I write this I am still in that group, learning how to have functional relationships, discussing and processing my issues with the other members who also had dysfunctional families. Also, around the age of thirty-five, I finally discussed my issues related to my appearance with my psychiatrist (I had shared these feelings with Bill from the very start of my therapy and had also shared within the group). I felt embarrassed and awkward talking to my psychiatrist about these things as the rapport wasn't really there. However, his diagnosis of BDD was a turning point for me, a realisation. Suddenly everything made so much sense. I was prescribed anti-psychotics along with my anti-depressant. This combination of the correct medication, the diagnosis and psychotherapy, and reading *The Broken Mirror* has made an enormous difference to my life.

I still suffer with BDD, but not to the extent that I once did. I can function and enjoy living my life most of the time. Below I have listed how I was in the worst period of my BDD and how I am now.

In the Past

- Hiding away – I couldn't go to many places on my own; public transport, cafes, college, etc.
- Severe mirror checking (not helpful that mum called me vain!).
- Constant preoccupation with how I looked, comparing myself with others, including my sister and also people in magazines.

- Unhealthy magazine obsession (see above).
- Skin picking, daily eyebrow plucking.
- Planning suicide.

How BDD Affects Me Now

- Feel very uncomfortable if I go out without make-up on, so rarely do go out without it.
- Don't buy celebrity magazines.
- Only pluck eyebrows every few days, but now pluck hairline.
- Camera phobic, only feel comfortable if I'm the one taking the photo, but then only do so when needed.
- Have mirrors in every room in my house, and in my handbag.

One of my biggest achievements – having my nose pierced!

Rachel Trewartha.

Tony

My BDD started a bit later in life than most other people. I was about twenty years old when I remember starting to feel really uncomfortable about my appearance, in particular the size and shape of my nose.

Having said that, I think my deep insecurities went back a bit further than that...

I remember being a ten-year-old boy and feeling ashamed of any freckles or moles on my body. No one had ever commented on them, and, in hindsight, I can now see that they were totally normal. Yet, at the time, I just saw them as an imperfection and wanted to get rid of, or hide, them. I remember having a large mole under my arm and always trying to hide it when I took my shirt off. I also remember trying to cut it out with nail scissors. This escapade has left me with a slight scar ever since.

But these feelings never really developed any further throughout my childhood and, looking back, didn't really cause me any serious issues.

At around the age of fourteen, I experienced a phase of bullying, and found out that some friends had been saying things about me behind my back. This led to me feeling ostracised from a group of mates with whom

I'd been friends my whole life. At that stage I felt very alone and questioned which of my friends I could actually trust. I remember feeling constantly paranoid about whether people were making jokes about me behind my back, not necessarily in relation to my appearance, but about anything and everything; about how I spoke, what I wore, how I acted, what I said. There was a clear degree of paranoia there. I became extremely self-aware, something that has stayed with me ever since. I always thought about how I must come across to others, rather than just relaxing and being myself.

I managed to stumble through the next few years, putting a brave face on, hiding my difficult feelings and trying to make the best of life. This attitude took me through the main years of growing up and I lived a very normal life. Despite having some insecurities, I was a relatively happy kid.

My first memories of realising that I had serious issues with my appearance started at the age of nineteen. I had just started a design degree at university. I think the type of degree is worth mentioning because I have always been obsessed with the shape and form that objects take – I love beautifully designed products, which includes the shape of buildings, cars, and, unfortunately, the shape of people's faces! I had been travelling for a year before university and had an incredible year. But when I returned home, I subsequently broke up with my childhood sweetheart. This all happened very quickly and really knocked me for six. I felt overwhelming guilt for what I saw as me ruining her life. In hindsight, I can appreciate that I was just a nineteen-year-old bloke who wanted to go out and sow his wild oats, but I felt so much guilt and subsequent fear of those feelings, I just couldn't live with myself.

I arrived at university and tried to distract myself from these deep emotions by drinking too much and smoking a lot of cannabis. Drinking helped me to forget about my issues. I had been drinking on and off for a few years and was embracing the culture of being away at university. I had used cannabis a few times before, but my gang of friends at university were smoking every day. I wasn't used to that, but it became normal to smoke a few times every week. I never really enjoyed the feeling. It was fun to begin with as I was always into music and smoking made listening to my favourite music sound amazing, yet I always felt incredibly paranoid when I smoked. But because of the crowd I was hanging out with, I couldn't seem to stop myself from doing it.

During that first year of university I was still feeling horrible about my failed relationship and suffered what I can only describe as an emotional breakdown. I became totally paranoid, felt insane levels of guilt about a variety of things, and was totally debilitated by fear.

Looking back, it's quite hard to explain and my guilt feelings seem very irrational. I think the combination of the emotional strain I was feeling from the break-up, being in a new environment with new people, and the sudden involvement with mind-altering substances really had a negative effect on me.

I distinctly remember going through a phase within which I would panic about really irrational stuff. I had one panic attack because I thought I might be gay – and started worrying incessantly about how I was going to tell my family and friends about it and what that would mean for my future. I have since learnt that there is a physiological issue known as 'homosexual OCD', where people feel a sense of panic about potentially being homosexual. Looking back, this could have easily persisted and been an issue I struggled with on a long-term basis instead of morphing into BDD. This perhaps indicates that I was in a very vulnerable state of mind. It was almost chance as to which symptoms developed from that period of time.

On another occasion, I remember being convinced that I was HIV positive. These were all ridiculous thoughts that overtook my mind and became all I could think about. Each time I found some relief from one fear, another fear would take its place. I would feel my heart sink and the blood rush to my head as I suddenly realised that there was something else, something equally terrible, to worry about. It was wave after wave of panic attacks and total stress. I was unable to function and remember going for days and days without eating due to the intense anxiety and sense of panic.

Somehow, I battled through the first year of university and came out the other side feeling a bit better. I saw a counsellor, who may have helped slightly, and read some self-help books on dealing with emotions. I had a good group of friends, had a fun job working in a bar, and a new girlfriend. Things were starting to look up. But then, in my second year of university, one of my new best mates made a comment about me having a big nose. I remember him creating a nose shape with his hand and doing an impression of me talking with his hand over his face. This wasn't a moment in which I suddenly thought, 'Oh God, I hate my nose' but, when I look back, that was the first time I felt deeply insecure about my looks. Before that I felt as if I was a pretty good-looking guy.

A year later I was on a work placement and broke my nose playing football. It left me with a deviated septum and I think this incident only caused me more paranoia about the appearance of my nose. This was around the year 2002, when digital cameras were becoming quite common. I was also, therefore, seeing a lot more photos of myself, which started to magnify my self-awareness.

Fast forward a couple of years and my insecurities about my nose slowly started to become worse and worse. I graduated from university and did lots more travelling, which I loved, but would often resort to drinking to mask my insecurities and attempt to get through life. I think it was around this period of time that I realised I had a psychological issue and discovered BDD while browsing online.

Many people say it is a positive moment for them when they discover that BDD is a diagnosable mental illness because it helped them to feel validated and less alone. I didn't feel that relief. I knew I had psychological issues but also believed that I had physical issues, too.

I hated photos of myself and would try to avoid people seeing me from my profile. Mirrors in bright sunlight were my enemy. I really hated looking in certain mirrors and having my photo taken from certain angles. I was generally demonstrating most of the classic symptoms that BDD sufferers present.

In 2006, my BDD got much worse. Another friend started making jokes about my nose and this really cut deep. Not only was I paranoid about how I looked, people were making fun of me and I reasoned, therefore, that I must look like a freak. All of those feelings of being a kid and people laughing at me behind my back came flooding back. Ironically, I actually thought I was a good-looking guy except for this horrible nose stuck on the front of my face. My nose became a separate entity to the rest of my face. I became obsessed with fixing it. By now I was a good graphic designer and would often spend hours photo-shopping images of myself so that I could see what I would look like if I fixed the problem.

This was also around the time that Facebook arrived on the scene, and so the combination of high quality digital cameras, travelling, and the internet meant that I was subjected to what felt like hundreds of photos of myself from all different angles being displayed all over the place. This really didn't help with how I was feeling. I felt that I was surrounded by beautiful people while I had a really embarrassing physical issue. I knew I didn't look disgusting. I knew I didn't look like a freak. I just thought if someone were to really look at me and scrutinise me, they would realise how ugly I looked. I thought it was the reason I was single and blamed every failed relationship and rejection on my nose.

Having said all of that, I was quite lucky. Although BDD has been a huge part of my life for fifteen years, it has never completely stopped me from living my life. I have always managed to get on with things. I have always found tactics to help get me through difficult situations. Some of these tactics have been unhealthy (drinking alcohol, looking at photos I liked of myself as reassurance that I looked all right) but, at other times, I managed to pull my socks up and get on with it. I feel quite blessed that BDD has never completely disabled me. Perhaps, however, this is one of the reasons I've let BDD linger on for so long and haven't fully attacked the problem, because I could live an 'acceptable' quality of life with the condition.

Don't get me wrong, there were times when I couldn't face going out and made my excuses and avoided socialising. I used to always avoid cameras from certain angles and sit facing people so they could not see my profile. I had some of the most classic BDD tendencies out there. But no one would have known I had these issues because I hid them so well and managed to have a full-time job, a few girlfriends, played a lot of sport, went out with my mates, etc. From the outside, it would appear that I basically lived a decent lifestyle.

After a particularly bad spell of feeling ugly, I decided to do something about it and booked an operation to straighten my nose and remove the hump. The operation was fine, I felt a bit better, but it didn't look good enough and quickly the feelings returned. A couple of years later, I decided to try again. I took out a huge loan and had a second operation with a top surgeon in London. This time I felt even better and the following six months were a bit of an improvement. The BDD feelings, however, came back ... slowly and less intensely ... but they were still there. I knew that I looked better than before, but still wasn't happy and had bouts of BDD at the same intensity as before my operations.

It was a few months after this second operation that I decided to seek help for my BDD. I actually promised myself that if the second operation didn't make me feel better I would pursue treatment for the psychological side of things, even though I also still believed I had a very real physical problem.

I started seeing a CBT therapist in North London. It was a huge relief to finally talk to somebody about my feelings. I continued to see this therapist over the course of a couple of years. Unfortunately, I was paying to see him privately and, therefore, it became a challenge to continue the treatment long-term and as frequently as I would have liked due to financial constraints. I did also go to my GP about it, but I don't think he was particularly helpful.

After maybe ten or twelve sessions of CBT with my therapist, I didn't feel as though I was making much progress and we decided together that I would try some SSRI drugs (fluoxetine) to see if that took the edge off my feelings. I began with 20 mg per day, but before long I was up to 80 mg per day.

I stayed on this level of medication for around a year, and while it definitely took the edge off my paranoia and feelings of self-loathing, I also put on a lot of weight, completely lost my libido, and felt like a zombie. I remember feeling a bit fed up because I didn't enjoy music any more; the numbness of taking these drugs had reduced any emotions I once felt (including happiness). It made sense that I wasn't enjoying life much. I just didn't really feel anything any more.

I don't think I realised at the time quite how much these drugs were affecting me, but the benefits were definitely equalled by the negative side effects. I was also still drinking quite a lot to hide my insecurities and to escape reality. I was generally not a very happy soul.

After twelve months of this, I decided to reduce my intake of the drugs, mainly because I was starting a new relationship and knew that this wasn't a long-term solution for me. I was feeling so lethargic, did not have any sex drive, and just generally didn't like the person I had become.

This takes us to about three years ago, and I have been drug free since. I'm now thirty-six years old, have recently started my own company, am living with my girlfriend, and we're also expecting our first child!! Big changes afoot for me!

While I'm not one hundred per cent better, I have improved in certain areas, yet I still have a long way to go. The feelings of BDD come and go, and sometimes they can be as bad as they were at their worst. I know that I need to confront the BDD head-on but have been suffering from some other serious health issues over the past two years and am currently focusing on these before I go back to BDD treatment.

One recent example made me realise that I am definitely not completely better. We were on holiday and I stood in front of a full-length mirror in a room filled with sunshine and the feelings of anxiety, panic, stress, and fear swept over me as I saw my face. I hated what I saw and immediately started thinking about having another operation. How else could I go on living my life?

So, there are clearly some BDD issues I have yet to overcome. And I know that I have to do the work myself to overcome these issues. Eventually I plan to continue CBT and really try giving the homework sessions one hundred per cent of my energy and attention. The few times I have tried the CBT techniques I have felt marginally better, so I know I need to continue with them.

Before I sign off, I would like to add that I have another theory on treatment for BDD that has intrigued me over the past few years – the concept of using psychedelic medicines to treat my BDD symptoms. I have never taken these types of medicine, and I call them 'medicines' because there is a huge amount of research being done on the use of drugs such as dimenthyltryptamine (DMT) and psilocybin in order to treat anxiety disorders including PTSD and addictions, etc. I am convinced that these drugs could help BDD sufferers but there is very little research being done on them and they have a bad reputation, hence the medical industry is ignoring them and is nervous to suggest their use without more research. If they could help us, why are they not being looked at more seriously? We all used to think the world was flat – we were proved wrong on that. How do we know that these types of medicines are all evil and have no use as a treatment for psychological issues? I just wish society had a more open mind.

Once my health issues improve and I am able to travel again, and if the CBT tactics continue to have little effect, I will look at testing these types of medicines myself. I see it as the only remaining option for me – a complete shift in how my mind sees the world and, I hope, how I see myself.

I would like to wish all sufferers of BDD and their families good luck. Let's keep sharing – it's the only way we are going to keep learning and chipping away at this horrible affliction.

Viktoria

I have a thirteen-year-old girl.

I'm not very kind to her at all.

She cries so loudly that I give in and let her have what she wants. I will do anything to stop the pain that she feels.

She's crying now and she doesn't want me to tell you about her because she is so ashamed, so racked with guilt at all the things she has done to herself and to others. She thinks that she's not worth talking about, thinking about, being cared for, or being loved.

I need to talk about this thirteen-year-old Viktoria. I know she won't like it but I need to.

Viktoria, you were the kind of girl who was too afraid to leave the house for three years because you thought you were too ugly for the world. The kind of girl who, because of her self-hatred, poisoned herself time after time with tablets and alcohol, who stabbed and sliced herself with anything she could. The kind of girl who would look in the mirror, cry uncontrollably until she was worn out, get up and do it all over again. The kind of girl who was locked on a children's psychiatric ward for three years for her own protection – protection from herself. The kind of girl who was stubborn and refused any kind of help, who wouldn't talk, who wouldn't interact with people or, in fact, with *life* of any kind. The kind of girl who could never sleep and would sit on the window sill and write under the moonlight, crying. The kind of girl who smuggled a screwdriver into her bedroom so she could open the windows properly and jump out into the night. The kind of girl who got to the bottom of the street, hoping to step in front of a car, saw some people walking their dog and was so distraught at the thought of them seeing her that she went back to the hospital and knocked on the door in the rain.

No one has ever been able to understand why you hated yourself so much. You were never abused and you never went without. You were bright, articulate, sociable, thoughtful, playful, imaginative, and funny ... but none of this mattered because you saw yourself as 'ugly', 'disgusting', 'vile', and 'worthless'. You were 'spotty', 'fat', with a 'huge nose', 'a hairline too far back', 'a misshapen head', 'a crooked smile with broken teeth'. So vile that you brushed your hair over your face and wouldn't even let your own family look at you ... and they wanted to look at you and they loved you and they were scared you were going to die. And you thought it would be better if you did.

But you didn't. You didn't die.

Because that same stubborn girl decided that couldn't happen. After all you had done to yourself, there must be a reason none of it had taken your life. You began to stand up.

Slowly, you went back to school for the last few months. You got called a freak, you got your tick for registration and then went home, coming back only for drama club on an evening or the school community centre, helping out with people with disabilities, the two places you felt safest. The self-hatred remained present as ever but became drenched in anger, creating fierce determination and ambition. You thought, 'Fuck it, I don't like me, I'll be someone else.' You decided you were going to be an actress. You pretended you were solid, hard, gutsy, another Viktoria, the tough part, the tough girl who would not take no for an answer. The girl who didn't go out for three years suddenly stood in front of people at auditions to get into college.

And you did.

You were the girl who auditioned for the National Youth Theatre of Great Britain and told the head auditioner, 'Of course I'll get in.' And you did. The girl who sat on buses at midnight to go to drama school auditions for 9 a.m. in London. The girl who was offered a place at one drama school and was then told, because of your history, that they didn't have the facilities to deal with someone like you. You were the girl who sat crying in Victoria Bus Station waiting to get the bus back to Sunderland. You were the girl who swallowed her tears and got up and went to other drama school auditions and got offered places.

And you went.

You were the girl who continued the tough persona throughout drama school. You were the sort of girl who refused to make friends because your mantra was that you weren't there to make friends, you were there to be an actress. Actually, you were the girl who was secretly terrified that no one liked her so she just got there first. The girl who had to explain her scars in dressing rooms to beautiful girls and felt so angry and distraught beneath an icy exterior of indifference. The girl who was so jealous of everyone because they were all better than her, more beautiful, more together, better educated, well-adjusted, and excited for life. The girl who could be someone else on stage and it was a fucking relief! The girl who, let's face it, no one had any idea how to deal with, because, let's face it, you had no idea of how to deal with yourself. You were the girl who graduated and didn't go to her own graduation ceremony because you 'didn't go for the bit of paper'; actually you didn't want to 'dress up'. The girl who wrote a million letters, got an agent and got her first job before she even left. The girl who, in that job, was barking mad, but so barking mad she was brilliant at playing a fourteen-year-old girl who hated herself. The girl who won a prestigious theatre award for that role and set off her career. The girl who, on winning the award, realised that she had no one to phone with excitement because she had always shut everyone out because she 'didn't need them'. The girl who had no one to share her success with. The girl who thought, 'I don't need anyone, I'll keep doing it'. And you did. The girl who was offered a part on a television soap and was terrified as she rang the costume department to say she couldn't wear a short skirt because of her scars. The girl who thought they would take the part away from her. But they didn't. And you were the girl who wouldn't be seen for three years and then ten million people watched you. And still you hated yourself. But you were someone else so it was all right.

The work got more and more intense and you collapsed psychologically. The denial didn't work as well as it once did and you couldn't pretend any more. You gave in and fell back into hopelessness.

But you got back up again.

And you went in a different direction this time. You see, you are a girl who has such empathy with suffering and couldn't bear to see anyone in pain. A girl who has sat, day in and day out, with hundreds of professionals, some of whom should never be allowed to work with pond life, let alone people. You wanted to help, to put the world's wrongs right. You did a counselling degree and drove yourself into the ground because you still had to be the best at everything and to get top marks. And you did. But more than that, you were truly good at being with people in their pain. But you felt it too much and every time you would trigger yourself over and over and over again.

And then you got a phone call from someone asking if you would like to be in a Shakespeare play. You did. And this time you were better than ever because you had worked so hard on yourself. And you ended up in the glittering West End of London in a play, with your face on a billboard. The girl who wouldn't be seen for three years. You kept going and going and working and working . . .

But then you fell down again.

You are still trying to get up.

I'm Viktoria, I'm thirty-three years old. It's twenty years on. I still have my thirteen-year-old with me and she's really suffering at the moment. But I'm Viktoria and I've realised that I've tried to so hard to battle my body dysmorphic disorder and maybe instead of trying to hide it, trying to cover it up, trying to pretend it's not there, I need to accept that it's always going to be there and that is that. Does that seem hopeless to those out there suffering? I don't think so. This seems honest to me and, believe me, honesty is one thing I have always craved from professionals, from anyone, in fact. Not, 'You'll be fine'; 'You will get over this'; 'You're not ugly'; 'It's what's inside that counts'; 'Beauty is in the eye of the beholder', etc., etc. What I need to say to myself is that I am me and that is that.

If I'd jumped in front of that car, or an overdose had worked or I had bled to death, I would not have felt such pain as I have over the years, but I would also have missed out on all the amazement, wonder, love, and excitement. I would never have climbed that mountain in the Lake District, stood at the top, looked out over the world and thought, 'Fuck me, I'm alive. I made it. I'm here.'

You have no idea of the power that you have. I know you don't want to hear it, believe me, I'm the worst one to hear it, but the truth is in what

I've just written. It's there in black and white and if anyone had told me back then that I would achieve an iota of what I have achieved, I would have furiously laughed in their face. All I would say is, if you don't believe me, the only way you'll know if I'm right is if you stick around to see for yourself.

RESOURCES

Avenues of Support and Further Reading

www.bddfoundation.org
www.ocdaction.org.uk/support-info/related-disorders/body-dysmorphia
www.skinpick.com – a skin picking resource
www.b-eat.co.uk – the UK's leading eating disorder charity
www.changingfaces.org.uk – support for people with visible differences such as burns or cleft palates.
www.depressionalliance.org – affiliated with MIND; www.mind.org.uk
www.anxietyuk.org.uk

Phillips, K. (2005). *The Broken Mirror: Understanding and Treating Body Dysmorphic Disorder*. Oxford: Oxford University Press.

Phillips, K. (2009). *Understanding Body Dysmorphic Disorder: An Essential Guide*. Oxford: Oxford University Press.

Veale, D., Willson, R., & Clarke, A. (2009). *Overcoming Body Image Problems Including Body Dysmorphic Disorder*. Quincy, MA: Robinson Press.

Treatment Manuals for Professionals

Veale, D., & Neziroglu, F. (2010). *Body Dysmorphic Disorder: A Treatment Manual*. New York: John Wiley.

Wilhelm, S., &, Phillips, K. (2013). *Cognitive–Behavioural Therapy for Body Dysmorphic Disorder: A Treatment Manual*. Surrey: Guilford Press.

BDD Leaflet for Taking to GPs and Other Medical Professionals

Information for health professionals about Obsessive Compulsive Disorder (OCD) & Body Dysmorphic Disorder (BDD) in children, adolescents and adults (based on the NICE Guideline on OCD & BDD)

What is OCD?

OCD is an anxiety disorder that can be very debilitating and can occur in children, adolescents and adults. It is characterised by obsessions or compulsions, but commonly both. An obsession is a repetitive, distressing, unwanted thought about things such as contamination or concern with order or symmetry. A compulsion is a repetitive, distressing, unproductive behaviour, which usually temporarily reduces anxiety and involves such activities as excessive cleaning, repeated checking or counting and hoarding. Repeated thoughts, such as fear of harming other people, are common symptoms of OCD and do not mean that people are at risk of acting on these thoughts.

What is BDD?

Body Dysmorphic Disorder (BDD) is characterised by a preoccupation with and anxiety about what is believed to be a major physical flaw. A person with BDD might spend an excessive amount of time concealing the perceived defect and looking at themselves in the mirror. Other disorders related to OCD - for example Trichotillomania (TTM/ Compulsive Hair Pulling) and Compulsive Skin Picking (CSP) - are not covered by the NICE Guideline, but further information is available from OCD Action.

ASSESSMENT & RECOGNITION

What shall I ask someone who may have OCD?

People with OCD have often had the condition for a long time before it is properly recognised. Consider the possibility of OCD in people with symptoms of depression, anxiety, alcohol or substance misuse or an eating disorder. People with OCD are often embarrassed about their symptoms. Therefore, if you think that a patient may have OCD you could ask:
 Do you wash or clean/check things a lot?
 Is there any thought that keeps bothering you that you'd like to get rid of but can't?
 Do your daily activities take a long time to finish?
 Are you concerned with putting things in a special order or are you very upset by mess?
 Do these problems trouble you? If so, to what extent?

OCD Action is the national UK charity for people affected by OCD and related disorders. Around 1-2% of the population are estimated to have OCD. The World Health Organization recognises OCD as one of the top ten disabling disorders.

Helpline: 0845 390 6232
Website: www.ocdaction.org.uk

ocdaction
it's time to act

Treatments recommended for primary care settings

Psychological Treatments

For children or adolescents with mild OCD, guided self-help is an effective treatment. For children, adolescents and adults, Cognitive Behavioural Therapy including Exposure Response Prevention (CBT including ERP) is an effective treatment for OCD, shown to significantly help about 70% of people with OCD. Depending on severity, it can be given either as a brief intervention with self-help materials or by telephone (up to 10 hours) or as a more intensive treatment for an individual or in a group (more than 10 hours). If it is appropriate it may be useful to involve the family or carer in this treatment. For adults in England CBT is available through the local Improving Access to Psychological Therapies (IAPT) service: www.iapt.nhs.uk

People with OCD might find the following books (available from the 'books on prescription' website) helpful
http://www.booksonprescription.org.uk/

- Understanding Obsessions & Compulsions: Frank Tallis
- Break Free from OCD: Dr. Fiona Challacombe, Dr. Victoria Oldfield & Paul Salkovskis
- Overcoming Obsessive-Compulsive Disorder: David Veale, Rob Willson
- Overcoming Health Anxiety: David Veale, Rob Willson

Please see our website for further information, including an up to date list of Support Groups around the UK and specific guidance on accessing National and Specialist OCD services: www.ocdaction.org.uk

Medications

An SSRI such as Fluoxetine, Fluvoxamine, Paroxetine, Sertraline, Citalopram or Escitalopram may be given to adults either in combination with CBT (including ERP), or alone, depending on severity, on whether the patient wants to have CBT (including ERP), and on whether CBT is working. Your patient should be closely monitored, particularly in initial stages for potential side effects such as agitation and suicidal thoughts, especially in young people.

There is a dose response relationship so that higher doses tend to be more effective e.g. fluoxetine 60mg. The medication may not have full benefit for up to 12 weeks. Your patient should be informed about the possibility of withdrawal symptoms if the medication is suddenly stopped. A child or adolescent with OCD may also receive similar treatment with an SSRI, but a specialist will usually be involved.

Prognosis and referral

With the right treatment 60-70% of patients with OCD will improve. If there is no improvement with CBT (including ERP) and/or SSRI after 12 weeks, NICE guidelines recommend that your patient should be offered a multidisciplinary review (in England with a consultant team of their choice) - where a range of healthcare professionals will assess their needs. For more information, please see www.ocdaction.org.uk/choice A different SSRI or Clomipramine may then be recommended. If the person has not responded to a full trial of an SSRI, or Clomipramine or combined SSRI and CBT (including ERP), they should be referred to a specialist team with expertise in OCD/BDD for further assessment and treatment planning.

Phone: 020 7253 5272 **Email:** info@ocdaction.org.uk
Suite 506-507 Davina House, 137-149 Goswell Road, London, EC1V 7ET
Registered charity no: 1154202

References

Bartlett, C. (2008). *Flickwerk: The Aesthetics of Mended Japanese Ceramics*. Cornell University.
Broyles, W. (2000). Cast Away: The Shooting Script. 20th Century Fox.
Cohen, L. (1992). Anthem. From the album *The Future*. Columbia Records.*
Feusner, J., Moller, H., Altstein, L., Sugar, C., Bookheimer, S., & Yoon, J. (2010). Inverted face processing in body dysmorphic disorder. *Journal of Psychiatric Research*, 44(15): 1088–1094.
Greene, V. Quote accessed online on 23.09.16. www.viviangreene.com.
Hrabosky, J. I., Cash, T. F., Veale, D., Neziroglu, F., Soll, E. A., Garner, D. M., Strachan-Kinser, M., Bakke, B., Clauss, L. J. & Phillips, K. A. (2009). Multidimensional body image comparisons among patients with eating disorders, body dysmorphic disorder, and clinical controls. A multisite study. *Body Image* 6(3), 155-163.
Monzani, B., Rijsdijk, F., Iervolino, A., Anson, M., Cherkas, L. &, Mataix-Cols, D. (2012). Evidence for a genetic overlap between body dysmorphic concerns and obsessive–compulsive symptoms in an adult female community twin sample. *American Journal of Medical Genetics B, 159b*(4): 376–382.
Nierenberg, A., Phillips, K., Petersen, T., Kelly, K., Alpert, J., Worthington, J., Tedlow, J., Rosenbaum, J. &, Fava, M. (2002). Body dysmorphic disorder in outpatients with major depression. *Journal of Affective Disorders, 69*(1–3): 141–148.

Phillips, K. (2005). *The Broken Mirror: Understanding and Treating Body Dysmorphic Disorder*. New York: Oxford University Press.

Phillips, K., Grant, J., Siniscalchi, J., & Albertini, R. (2001). Surgical and nonsurgical medical treatment of patients with body dysmorphic disorder. *Psychosomatics, 42*(6): 504–510.

Phillips, K., McElroy, S., Keck, P., Pope, H., & Hudson, J. (1993). Body dysmorphic disorder: 30 cases of imagined ugliness. *American Journal of Psychiatry, 150*(2): 302–308.

Phillips, K., Siniscalchi, J., & McElroy, S. (2004). Depression, anxiety and somatic symptoms in patients with body dysmorphic disorder. *Psychiatric Quarterly, 75*(4): 309–320.

Rosen, J., & Ramirez, E. (1998). A comparison of eating disorders and body dysmorphic disorder on body image and psychological adjustment. *Journal of Psychosomatic Research, 44*(3-4): 441–449.

Veale, D. (2000). Outcome of cosmetic surgery and 'DIY' surgery in patients with body dysmorphic disorder. *Psychiatric Bulletin, 24*(6): 218–221.

Veale, D., & Lambrou, C. (2002). The importance of aesthetics in body dysmorphic disorder. *CNS Spectrums, 7*(6): 429–431.

Veale, D., & Riley, S. (2001). Mirror, mirror on the wall, who is the ugliest of them all? The psychopathology of mirror gazing in body dysmorphic disorder. *Behaviour Research and Therapy, 39*(12): 1381–1393.

Williamson, M. (1996). *A Return to Love: Reflections on the Principles of 'A Course in Miracles'*. London: Thorsons.

Printed in Great Britain
by Amazon